Published by East Asia Literacy Agency.

Printed in the United States of America

ISBN 978-0-9913198-0-0

RIDE THE EAST WIND

Private Payne

privatepayne.com

CONTENTS

PART I

Kings Creek

PART II

THE CHOCOLATE BAR DAYS

PART I

KINGS CREEK

Geri Payne and Elvis Presley with classmates in Miss Camp's sixth-grade class photo, Milam Junior High School.

RIDE THE EAST WIND

The War is Over

The war is over; I find myself walking the streets of Yokohama as an eighteen-year old soldier, looking in awe and wonder at a world of devastation and despair that I see before me. Japan is an intriguing and different world. A world I had only seen while watching newsreels at the Strand Theater in Tupelo. I have never been far from my home in Mississippi. I glance at homeless people gathered in small groups near train stations looking forlorn and destitute. I see makeshift houses built along the riverbanks and shacks under bridges to help block the cold winter weather. Adults and children hug tattered blankets to keep warm. As I slowly walk in the city, I stop and stare with wonder at the bombed out buildings- many now call home.

At the entrance of a temple, I see a cluster of former Japanese soldiers missing arms or legs. Some have bandages- leaving their wounds festering, hoping for donations of food and money.

A few months ago, the Japanese were my deadly enemies. Now, I see them through different eyes- eyes of compassion. I realize the impact of war on families and children. As I ponder this, I think of my family in Lee County, Mississippi and the difficult times our family endured during The Great Depression.

Lee County Mississippi

1928 Year of the Dragon

Hello Mississippi, how are you! This lucky day is my birthday! The number eight is my lucky number. I greet this world as the eighth child on the eighth day, of the eighth month, the twenty-eighth year of the 1900's - *The Year of the Dragon.*

In East Asia, to greet this world, as a dragon with four eights is extremely lucky- eight is the luckiest number in East Asia! In the Asian zodiac, all signs are animals with one exception, the dragon. The dragon is a mythical creature. East Asians believe dragons are incredibly lucky, blessed, charismatic, and even gifted with great powers. They say a dragon's self-confidence will rarely go unnoticed. In the years to come, running the streets and jungles of East Asia, I will need all of the self-confidence and luck that I can get.

"The lucky rabbit foot that you carry around
was not so lucky for the rabbit."
Joshiki

Mama always says, I was the easiest and fastest birth she has ever had. I am certain it is, because I was in such a hurry to get out into this world to see what is going on in our Lee County, Mississippi.

It is one of those hot summer Mississippi afternoons. My older brothers and sisters return from picking blackberries. They come up the porch stairs and wave to Doctor Holland who is leaving the house; they quickly run inside to greet mama and daddy. Seeing a new baby in the cradle, they gather around with open mouths and look at each other. Little two-year-old Hugh takes a step forward poking his head over the cradle and says,

"Who's that?"

"That's our little baby brother," replies Elizabeth.

"What's his name?" asks, Hugh.

"We haven't named him, yet" replies daddy.

"Why he don't have no name?" pipes up, Buddy.

Our mama speaks up, looks at my brothers and sisters and says,

"We shall name him Noel after our good Mississippi Senator Noel."

"We are gonna' name him after Mississippi's Private John Allen," proclaims daddy.

"He looks like that little baby boy in my school primer book, *Baby Ray*. Let's call him Baby Ray," says Buddy.

"Look! He is looking all around staring at us.

"Who does he think we are? Aliens from Mars?" asks James.

"He knows who we are. He knows we are his family," says Opal.

"I think Baby Ray is cute," says Elizabeth.

My mother holds me up, cradles me in her arms and my brothers and sisters come in closer. My father tickles me; I smile as they all break out in laughter. I was born into a loving family. I was too young to know that one year after my birth we would be in the midst of the Great Depression.

"Time spent laughing is time spent with the Gods."
Japanese Proverb

Our Father

Daddy is a handsome young man out of the hill country of northeast Mississippi. He is strong and high-spirited. Daddy is a good horseman and a crack shot. He rode down from the hills and that is where he met our mother, a young beautiful plantation lady. Daddy is in love; he knows what he wants. *He wants our mother!*

Our mother met Hugh Payne at a barn dance and that is where on a special evening they fell in love. A man from the hills and a young lady from a well-known plantation family of gentry are in love- a love that is not meant to be, but it did happen. There is just one big problem with this new romance . . . our mother is already betrothed to a southern gentleman. *Now, can you see there is going to be trouble*? Up in those hills daddy doesn't get much schooling, but he has a lot of common sense. Hugh Payne has a well-laid plan to secure the wife of his dreams, Nell High- the woman who has stolen his heart. Hugh Payne will take the most practical and direct route to get the woman he loves.

Nell High's aristocratic fiancé, heir to a large plantation in Palmetto, is taking her out for a Sunday buggy ride. The gentleman's buggy is a fine buggy indeed- with painted gold trim accentuating the body and leather seats for comfort. The harness is highly polished with bees wax. The bright brass knobs above the collar are adorned with small bells. The tiny bells are ringing out tinkling music, as the little gated sorrel mare trots along- a perfect setting for a romantic drive.

Nell's fiancé, a man of gentry, is well dressed- a small derby hat, a white well-starched shirt with frills, and attached to his brown suede vest is a gold watch chain. His riding jacket is trimmed with soft brown leather. His pants snuggled down into highly polished knee- high riding boots complete his Sunday best.

Nell High sits high up in the buggy gracefully holding a pink parasol. Her rich patterned velvet dress has long laced sleeves- lined in rose-colored silk with fringed edges. Draped over her shoulders is a velvet-collared cloak with raised patterns in gold and silver brocade. Nell High is the most desired beautiful young girl in all of northeast Mississippi. On this bright Sunday morning, there are two men . . . that know this well.

On this fateful morning, Hugh Payne puts his plan into action. Daddy lies in wait. Off in the woods, out of sight, he sits astride his big black blaze-faced mustang, well known for his stamina and noted for winning races. That there mustang is as wild as daddy is!

Soon, the buggy appears in sight. He watches as the buggy passes by. The little sorrel mare with bells jingling is going down the road at a slow trot. Maneuvering between the trees, jumping the ditch on the side of the road, daddy nudges his heel on his mustang. The spirited horse goes into action, and bounds into a full gallop. The gentleman in the buggy, hearing a galloping horse approaching, looks over his shoulder and sees the mustang racing down the road, bearing down on the buggy. He whips the little sorrel mare into a fast run- the mare is no match for daddy's mustang.

Hugh Payne grabs the halter of the buggy horse- bringing the buggy to a halt, shoots his pistol up in the air- scaring that other fellow almost half to death. Quickly, he grabs Nell High, swings her over on the back of his horse- together they ride off at a fast gallop- away from the lowlands of northeast Mississippi. Mother's smile shows she could not be happier; she holds tightly on to Hugh Payne- as they race for the hills.

"Where so ever you go, go with all your heart."
Confucius

Our Mother

Our mother, Nell High, is a daughter of the High Plantation. In the years following her marriage to daddy, with eight children to raise and not much money, mother learns to be very resourceful. It is not easy caring for eight children; mama works tirelessly- preparing meals for us and washing our clothes up and down on the ol' tin washboard in a tub of soapy water. Rinse tubs complete the cycle. Sometimes there is not much food in the house, but mama always seems to find some way to make us something to eat.

Nell High and Hugh Payne love each other dearly. Not only are they husband and wife, they are sweethearts and lovers. They are the best of friends and very close. Throughout their short lives they support and comfort one another and their children. Life is hard; in the midst of all the hardship, she is a very warm and caring mother to all her children.

Mama and daddy stand side by side facing life bravely, as we move from house to house in Lee County during The Great Depression.

The High Plantation has passed through family hands from generation to generation. The entrance of the drive to the home is gracefully lined with large oak trees. Beautiful white columns support the home's wide porches and balconies. Our lovely, southern magnolia trees accentuate the expansive lawn surrounding the home. The plantation is so large that one can get on a horse, ride all day and still be on the High Plantation.

Velma Filgo, daughter of our eldest sister, Opal Dew Drop, and I make a visit to the Lee County Court House. She shows me the record of the land that was once the High Plantation.

In my mind I can see rich bottomland with miles and miles of cotton fields, rolling hills, horses and cows grazing in lush pastures. Nearby pools for watering the livestock are graced by weeping willows and are well stocked with fish.

Over the years the plantation has been divided among family members. Much of the land is lost to the Citizen State Bank and Trust Company during the Great Depression. The remaining land went to my mother, her sisters and brothers.

Sadly, the High Plantation land is not to remain in my family.

"When we feel love and kindness towards others, it not only makes others feel loved and cared for, but it helps us also to develop inner happiness and peace."
Dalai Lama

Family

In the hills of northeast Mississippi, mama and daddy settle in a small one-room cabin with a lean-to attached to the side for daddy's mustang. Mama soon finds out that life is hard for hill people. For food, daddy shoots squirrels out of trees near the cabin. This is not hard for daddy to do with the help of his partner- his little squirrel dog, Benjamin. When a squirrel sees daddy, the squirrel runs around to the other side of the tree- Benjamin goes into action, Benjamin also runs around to the other side, starts barking and that makes the squirrel run back to daddy's side- squirrel for supper . . . Benjamin gets his share.

At one end of the cabin is a stone fireplace. An iron hook centers over the fireplace from which hangs a cast iron pot. In this cast iron, pot mama cooks black-eyed peas with pork fatback, wild mustard greens, and sometimes squirrel stew flavored with wild onions that have the aroma of garlic. This delicacy daddy gathers from the nearby forest. Mama and daddy must have had other food, like corn bread, butter beans and grits which no southerner can live without.

Hanging on the wall next to the fireplace is a short handle hoe that is bent in the shape of a paddle. On this hoe, mama often cooks cornmeal hoecakes over hot coals. She serves them with sorghum molasses to daddy's delight!

Close by the cabin is a small pool to water the mustang. The pool has catfish that daddy often catches with a cane pole, some string with a lead weight, and dangling from a hook is a freshly dug wiggly earthworm to attract the fish. After catching a few fish, daddy nails the catfish through the head to a tree, then skins, guts and cleans them for mama to fry, accompanied by hot hush puppies right out of her cast iron pot. *Daddy thinks there is no better living than the hill country.*

One of daddy's daily chores is to bank the hot coals at night by covering them with a goodly amount of ashes. Early the next morning, he jumps out of bed, uncovers the coals, throws on some kindling wood. When the kindling is blazing, daddy puts on a few larger sticks of wood, runs back **. . .** jumps into bed. Soon enough, the cabin has warded off the frosty air and begins to glow with warmth for them to start a new day of . . . *life in the hill country.*

The first born for Hugh and Nell soon arrives. He is mama's first baby, a boy; he dies at birth. Their second child is a girl that mama names, Virginia. *Isn't that a beautiful southern name?*

Unfortunately, baby Virginia lives only three weeks. The loss of their first son and daughter is heart breaking for the two of them. Life is difficult in these hills without medical assistance or the help of family nearby.

The bitter winter moves into springtime in the hills, and the dogwood trees are beginning to flower **. . .** this is when our mother says,

"Hugh, we are leaving these hills and we are going home to Palmetto!" Mama packs their few belongings and says,

"I am ready, Hugh."

Our father saddles up his horse and they ride down from the hills, down into the low lands of Lee County. The kidnapping is over looked; no questions asked. On the other hand, is it because daddy is such a crack shot, as most hill boys are?

They settle down on mama's eighty acres of inherited land and raise cotton and kids. *Daddy would go through hell and high water for mama.*

"He acts before he speaks, and afterwards
speaks according to his actions."
Confucius

The third child born in the Payne family is a daughter.

She is given the lovely name of Opal Dew Drop. *Have you ever heard of any one naming a kid Dew Drop?* She is mama and daddy's first living child.

Since Opal Dew Drop is the eldest, she is hard on us at times. When I am mischievous, she tells mama to make me go outside and get a willow switch. I will have to find and cut my own switch for mama to switch me.

Once, I cut little notches in the switch and mama draws back to switch me. The switch cracks into pieces on contact with my bottom; mama laughs so hard that she doesn't want to switch me no more, but Opal keeps yelling,

"Mama, make him get another switch! Go on! And, she does.

After daddy and mama die, Opal, their first-born, mothers the younger ones.

Mama and daddy's fourth child is a boy; James Travis joined the Marine Corps before World War II and went on to serve throughout much of the war. He was in the third wave when the landing craft arrived at Guadalcanal. He said the Japanese rice pots were still warm.

They say everything changed when our brother, L.J. the fifth child was born- *Yep, that is his name, but we all call him 'Buddy'. It is not unusual in the south to name boys with initials only. One of our cousin's name is R.B.*

Buddy is born with his little feet turned backwards. He didn't really know the way he wanted to go, forwards or backwards. Was he ah coming or was he goin'? Anyway, our mama tells our daddy,

"My little boy is going to run and play like all the other little boys." Mama makes up her mind- there is no turning back! She sells her land to Uncle John.

When Buddy is old enough for the operation, the doctors break Buddy's little ankles and turn his feet to the front and mama makes sure the doctors are paid.

Buddy wears steel braces and his feet heal to the front and when those braces finally come off, he knows which way he is ah goin'! Sure enough, Buddy can now run and play like all the other little boys. It is wonderful to see him go . . . whistling, running and jumping back and forth across the yard. Buddy is one happy little boy! Daddy says,

"Just look at him go!"

Mama no longer has any of the High Plantation land, but she has peace of mind. She has a little boy that she loves and cares about with all her heart, who now runs and plays like other boys. She is mighty grateful to those doctors for making sure her little son is going to have a good life.

Our mother and daddy continue to increase their little family in Lee County, and soon our sister Elizabeth who was always called Betty is born. Betty is number six in the order of the Payne youngsters. In later years, we all pile in daddy's car and drive over 500 miles to see Betty's husband who is in the hospital in Chicago. We become lost in the unfamiliar streets, crowded and noisy with heavy traffic.

We pull into a gas station to ask directions. The gas attendant says,

"Well, you are going right opposite of where you should be going-so you'd best turn this car back and head the other way." Buddy just kept driving. We tap his shoulder,

"Buddy, he just told you to go the other way!"

"I know he did. He ain't tellin' the truth, though! He didn't like the way we talk, so the Yankee done sent us on a wild goose chase."

Betty is mighty glad to see her family after our long trip from Tupelo to visit her and her husband who was very ill in the hospital.

The next little child to come into the world in Tupelo was a boy. Hugh Holland- named after our father Hugh, and Doctor Holland who brought all of us into this world. He is two years older than I am. Hugh is a good, kindhearted big brother. Hugh always feeds stray dogs that come around our house. Once, someone gives Hugh and me two young shepherd dogs.

Where we are from, most everyone calls them "German police dogs." Mama and daddy do not let us keep them, so we return them to the people that gave them to us. Hugh and I cry and cry, not knowing that more often than not, there is not enough food to feed our family, much less two large, growing dogs.

It is my turn to be born. I am next in line ushering in the Great Depression. Soon after I was born, we lost our farm. The Great Depression hit hard for farmers everywhere.

Mississippi sure is hard hit. *Banks fail daily. The nation's economy stagnates beyond belief. Unemployment is at an unprecedented high. Many sink into despair and shame after they cannot find jobs. Families lose their homes and businesses because they cannot pay their property taxes. In a single day, the day of Franklin D. Roosevelt's inauguration, in April of 1932, one fourth of the real property in Mississippi, including 20% of all farms and 15% of town property go under the auctioneer's gavel and are sold to pay taxes.*

Like many others, we lost everything. My older brothers and sisters laughingly say life was good . . . until I came along!

Mama and daddy welcome two more little girls into their

growing family, our younger sister, Bonnie and last of us all, our baby sister, Geri. Her real name is Geraldine, but I will let her tell you all about that. *From 1946, in the early years living out of the states, I did not stay in touch with the family much and I rely on my youngest sister, Geri for a lot of the information that happened to our brothers and sisters during that time.*

Like many sons of America from the south, as soon we get old enough, we enlist into the military, and so do a few Yankees. Buddy serves in the Army Air Force; although, he could have been exempted and declared 4F, because his feet were still a little crooked. Hugh is in the Army, and fights in the Pacific.

When I went into the Airborne, mama put a little flag in the window with four red stars. People put these little flags in the front window of their homes to show how many sons they have in the military. Mama is mighty proud of her four stars. A gold star signifies a son killed in action. After the battle of Tarawa in the Pacific, James is sent to a hospital in Australia. Mama says,

"We are lucky! James' star remains red."

James is at Pearl Harbor when the Japanese attack early on a Sunday morning in December. Although James is off duty, he is still on base. He tells us,

"As the bullets are flying from the Japanese fighter planes, me and Les Irish try to hide behind the same telephone pole."

The war continues, and James is sent to the hospital from the battle of Tarawa. James says the hospital in Australia is nice and the nurses are all mighty pretty.

Elizabeth (we all call her Betty), marries a Yankee and moves north. Geri also marries a Yankee and moves north. We finally forgive them both . . . after about 30 years!

"Naw', y'all know, I'm ah just jokin', but it did take ah spell."

Bonnie, two years older than Geri, remains in Mississippi. Bonnie and her husband Monk raise a good southern family.

As the years go by, our older brothers and sisters are no longer with us. My younger sister Geri and I are here to tell the story of a dashing young man out of the Mississippi hills by the name of Henry Hugh Payne who kidnaps and marries a young pretty plantation girl by the name of Nell High.

"Life's fulfillment finds constant obstacles in its path; but those are necessary for the sake of its advance. The stream is saved from the sluggishness of its current by the perpetual opposition of the soil through which it must cut its way. The spirit of fight belongs to the genius of life."
Sir Rabindranath Tagore

Geri and I have spent some time in Okinawa (where I live to this day) together, and we see each other in the states as often as possible. I have lived outside of the United States for more than sixty-eight years. I go home to Mississippi often and when I do, I talk just like the rest of 'em.

"How y'all ah doin'? (How are all of you doing?)

"How's yo' mama nem'? (How are your mama and them?) (Literally, this means, how is your family?) *You can take the southern boy out of the*

south, but you can't take the south out of the southern boy.

Geri has a great memory and answers my questions about many things that I have long forgotten. Geri and I enjoy talking about growing up in Lee County, Mississippi. Tupelo is the county seat of Lee County. My story telling has her descriptive additions, and I am ever so thankful for my little sister, Geri and her great memory that helps complete my story of those happy days gone by in Lee County, Mississippi.

Southerners take great pride in their heritage and we talk about this all the time. If you travel through our southern states, you probably notice that on the corner of county court houses there is a statue of a Confederate soldier. Southern pride runs deep. Generations of people in the south have handed down stories, customs, and traditions thus giving southern authors much to write about, often drawing from their own treasure of family stories.

"A bird does not sing because it has an answer,
it sings because it has a song."
Chinese Proverb

Palmetto

Our World As We Know It

The splendor of Palmetto's summers is like a dream . . . rolling hills; lush valleys, clear running streams- jumping with fish. Fields of beautiful wild flowers border magnificent forests of gum and oak trees. Soaring high up in the sky- the scream of the red-tail hawk as it circles under soft white clouds. Fragrance of honeysuckle vines fills the air during hot humid nights. The call of the hoot owl echoes off in the distance.

In the wild, are delicious pecans, hickory nuts, chestnuts and persimmon trees, wild blackberries, large yellow plums, summer grapes, possum grapes and our southern Muscatine grapes. Throughout the countryside are fields of large luscious watermelons basking in the early morning sun. Across the land for miles and miles are the cotton fields. Listen to the colored folk singing as they walk to the fields . . .

Swing low, sweet chariot,
Coming for to carry me home
Swing low, sweet chariot,
Coming for to carry me home
I looked over Jordan
And what did I see,
Coming for to carry me home?
A band of angels coming after me,
Coming for to carry me home
Sometimes I'm up, and sometimes I'm down,
Coming for to carry me home
But still my soul feels heavenly bound.
Coming for to carry me home
The brightest day that I can say,
Coming for to carry me home
When Jesus washed my sins away.
Coming for to carry me home

If I get there before you do,
Coming for to carry me home
"I'll cut a hole and pull you through,
Coming for to carry me home
Tell all my friends that I'm coming to,
Coming for to carry me home."
American Negro Spiritual

Before moving to Tupelo at the age of eight, I remember each house where we lived in Palmetto The old wooden house I was born in is still there. It is painted white with a brick foundation.

The next house we lived in is the little house in Palmetto with a peach tree in the front yard. Mama would tell us,

"If y'all chase that old cow out of the pasture and into the barn, I will milk it and make you some peach ice cream."

I spend many ah day trying to corral that ol' cow into the barn. Mama says,

"What a sight you are to see!"

My mama makes good peach ice cream.

Another house I remember well had an upper floor. I remember the day our older brothers, Jim and Buddy's goats went upstairs. Mama got mad when she found the goats jumping up and down on the beds.

"Y'all get those goats off those beds, down those stairs and out of this house or I'm ah gonna whup' the daylights out of you!"

Hearing all of this, I want to know what in the world is going on. I'm gonna laugh an' make faces when I see my older brothers get ah whupping'. This is gonna' be fun, as I stand at the bottom of the stairs- I don't want to miss nothing, and I don't!

Goats and brothers come rushing, tumbling down the stairs. Guess, who is in the way of this mad rush **. . .** me. After being trampled by scrambling goats and brothers- looking at my bruises, I agree with mama- no more goats up those stairs!

Times get worse for our family. We move into a little wooden shack of a house in Palmetto. The old unpainted wooden boards on the sides of the house are weather beaten. Not to be outdone with the look of time is a roof of well-rusted galvanized tin.

Our little house sits off to the side of a dirt road. Behind the house, there is a small stream with shallow running water. In the stream, we catch crawdaddies. My daddy tells me that Yankees call crawdaddies, 'crayfish'.

We have an old rusty water pump in the backyard; the handle is wired to the pump with bailing wire. We hand pump water for drinking, cooking, washing clothes, and our weekly Saturday baths in the washtub.

The front part of the house is what we call the 'living room'. It has two beds. We spend family time around our pot-bellied stove trying to keep warm during cold winter nights.

On the stove top mama also heats her flat irons for ironing our clothes; we may not have much in the way of nice store bought clothes, but Mama makes sure our clothes are clean and neatly ironed. On cold winter nights, she heats her flat irons, wraps them in old clothes that she places at our feet when we children go to bed. Before going to bed, we sit around as a family, roasting peanuts on the stovetop while talking to each other. We talk about our world, as we know it in Lee County, Mississippi.

Adjoining the living room is a small room with two beds. In this room, a wood ladder nailed to the wall, leads to a loft over the living room where the little children like me sleep. There is only enough room in the loft below our roof for us to crawl into and under our blankets. The pitter-patter of the raindrops falling on the tin roof is like a gentle waterfall . . . music to our ears as we fall asleep.

To the back of our little home, is a small lean-to kitchen with a wood-cooking stove. There is a table with a wood bench and some stools where we sit together to eat what little we have. It is winter.

As children growing up during the Great Depression, we do not know or understand how bad things are. We just think that this is the way . . . the world is supposed to be.

On days that we can go to school, for our school lunch, Mama bakes some biscuits; she cuts them open and puts some sweet milk-white gravy inside the biscuits and then she sprinkles on a little black pepper for taste. During the time when we live in a little wooden house we call home, our family endures extreme hardships.

One-day daddy brings home two large boxes of used clothes and shoes-donated for poor people. I dig around in the boxes with my brothers and sisters for some clothes that might fit; I find a pair of old brown shoes that are a little large for me. Each shoe has a large hole worn in the sole. On the days that I can go to school, when playing, I run flat-footed so as my heels will not kick up to show the holes. I got some cardboard paper and cut it to fit the inside sole of the shoes. This helps some . . . until it rains. We lost our farm during the Great Depression; we lost most everything, except our love and concern for each other.

The long hot summers of Mississippi help make for a good growing season in mama's small vegetable garden. In the nearby woods, we pick wild berries, plums, summer grapes, possum grapes, and small sweet persimmons. We all run around with bare feet. Our clothes are simple; we younger boys have hand-me down overalls and the younger girls wear hand-me down cotton dresses.

Work is scarce. Mama and daddy find a little work with the WPA in Tupelo. Sometimes the whole family picks cotton in the hot Mississippi sun. This brings in money to buy clothes for that dreaded school that will once again start in September.

School begins late in the year so the kids can help with the cotton picking; it is usually early September. If cotton picking is not over when school starts, our family usually keeps us out until it is finished. My summer days in Mississippi are full of fun with my friends, and like I say, making money!

When we go to the cotton fields, we take along sacks made of heavy material. Mama buys material and makes us sacks that are in various lengths from three feet to twelve or fifteen feet long- there is a strong strap at the open front end that goes over the neck and rests on the shoulder with the sack trailing behind us on the ground as we walk down the rows.

The younger kids use the small sacks and the older boys and girls use the larger ones. Our sacks are very heavy to drag when they are about full. My brother Hugh and I with our smaller sacks carry or drag them to the scales. We are always excited to see how much we get for our bags. We give the money to mama to save for our clothes.

Everyone brings a lunch to the cotton patch (sometimes, if the field is not too far, our family walks home for dinner). The cotton sack makes a soft seat for eating our food and even a nice bed for a short rest before going back to picking cotton. Mama sometimes builds a fire and boils coffee in a bucket, or a big pot for the older ones.

There is a water bucket in the shade of the wagon with a dipper hanging on the rim. Everyone drinks thirstily from the same dipper and when the bucket is dry, one of us kids fetches some more water. On other days, mama and daddy go alone to Tupelo to get what work they can find. They stop and buy something for our supper, which we very much look forward to.

At the end of the day in the twilight of the evening, all eight of us kids sit out in the yard by the side of the road. While we are waiting for mama and daddy to come home, we sing songs that daddy sang up in those hills when he was a boy.

"How does my Lady's garden grow?
How does my Lady's garden grow?
In silver bells and cockle shells
And pretty maids all in a row.

How does my Lady's garden grow?
How does my Lady's garden grow?
In silver bells and cockle shells
And pretty maids all in a row."

As we sing, my brothers and I point to our sisters and they turn their heads to the side and giggle like everything, as silly girls do.

As the evening falls, all our eyes are on the road looking for the lights of the old car that will bring mama and daddy home with food. We are like baby birds waiting for their mama and papa to return to the nest.

"Faith is the bird that feels the light and sings when the dawn is still dark."
Sir Rabindranath Tagore

As we sit on the side of the road, waiting for our parents' return, we are so happy just thinking about the carefree days ahead. We sure are excited about this coming Sunday's trip to the Palmetto Methodist Church. It is a great time for us and for our neighbors alike. It will be the yearly meetin' time of all day singin' and dinner on the ground.

All Day Singing and Dinner on the Ground

It is a beautiful summer Sunday. A gentle breeze rustles the leaves on the willow trees while little children hold hands and play London Bridge in the warm sun. Our church in Palmetto is having an "all-day singing and dinner on the ground." *Let me explain again for the Yankees- for us Southerners, it is breakfast, dinner and supper*. It is an exciting day for all, especially us young'uns. We are going to the Methodist Church graveyard in Palmetto. We are simple folk; we believe in God, family, and in being good neighbors. A man's word and his handshake are as good as gold. Taking care of family is our God given promise. This is our southern way of life in small town Mississippi.

Mama always makes sure we are clean; we all take our Saturday night bath in the washtub out back of the house . . . we are a well-dressed family. Our sisters are wearing light cotton dresses that mama has made. We boys have clean shirts and store bought overalls. My brother Hugh and I wear hand me downs from our older brothers. By the time we get them, they are pretty worn. The buttons are missing on the top of my overalls, but a couple of small nails take care of that. I place the nails through the holes where the metal buttons once were, and bring the straps over my shoulders. The nails fit into the metal rings at the end of the straps. I look nice . . . mama says so. Barefoot, we walk to the graveyard, happy and excited looking forward to the festivities of the day.

Mama has made some Amalgamation cakes (*It's a southern thing from rural northeast Mississippi.*) All the women have made their special foods with much pride. In the hot summer sun, the men wear hats and the women homemade bonnets. The bonnets are so pretty- each woman trying to outlook the other with colorful ribbons and designs.

Earlier in the year, the men have cleaned the graveyard for our loved ones, the present generation, generations before and the generations to come. Our preacher man has been preaching most of the morning to save our souls. Uncle John along with others who have brought their guitars and fiddles play the old familiar hymns: We stand and sing:

There's a church in the valley by the wildwood
No lovelier spot in the dale
No place is so dear to my childhood,
As the little brown church in the vale.
Come to the church in the wildwood.
Oh, come to the church in the dale,
No spot is so dear to my childhood,
As the little brown church in the vale.

How sweet on a clear, Sabbath morning
To list to the clear ringing bell
Its tones so sweetly are calling,
Oh, come to the church in the vale.
There, close by the church in the valley
Lies one that I loved so well
She sleeps, sweetly sleeps, 'neath the willow,
Disturb not her rest in the vale.

There, close by the side of that loved one
To trees where the wild flowers bloom
When the farewell hymn shall be chanted
I shall rest by her side in the tomb.

From the church in the valley by the wildwood,
When day fades away into night,
I would fain from this spot of my childhood
Wing my way to the mansions of light.
Come to the church by the Wildwood
Oh come to the church in the vale.
No spot is so dear to my childhood,
As the Little Brown Church in the vale

It is now time for dinner. *(Yankees say lunch.)* The women spread colorful quilts on the ground and put out the most wonderful assortment of food that one will ever see-good ol' southern home cooking. We have fried chicken from cast iron skillets, so tender it falls off the bone. Pork chops, fried okra, fried green tomatoes and country-cured ham are also on the quilts. *Chow Chow* is a hot sweet and spicy relish. It goes so well with the salmon patties and catfish. The large luscious watermelons look as big as I am . . . and I am ah gettin' hungry.

Cornbread and biscuits, with sweet milk gravy . . . lots of black-eyed peas with ham hocks, snap beans, butter beans, summer greens, corn puddin' and spiced peaches that make our mouths water . . . not to be outdone by delicious southern deserts and our mama's *Amalgamation* cakes. The other women's coconut cakes, chocolate cakes, pecan pies, sweet potato pies, lemon meringue pies, chocolate cream pies, and coconut pies are mighty tasty-all washed down with gallons of sweet tea.

It is late in the afternoon as mama gathers her dishes, and we help her pack the baskets and fold the quilts. Everyone is tired after singing, playing and eating all day.

As we slowly walk home on the dirt road, I think with a happy heart and full stomach, that I can't wait for our next going to the graveyard for *"All day singing and dinner on the ground!"*

Many a days in those warm summer months, my mouth is ah hankering for some of my mama's southern down home cooking. I especially look forward to mama's *Amalgamation* cake: Now, for those of you whose mouths are also hankering for some of that good ol' southern down home cooking, I present mama's *Amalgamation Cake:*

Mama's Amalgamation Cake

With a Little Revision by Daddy

Our wonderful *Southern Amalgamation Cake* originated right here in the heart of the deep south, northeast Mississippi. This cake is loaded with good things and is time consuming to prepare; it takes a lot of work to turn one out to perfection. That's why my daddy says . . .

"That cake needs tender loving care in order for it to come out real good. It needs some revision for a little relaxation!"

If y'all are gonna' try to make Mama's *Amalgamation Cake*, this is what y'all are gonna' need.

Cake

One bottle of moonshine (Preferably Anderson's Lee County)
(*Daddy's Revision*)
One cane bottom rocking chair or similar.
(Another of Daddy's Revisions)
Daddy says:
"That there chair works well with the moonshine."
2 cups white sugar to start with....
(*You may have another taste of the moonshine and try brown cane sugar.*)
1 1/2 cups butter (*Only Yankees would use un-salted butter*)
1 cup buttermilk (*Buttermilk-Daddy says, "This just blows the mind of Yankees.*")
1 teaspoon baking soda
4 cups all-purpose flour
1 cup chopped walnuts
1 cup of chopped pecans
1 cup of raisins soaked in Sherry (*Another one of daddy's revisions.)*
1 cup flaked coconut
1 teaspoon ground cloves
1 teaspoon ground cinnamon
2 cups any flavor fruit jam (*I like Black Cherry Jam.*)
4 egg whites

This is how mama makes her wonderful *Southern Amalgamation Cake:*

Preheat oven to 325 degrees F (165 degrees C).
Grease and flour 3 8-inch cake pans.
Mix flour, soda, cloves, and cinnamon
Add 1 cup raisins, 1 cup walnuts, 1 cup pecans, and 1 cup coconut
Y'all keep stirring until you mix in well the good things: pecans, walnuts, raisins, coconut and two drops of moonshine.
Set this mixture aside . . .
Cream 2 cups sugar and 1 1/2 cups butter.
Stir in the jam.
Add buttermilk alternately with flour mixture, blending with a spoon, until all is used up, ending with the flour mixture.
In a separate bowl, beat egg whites until they hold a peak.
Fold into the batter mixture. Pour into prepared cake pans. Bake approximately 30 minutes or until top springs back when lightly touched. Turn cakes out of the pans on wire racks to cool while you have another sip of *Anderson's Lee County Moonshine. . .*

Frosting

2 cups white sugar
4 egg yolks
1/2 cup butter
2 cups chopped walnuts
2 cups raisins
1 1/2 cups evaporated milk
2 cups flaked coconut

Mix 4 egg yolks until they are broken up and smooth.
Add ½-cup evaporated milk and mix together until the eggs yolks are mixed well with milk.
Add the rest of the evaporated milk, 2 cups sugar, and 1/2 cup butter.
Cook until thick and remove from heat.
Stir in 2 cups nuts, 2 cups raisins, and 2 cups coconut.
Cool slightly while beating mixture with a spoon.
Spread on cooled cakes.

Daddy says,

"While waiting for the cakes to cool down, you should try to relax. Sit in the rocking chair . . . pour yourself another few sips moonshine and . . . you will relax!"

Good luck!

"I would rather have tried and failed than never to have tried at all."
Joshiki

I told you about daddy's revisions to mama's *Amalgamation* cake. Now, I'll tell you there are things that daddy does that mama will just not put up with . . . daddy's table manners.

Daddy's Table Manners

Mama is always a trying to teach daddy table manners. Daddy never takes much stock in that, and mama never has much luck, neither!

Daddy likes his coffee black, strong and steaming hot. When daddy makes coffee, he boils water in his old beat up enameled gray coffee pot. When the water is at a good boil, he throws the coffee into the pot. I am sitting there with big eyes and open mouth; I am fascinated as I watch the steaming brown foam and smell the wonderful aroma of his coffee. I can't wait for the next part of the show. Daddy pours the scalding coffee into his cup. After that, he pours some coffee from his cup into his saucer, and then he puts the saucer to his lips and slowly sips his very hot coffee. This drives mama crazy! I can never figure that part out, pouring coffee into a saucer. I guess it is to cool the coffee down some, or is it to keep the grounds in the cup so that the coffee grounds won't go into the saucer? Maybe it is just so he can watch mama frown- daddy always whispers to me after mama scolds him,

"Yo' mama is just as pretty when she is angry."

My sister Geri says, "Sipping hot coffee from a saucer was an English custom, they would sip their hot tea from a saucer." Saucers were different in those days - deeper than saucers of today (almost bowl like). At the turn of the century, people were still eating with case knives and using deep bowl-like saucers."

Daddy smiles at me as he takes another sip from his saucer. Anyhow, try as much as mama does, she can never get daddy to drink his coffee from a cup.

Daddy eats his food with nothing but a case knife. For y'all who don't know what a case knife is, it is a flat knife with a round end. Geri continues explaining,

"This was the English way of eating. The Payne family's ancestry is from England. This eating custom is handed down from previous generations. The reason the case knife is called a case knife is because

back years and years before, the wealthy nobles of England would take their eating utensils with them in a case when they traveled. Often visiting friends and family, they would stay sometimes for months. So, therefore, the knife was called a case knife."

Daddy does not use no fork! Hill people eat that way. Daddy even scoops peas up on that flat knife.

I am always big-eyed watching daddy eat. I want to eat the same way he does, but one look from mama says it all- I had better not even think about it! Mama just grits her teeth. It is true; daddy has his own style of eating- she just puts up with it in her own way. Mama sure loves daddy!

Our daddy, Hugh Payne raises us kids through The Great Depression. We may not have much- like shoes to go to school some winters, but he makes sure we have food. He is a good daddy with a big heart- the best daddy any kid could ever have. He is the only daddy that us Payne kids ever had!

The Great Depression days are trying times for men and women's spirits. They struggle to find ways to support their families. Some people are worse off than we are.

Moses

In Palmetto, we Payne kids have a good friend; he is an old colored man- his name is Moses. We love Moses; he sings to us and tells us exciting stories such as Brer Rabbit and the Tar Baby. We don't like that bad ol' Brer Fox! He is evil- wantin' to kill Brer Rabbit!

It is a warm sunny afternoon; we are sitting outside on cane chairs talking and laughing about the time Geri got a bath in the washtub, when we see Moses slowly walking down the road. We jump up and run up the road to greet Moses, wanting to be the first to hold his hand. As we walk along getting closer to our home, mama can hear us happily calling out,

"Mama, mama, Moses is here!"

Mama comes out the front door with a cheerful smile on her face- always happy to see Moses as she says,

"Moses, it is good that you are here- the children have missed you. Please sit down; Opal, go bring Moses a nice glass of iced tea."

We are all jumping up and down- "Moses, Moses, tell us more about that mean ol' Brer Fox. Is he gonna' try again **. . .** to catch Brer Rabbit?

Moses relaxes in the shade of the house, sipping his cold sweet-tea, as he says to mama,

"Misses Payne, can I eat one of them cucumbers in yo' garden? I sho' is powerful hungry."

"You wait right here Moses, you need to rest; drink your iced tea and talk to the children; I will be right back."

Mama soon returns from our garden with a flour sack full of cucumbers, string beans, butterbeans and okra.

"Moses, take these vegetables from our garden home to your family."
Our mother had inherited from her plantation family a deep sense of responsibility and concern for others.

Then as always, Moses stands, holding his cap in his hands and says,

"Thank you, Misses Payne. Now, I'se gonna' sing ah song for yo' little chillun'. Now, you little chillun' come over here; we gonna' sing together."

We happily gather around Moses, holding hands as we swing from side to side . . . we sing:

"I'm sitting on top of the world
Just rolling along
Just rolling along
I'm quitting the blues of the world
Just singing a song
Just singing a song."
Sam Lewis and Joe Young

God bless you Moses! You bring us . . . happiness. You leave us . . . with a song in our hearts.

Life is difficult for many during these trying times, a miserable way of life for many. In these days of our Great Depression, Moses adjusted his way of life.

"*Life at any time can become difficult. Life at any time can become easy. It all depends upon how one adjusts oneself to life.*"
Morarji Desai

For the family- life gets better . . . we move to Tupelo.

Sister Geri Gets a Bath

Life is not easy for most folks in these troublous times; however, our mother does get help some days with the wash and other things. Geri is playing in the yard the day they set up the washtubs. Here is what Geri remembers:

"Even though life is a struggle for most everyone, mother and daddy are always doing things for people- sharing . . . what little we have. The colored ladies who help our mama . . . do whatever they can to make life easier for everyone.

Mother has help at times with the washing and ironing. I am walking and talking the day that they set up the washtubs. I am outside playing in the dirt. One of the colored women picks me up and says, 'This baby is dirty!'

She sticks me in the tub that has the last rinse water and gives me a bath. She doesn't ask mother if she can bathe me, she just does it, knowing that it is all right. *Colored people in Lee County are just like part of the family!"* Geri recalls,

"After we move to Tupelo, as a young girl, I remember walking downtown with mother. Mother is always friendly, and we often stop and talk to some of the colored women from Palmetto. They ask me,

"Do you remember me, chile'? I used to take care of you when you was a baby."

Mother always takes the time to talk to the colored people of Lee County. She truly cares about how they are getting along during these hard times. She tries to help out in any way that she can. The colored people in return show that they care about us with acts of kindness and loving words of encouragement. Our parents teach us to show our respect and kindness to all people

All of our life . . . we have always done so."

"All that we are is the result of what we have thought."

Buddha

I question Geri: "Do you recall the house in East Tupelo on Canal Street? Some colored folks now live there."

Many years later, I went back to the house on Canal Street where we used to live, I introduce myself to them and tell them that our family lived in their house. They invite me to sit on their front porch and I say to them,

"Y'all wait hea' I'll be back in two whoops and ah holler!"

I go to a store and buy some fried chicken and a bottle of Wild Turkey. We spend a wonderful afternoon talking and laughing about growing up in Lee County . . . eating fried chicken and drinking Wild Turkey. The colored folks and I had a lot of empathy for one another. In the pleasant afternoon we spent getting to know one another better; we find common ground in southern living at its best.

"Fourscore and seven years ago our fathers brought forth on this continent, a new nation, conceived in Liberty, and dedicated to the proposition that all men are created equal."

Abraham Lincoln

Two Different Worlds
Shake Rag

Shake Rag is on high ground at the north end of Tupelo. If the city cuts down the heavy growth of trees, we can see Highland Circle, which is one of the wealthiest, if not the wealthiest residential areas for whites only- so near, yet so far apart- two different worlds.

Geri says, "Shake Rag is one of the largest residential areas for colored families in Lee County. The wealthy and not so wealthy townsfolk want their domestics to live within walking distance- Tupelo does not have a public transportation system. Taxis do not have meters. Anywhere within Tupelo city limits, the fare is ten cents. This adds up to a lot of money each month for most colored folk; money they either do not have or cannot afford to spend on transportation.

More important for the families is food and milk for their children. Milk is now expensive . . . ten cents a quart for sweet milk, five cents for buttermilk. A loaf of bread has gone up to five cents. Hamburger meat is ten cents a pound; most beef is fifteen cents a pound or higher. Ten pounds of potatoes now cost ten cents. Eggs have risen to the ridiculous price of eighteen cents a dozen.

Sylvia says. "There ain't no end to these high prices! What is a body gonna' do just to stay alive! What will this world be like tomorrow?"

Shake Rag's women work as domestic maids and cooks. They do laundry and ironing for rich white families, and those not so rich. The men work in Tupelo as restaurant and hotel cooks- anything to get a job to support their families.

Most of the men walk to work- rarely do they work outside of Tupelo for the lack of transportation. Around town, they are in heavy labor such as warehouses, construction, and the cotton gin.

One of the most common things the colored women of Tupelo do is to take care of little white children. Anything the colored women do . . . they do well.

I have a colored woman by the name of Sylvia Johnson taking care of me from time to time in our house on Court and Green Street. Bonnie, two years older than I am, is in school. Mother is working at the hospital across Green Street.

One day fooling around, I get a big wad of chewing gum in my long hair. The more I try to pull the gum out, the more it gets stuck. Sylvia is trying to get it out, but she, too, can't get the gum out; I am yelling my head off . . . so she takes me across the street to the hospital where mother is. WOW! Some of the nurses are holding me down while mama and other nurses take out bandage shears and start cutting the gum out of my hair. I am screaming loud enough to be heard in the rooms down the hallway . . . Mama takes my hand trying to calm me down. Everything becomes just fine when one of the nurses hands me a big ol' candy sucker.

Every afternoon Sylvia takes me for a walk. We go to this big house on the corner of Main and Church Street that is the home of a well-to-do white family. The house has a large yard with benches; there are other colored maids taking care of white children. The colored maids visit with each other while the white children play together.

On one of our walks up Green Street to Shake Rag, Sylvia takes a paper bag with her. She finds the right hillside, digs out some dirt and gives me some to eat. I cannot believe that I am eating it. It is not all that bad. I guess she thinks that I need it. Little do I know the colored people believe that eating this soil is a good preventative medicine.

Mother often works at night in the hospital. Sylvia frequently comes and spends the night with Bonnie and me. She bakes my birthday cake for me. It is fascinating when she takes out a hard-earned dime, wraps it in wax paper, places it in the bottom of the pan- then she pours in the cake batter. She says to me,

"Honey Chile, whoever gets the piece of cake with the dime in it, is ah gonna have lots of good luck."

I am hoping it is going be me; if I am the lucky one to get that piece of cake with a dime in it, I'm going to buy two big ol' Moon Pies, one for me and one for Sylvia.

Sylvia lives in Shake Rag- not so far inside, a little down near our home. Her husband's name is Jess. Jess works for the railroad, and boy can Jess sing! I can hear him singing all the way to our house. I love to hear him sing:

I been wukkin' on de railroad
All de livelong day,
I been wukkin' on de railroad

Ter pass de time away.
Doan' yuh hyah de whistle blowin'?
Rise up, so uhly in de maw'n;
Doan' yuh hyah de cap'n shouin',
"Dinah, blow yo' hawn?"

Looking for Sylvia

The years go by, Geri continues,

"It is a cold late winter afternoon in down town Tupelo. It is getting late and beginning to drizzle rain- I am in a hurry to get home; Johnny Payne, my toddler is in my arms, tired and sleepy. As I walk, back to where I parked my car, a colored lady stops me and says,

"Good evening, I know you. You are Miss Geri Payne- a friend of Sylvia. Sylvia took care of you when you was ah chile'. My name is Nora- Nora Barnes. It is so sad to tell you this- I guess you don't know, Silvia is very sick and has not much longer to live. She has cancer real bad. Miss Geri, if you would like to see Sylvia, she is in a house in Shake Rag on the lower end, near Front Street. Sylvia is living with friends, you know- Sylvia never had chillun'."

To hear that Sylvia has not much time to live, I am shocked with sadness- I lower my head, close my eyes and softly say,

"Oh my goodness gracious, I didn't know that- thank you Nora; thank you for telling me this. I will go looking for her right away!" I gently squeeze Nora's hand, touch her arm and say goodbye. She briefly holds onto my hand, releases as she looks into my eyes, nods her head and slowly walks away. With tears in my eyes, I hurry to my car.

My only thought . . . I must find Sylvia, the sweet woman that I love so much. It will soon be dark- rain is falling on the streets as I hurry to my car. I quickly get in the car- place little Johnny Payne in his car seat, and drive to a store to buy Sylvia some fruit. It is now dark and rain is sprinkling a little harder. I must find Sylvia, so I begin my search in the area.

Arriving at Front Street, I stop the car in the area Nora has told me to go. At the first house that I come to, without fear, I walk up the steps and knock on the door; a colored man comes to the door. He is surprised to see me- taken back by my presence, so I quickly introduce myself,

"My name is Geri Payne, I am a friend of Sylvia Johnson who is ill; it is important that I find her; does she live here- if not can you tell me where she lives?"

"Sorry, young lady, I do not know Sylvia, but I would think, if you keep trying doors, someone will know her."

He is so polite and helpful. As I turn to leave, he says to me,

"Misses Payne, be careful of the steps; they are wet and slippery- I will pray that you find Sylvia."

I am now going from house to house knocking on doors. I do not remember how many doors I knock on, but it is many doors this rainy night; finally, a door opens. Again, I ask,

"Do you know Sylvia?" A lady steps out on the porch and points to a house up the street . . .

"That house over yonder is where you will find Sylvia."

I thank her and move my car to the house with Johnny Payne still asleep. I am not afraid to leave my sleeping child in an unlocked car in Shake Rag.

The house is the usual unpainted small house one finds in Shake Rag with a narrow front porch that leads to a front room that is the living room. Often there is a radio playing. Telephones are unthought-of. Living is simple in these trying times. In the back part of the house, there are one or two small bedrooms and a small kitchen. Out back of the house is an outhouse toilet.

As I stand at the door with my hand raised to knock, I pause, feeling the suspense within me. Gently, I tap on the door- lowering my head- I breathlessly wait. I see the doorknob is turning and the door slowly begins to open. The door opens further. Standing before me is a lady wearing a gray housecoat. I see a look of surprise in her eyes; we are speechless as we look at each other. My thoughts are of Sylvia; no doubt, she is thinking:

"What is a white woman doing at my front door this cold rainy night?"

I interrupt our thoughts by saying,

"Please forgive me for coming to your home so late in the day- but I must see Sylvia. My name is Geri Payne."

"Did you say Geri Payne?"

"Yes, I am Geri; Sylvia took care of me when I was a little girl."

"Oh yes, Sylvia has told me about you. My name is Sarah Calhoun; it is nice to meet you; please come on in. Sylvia will be happy to know that you are here. Honey, you just come with me, I will take you to her room."

She takes me to Silvia's room; on entering, she turns on a soft ceiling light. At a glance, I can see the room is neat and clean. Sylvia is lying in a neatly made bed; covering her is a colorful homemade quilt. I can see that Sylvia is being well taken care of. Sarah brings me a chair and places it by Sylvia's bed. I sit down and take her hand; softly saying,

"Sylvia, it's me Geri-you remember me? I'm Geri. Remember, you took care of me when I was a little girl."

She slowly turns her head; I see a little nod of happiness with recognition. Her eyes brighten as she tries to smile. I lay my head on her on her shoulder and hold her. She lies so still, unable to talk. I tell her she looks nice with her beautiful warm quilt, as it is damp and cold outside. I tell her how much I love her and I have thought of her often, as to how she had taken such good care of me. I can see that Sylvia is tired and weak-she drowses off to sleep. I lean over and kiss her on the cheek. I turn off the light and leave the room. Sarah is waiting for me in the living room-giving me time to be alone with Sylvia. I thanked Sarah for her kindness in taking care of Sylvia.

When I get back to the car, Johnny Payne is still asleep. It is a long, sad drive home in the drizzling rain, as I think of Sylvia lying so still under her patchwork quilt. A week later, I go again to see Sylvia. Sarah Calhoun invites me in,

"Come on in honey, let's sit in the kitchen and have a nice hot cup of coffee, we need to talk."

With concern, I suspect the worst. As we drink our coffee, Sarah softly says,

"Sylvia is no longer with us; she has gone to be with God."

I drive away from Shake Rag, and hear the radio announcer say,

"Severe weather warnings are issued for northeast Mississippi!" As I drive along, I sadly ponder the loss of Sylvia- a loss that takes me back to my childhood... when many of us lost our loved ones... in the frightful tornado of 1936- a tornado that brought havoc to our quiet little town of Tupelo, Mississippi.

"The little reed bending to the force of the wind, soon stood Up right again, when the storm had passed over."

Aesop

The Tupelo Tornado
1936 Year of the Rat

Geri has this to say about the tornado that hit Tupelo:

"I remember well the day of the tornado; Daddy has a bunch of us kids in the old car. We are returning from visiting our cousins in the nearby town of East Tupelo. He stops at a gas station to get some gas. He just pulls in when a man walks up and says,

"Howdy, how y'all ah doin'? How much gas y'all want?"

Daddy says, "I need about ten gallon-how much is it for a gallon?"

"Today, it's nineteen cents a gallon. I heah'; though, it may go as high as twenty cents a gallon tomorrah'."

As I watch the gas flow down from the glass container on top of the pump, I hear Daddy say,

"My goodness, ah dollar ninety for only ten gallons of gasoline-that's almost a week's pay. What is this world ah coming to? I'll have to pick three hundred pounds of cotton that make that kind of money!"

Daddy pays the man, turns around and points to the sky. I stick my head out of the car window and look up; I can see the moon and stars disappearing behind big dark clouds.

"Come on now," Daddy says.

"Those dark clouds rollin' in don't look so good. It looks like ah bad storm is ah comin'; we best be gettin' on home."

Daddy drives us home, and we all tumble out and run to the kitchen. We hear the terrible roar of the winds. The back door to the kitchen slams wide open. Buddy, James, and daddy shove an old icebox against the door to hold it shut.

All eight of us children are put to bed with the winds howling around our little house. Girls and boys sleep together in the two beds in the front room. We huddle under the quilts and hold on to each other. The powerful winds have a ghostly rumbling sound of a fast moving train as the house shakes and creaks. We share our fears with each other and try to comfort the younger ones. Mama pulls up a chair between the beds and says,

"Don't worry; this will be over soon; pray the Lord." And sure enough, it begins to quiet down into an eerie silence as the tornado moves on. The question the family has asked ourselves many times: *Why were we spared when so many around us lost their lives?* It is a miracle; the tornado cut a path around our little wooden house and spares our family. So many others in Lee County were not so fortunate.

Daddy gets up early the next morning to join a search party-neighbors helping neighbors gather the dead, white and colored. It is hard to accept the great damage and emotional pain the tornado caused in our little community of Palmetto. Daddy is gone all day.

"Life's most persistent and urgent question is,
'What are you doing for others?'"
Martin Luther King Jr.

Tupelo is hard hit, with two hundred and sixty miles per hour winds. Many homes are destroyed, killing entire families. The actual count of the storm's fatalities is unknown. Shake Rag is hit the worst; homes are devastated as entire families are swept into Gum Pond. After the tornado, many bodies of colored people are found in the pond. It is not known how many people lost their lives as the newspaper reports only the deaths of the white community. The Tupelo tornado could very well be the most deadly tornado in American history.

I say to Geri,

"I hear they found a colored baby alive floating on a mattress in Gum Pond and I am happy for that miracle."

Geri replies,

"Yes, Ray, I am so happy that baby was discovered floating on the mattress that morning after the tornado left our town so torn apart . . ."
Aunt Grace says it is a miracle that I am here.

Aunt Grace
Here I Am!

Sometimes during the summer, I go to Palmetto to stay with Aunt Grace and her family. Uncle Thomas and Aunt Grace have only one child. Her name is Mary Edith and we are the same age. Geri and our sister, Bonnie sometimes also go out to the country to be with Mary Edith so she will not get so lonesome.

Geri asks,

"Ray, do you remember this? Mother sends our sister, Bonnie, and I out to Palmetto on the milk truck. We walk to the Carnation Plant. Mother tells us the milk truck driver's name, with whom we will be riding. He knows who we are and where we are going. We sit up in the cab of the truck and the nice man talks to us as we make all the stops. Aunt Grace more than likely knows we are coming. She is always waiting down by the roadside next to the milk cans that he will be picking up when we get there. It is very common in our days for people to ride the milk truck from town and back, or from farm to farm. Everyone knows everyone along the way.

Aunt Grace is so good to Bonnie and me. She sends us to the country store to buy something she doesn't need. She gives us each a penny to buy a sucker. There are good times at Christmas when we go out to Aunt Grace's farm, and again in the summer when school is out.

Mother says,

'It is time for you to go to Palmetto to play with Mary Edith.'

She knows that Bonnie and I have each other, and Mary Edith has no one to play with.

It snows in the cold Mississippi winter and Aunt Grace put heavy socks on our hands to let us go out to play in the snow. . Aunt Grace takes us down to the frozen pool, with a chair from the kitchen to use for a sled. We slide all over the ice covered pool. I do remember Mary Edith doing that with us. It was a lot of fun for all of us; and Mary Edith seemed to be so happy we were there with her."

Geri says,

"Ray, I think we are closer to Aunt Grace than mother's other sisters. I heard from Aunt Grace about the night that I was born, as she was there and that it seemed inevitable that I might die. They worked with me trying to get me to breathe. She said they were making every effort. Everyone in the room kept trying ways to be assured I was going to live . . .

They stuck me in hot water and then cold water to shock me. Aunt Grace said she was so scared. She was thinking that I might actually die. Nothing seemed to make me come around as I fought to "wake up" . . . Thanks to their extreme efforts for me to live using all the ways that they knew that night . . . here I am!"

"Thinkers do not accept the inevitable; they turn their efforts toward changing."
Paramahansa Yogananda

Geri and I both have a lot of energy and share a common enthusiasm for life. I am glad that Aunt Grace made every effort to save Geri's precious little life the night she was born.

I hear Aunt Grace calling me. She wants me to ride ol' Dolly over to the gristmill to have some corn ground, so that we can have cornbread for supper. I like hearing this as I love cornbread and milk and . . . riding Dolly!

A Business Trade

It is early 1937 - The Year of the Ox

It is in my eighth year of the cotton blossoms of Lee County, a beautiful sight in full bloom, when we move from Palmetto into the town of Tupelo. We do not have much of anything to move. Moving into Tupelo gives me many opportunities to make money. At the age of eight, I have already learned how to trade like a businessman. That is when I bought my little banty rooster in Palmetto on a visit to Aunt Grace's farm. *For you Yankees who don't understand that in the south we call bantams, banties.*

One afternoon, Aunt Grace calls me over to her and says,

"Baby Ray, here's a sack of corn; here, let me help you up on ol' Dolly. Go over to Mr. Miller's gristmill and have him grind this corn so as we can have some cornbread for supper." With a sweet smile she adds,

"Honey, here's a penny for you, so's you can buy yourself one of them big ol' candy suckers."

With the sack of corn sittin' up front, I ride ol' Dolly over to Mr. Miller's gristmill. Dolly is a large workhorse with big hoofs. I am one happy little boy- I sing a little tune as she just plods along. I think Dolly is happy, too.

On the wide veranda white
In the purple failing light
Sits the master while the sun is
Slowly burning;
And his dreamy thoughts are drowned
In the softly flowing sound
Of the corn-songs of the field- hands
Slow...retuning
Oh, we hoe de co'n
Since de ehly' mo'n. . .
Now, de sinkin' sun
Says de day is done.

I see Mr. Miller standing in the doorway of the gristmill throwing corn to his little banty chickens running around the yard. I see one pretty little baby banty rooster with black and white tail feathers that I want to have real badly. That little banty and I keep looking at each other eye to eye as is if we belong to one another. I ride Dolly over to a tree stump and swing down hanging onto Dolly's mane.

"Mr. Miller, suh, how much do you want for that little ol' *ugly* banty rooster?"

That little rooster looks back at me as if he knows something that Mister Miller does not know. Now, I am ah guessing that Mr. Miller is gonna' trade that little banty rooster for whatever the price will bear and that price will be . . . all that he can get. So, he says to me,

"Son, that there is ah mighty fine little rooster; listen at him crow; ain't he pretty? I will let you have him for only a nickel."

He smiles at me and reaches over to pat my head. I step back, dodging under his hand and say,

"Oh, my goodness gracious, ah whole nickel! Mr. Miller, for a whole nickel I can buy a big ol' Moon Pie. Mr. Miller, that little rooster is the *uglies*t chicken I ever did see and besides he crows like a screech owl."

"Mr. Miller," as I look out of the side of my eyes, with feinted hesitation,

"I ain't got no nickel! I only got a penny and I was not gonna' spend that penny today, as I was gonna' wait til' I go into Tupelo and buy me one of them big penny candy suckers."

I can see that with the squint of his eyes, Mr. Miller is holding his breath. He can see his sale is slipping away, so I get a little more daring with the trade.

"Mr. Miller, that little hawk-eyed banty rooster is ah eatin' yo' corn and he don't lay no eggs, and he sure is *mighty ugly*."

Surprisingly, that little rooster turns his head, gives me a hawk-eyed mean look and furiously scratches the ground.

Mr. Miller says,

"Well, alright boy, as I see you really want that little rooster and knowing candy is bad for yo' teeth, I will trade you that little rooster for that penny."

With a dumb-founded expression on his face, as if he had been had and excitement in his voice, he looks at me and says,

"Boy, where in the world did you learn to dare to make trade like that!"

"One in this world, who doesn't learn to be daring in trade,
often misses the excitement of the trade."
Joshiki

I now own this little banty rooster that I name, Biddy because he is so small. My Biddy is one tough little bantam chicken- one of my most important business deals.

Yes siree! You can bet your bottom dollar that Biddy is one smart little baby banty rooster. Maybe he thinks that being smart will keep him out of the chicken pot . . .

Biddy and the Airlift

It is a real hot summer in the middle of *dog days,* when nothing moves but Yankees and flies . . . *so Uncle Thomas says!* I sit on aunt Grace's front porch eatin' a peanut butter banana sandwich and drinkin' a glass of cold sweet tea. I am ah fannin' myself and swattin' flies. Each time after I swat a fly, Biddy runs to it and gulps it down. This gives me an idea. I am going to teach Biddy to ride through the air on the fly swatter and over to the swatted fly and if he does not ride, he don't get no fly. I swat a fly and Biddy comes ah runnin'. I hold him back by pushing against his little chicken breast with the fly swatter. After he gets tired of pushing against the fly swatter, I slip it under his little feet, lift him up, and carry him through the air just like them there stunt pilots ah ridin' on the wings of an airplane. Biddy flies over to the dead fly where he jumps off and grabs his fly.

After a few trials, Biddy learns that the only way he can get to his tasty fly is to be airlifted. Now, he waits to hop on the swatter to be airlifted and gently landed before he runs back to his delicious fly. *I have raised little banty chickens just about all of my life and it all started with Biddy.*

I always have a lot of banties running around our little shotgun house, alongside Kings Creek in Tupelo, Mississippi

I want Biddy to have some company. Biddy too, wants company. He wants some of those little banty hens, so I buy some little hens for Biddy to play with. I also buy a couple more little banty roosters. Biddy does not like any more little roosters in the yard. The little roosters fight all day long over my little banty hens until the little roosters just get all tuckered out . . . and the little hens get all tuckered out from being tuckered out by the little roosters. *You know what I mean!*

To this day, here at Rose Hill Plantation in Okinawa, Japan, I have banties running around my gardens. Banties are part of my youth, my life right out of the south. A little mother banty hen is the best mother in the whole animal world to take care of and protect her little ones. I saw a little

banty hen fight off two sparrow hawks at the same time to protect her little ones.

In the middle of the Great Depression, for us there is no TV, no Nintendo . . . Life is simple, and in our world of Lee County, Mississippi, life is often extremely challenging, yet most entertaining.

With the innovation of my new human-powered stunt plane ride for Biddy, he has learned teamwork with follow through to get what he wants.

Things did not go as well when one day, playing with Mary Edith, I decide to ride her bull, Ferdinand . . .

"One person can have a lot of ideas and innovations, but without the teamwork to follow through, these cannot be implemented."
Stan Shih

Dolly and Ferdinand the Bull

Uncle Thomas' big mare, Dolly loves for me to ride her. So, I go as often as I can to visit Mary Edith and ol' Dolly on Aunt Grace's farm in Palmetto. For the fun of it, I ride Dolly around the house and under an old chinaberry tree. I swing off of her onto a limb and old Dolly just keeps plodding on around the house. When she comes back around again under the chinaberry tree, I drop off the limb onto her back and around we go again. Dolly seems to like it and so do I.

Uncle Thomas has a young red bull that Mary Edith and I name Ferdinand. He lets us pet him while he licks salt from the palms of our hands. Ferdinand is a gentle little bull, until one day I say to Mary Edith,

"You hold onto that halter, lead Ferdinand over to that tree stump as I'm gonna' jump on and ride 'em'."

Mary Edith says as she leads him to the stump,

"Goodness gracious, you gonna' ride Ferdinand?"

Ride Ferdinand I sho' do . . . for about twenty seconds. That little bull isn't so gentle after all. He is a whirlwind of a tornado! He takes off running, jumping, bucking, and twisting from side-to-side as I hold on for dear life. With a hard buck and a fast twist, he must have thrown me for a country mile, so I thought . . . I land on my back and the hurting is terrible around my tailbone for about a week. Ferdinand the bull and I both agree for sure that I will never do that again!

Something else more exciting is soon to happen. Would you believe it- I'm ah goin' to ah weddin'.

Cousin Elbert's Weddin'

My daddy says, "Baby Ray, my cousin Elbert Payne is having a gittin' married celebration. Cousin Elbert is ah marryin' Lauren McGillicuddy and this is gonna' be some gittin' married party- you come go with me to meet some of yo' cousins!"

The small winding dirt road is taking us higher up into the hills. Along the side of the road, the dogwood trees have taken on shades of red and purple. Chattering squirrels dart among the branches feeding on the small red berries. Every now and then, I see a small, unpainted wood house or log cabin with a wisp of smoke rising from a smokestack into the autumn air.

After what seems like to me a never-ending road into the hills, we arrive at cousin Elbert's house. There are wagons with the horses and mules tied to trees. A few old Model-T open cars and trucks are scattered along the side of the road.

I see they have moved the rocking chairs from the front porch and made room for the band- including guitars, fiddles and a washboard. A man wearing a store bought straw hat- his pants held up by wide well-worn brown suspenders- is tapping with sticks on a crosscut saw making a clanging rhythm. A large woman with a bright red bonnet- smoking a corncob pipe looks like she has sampled too much from the jugs of moonshine is slapping large spoons together on her knees and her hands. Some ol' man with a long beard is rubbing the washboard up and down sompin' fierce- the fiddles are ah whining away. Gnawing on my *roastaneer,* sitting on the edge of the porch, I am bug-eyed!

The music is fast and the fiddlers are high in pitch. Cousin Elbert, daddy and all them others are now ah dancing around in front of the band. The women are twirling around and ah clapping their hands; Cousin Elbert's coon dogs are sitting up and ah howling like mad. The men are stompin' their feet and jumpin' around like cats on a hot tin roof. They are keepin' time with the music; some ol' man is standing on the porch stompin' his foot sompin' wild as he is ah hollerin' out a song ... about mountain dew.

"Down the road from here
There's an old hollow tree
Where you lay down a dollar or two
If you hush up your mug,
They will fill up your jug
With that good old mountain dew.
They call it that good old mountain dew
and them that refuse are few
You'll go 'round the bend
But you'll come back again
For that good old mountain dew."
Bascom Lamar Lunsford

Daddy and the others are passing around a jug of corn likker' taking big long swigs. The more of that mountain dew they drink, the more that ol' man on the porch hollers out songs, the faster the fiddles whine; the faster they sing and dance, and the more the dogs howl!

"Dance as if no one's watching, sing as if no one's listening, and live everyday as if it were your last."
Irish Proverb

Being from a large family guarantees we will have a goodly supply of playmates and a week after the wedding I meet up with two of my other cousins for some fishin' fun.

What a Wonderful World

As children growing up during the Great Depression, we live in our own world. It is a world of hardship, a world with little money, a world of fantasy and make-believe, yet we bring much happiness to our world as we make our way with creative minds- grasping every opportunity that presents itself.

In Palmetto, I often go fishing with my cousins, Buddy and Billy Anderson. We catch the freshest fish that taste just right when we fry 'em right there next to the pool. Our fishing poles are simple, but they work- a thin bamboo cane, some string, a cork from a vinegar bottle, and a fishhook. If we don't have store bought fishhooks, we make our own by twisting a straight pin into a hook. We add a small lead weight below the hook.

We bring with us a small skillet, some lard for frying (I will tell you more about lard after we do some fishin'), salt, pepper, and cornmeal. We are good at catching little perch and sun bream. After we catch enough, we gut them and then with a few shakes into the pool to clean them, we sprinkle them with salt, pepper, and cornmeal. We make a small little fire and we fry up our fish on the bank of the pool. The crispy fish taste so good with our store bought Moon Pies and RC Colas.

The lard we fry our fish in comes in either half-gallon or gallon tin pails. We use the pail lids as our racing wheels. We hammer a piece of tin into a small flat shape with two wings tips turned up. This piece we nail to the end of a thin strip of wood. This is to guide the lid as we go racing down the dirt road pushing and guiding the rolling lid ahead of us to see who can go the furthest without losing the wheel.

We also turn our lard pail lids over with the edges down to catch the wind and fly them high up into sky to see who can fly the highest and the furthest. We have flying disc wars to knock another's space ship out of the sky. Using our exciting imaginations, we are Buck Rogers and Flash

Gordon racing through the skies.

"It is possible to fly without motors, but not without knowledge and skill."
Wilbur Wright

Lard also comes in small heavy waxed cardboard cartons. One would be surprised at our knowledge as to how skillfully we cut those waxed cartons into the body and tail of a glider. We cut the body of the glider, wings and rudder and then insert the wings and rudder into the body of the glider. When thrown into the air, the glider plane flies so well, and it brings joy to our lives as we watch our gliders soaring at tree top height.

"Those who, relying upon themselves only, not asking for assistance to anyone besides themselves, it is they who will reach the top-most height."
Buddha

Now, one of my aunts can draw back her tongue and squirt snuff juice thirty feet! She can knock a blue-tail fly off the rear end of a northbound mule . . . *without squintin' an eye!* Her

Favorite snuff is *Straight Shot*, although I must say . . . it is not a favorite of the blue-tail fly!

Snuff comes in little tin cans or brown square glass bottles. Matches come in penny boxes or nickel boxes. We harness a snuff bottle with small strips of cloth; the snuff bottle becomes our tractor. We hitch our tractor to an empty five-cent matchbox; the matchbox is our wagon. We haul dirt and build roads not knowing we are also building young creative minds.

No, we kids did not dip snuff; only some of the adults did, but no doubt, it had an influence on some kids in their later years . . . like professional baseball players.

We are good at using our imagination and making our own toys. In those days one had to rely on one's creative thinking and ingenuity. It takes some skill to make sling shots that can hit a cottonmouth on the head from a distance . . .

The Wild Wild West
Cowboys and Indians

Before we are old enough to make enough money to buy guns, we make slingshots for hunting doves and rabbits for the supper table. Since there are always a lot of old used automobile rubber inner tubes lying around, we kids all have useful slingshots which we can easily make. Nearby we find a tree limb with a small forked branch. We cut the forked branch about two inches from the stock about hand-held size.

Next, we carve a small narrow indentation just below the tops of the forks and fold the ends of the strips of rubber, one-at-a-time on each fork; then continue by tying with string that holds the rubber strip tight with the indentation carved into the wood. On the other end of the two strips of rubber, we cut and tie a small oval-shaped piece of cut leather in which we can place a small stone. Placing a stone in the leather holder and pulling strongly back on the rubber strips, we release the leather and giving a little wrist spin, the stone shoots strongly through the air for a long distance.

One would be surprised as to how accurate we are with our slingshots. Our slingshots can make a cottonmouth real mad! *Wait til' I tell about them there cottonmouths!*

Not only are we accurate with our slingshots, we have other ways to hunt. We make our own bows and arrows. We cut a branch of a tree for the bow. A strong limb that will bend when pulled with a cord tied at each end. Our arrows have small metal points that we hammer out and affix to the end of slender reeds. We tie small feathers to the other end notched to fit the cord. Our arrows are accurate for hunting rabbits and shooting fish in the shallows of a creek. Robin Hood would be mighty proud of us.

Before we know it, we are putting our bows and arrows to even better use . . . playing Cowboys and Indians. We use our bow and arrows, our self-made pistols and our imagination to bring our games to life.

On some occasions, daddy drives us out to a cow pasture, where someone has set up a screen and projector. *Could this be the start of drive-in movies?* What we like the best is the Cowboy and Indian picture shows.

I enjoy seeing the good guy on his horse chasing the bad guys who are in a pick-up truck. The good guy's horse outruns the truck and jumps into the open back bed of the truck. "*That was some horse and after that, I think that movie directors have wild imaginations!*"

To play cowboys and Indians, we make our own guns. We take a kitchen knife and cut a small tree branch that has a curve, which becomes the handle of the pistol, the longer part- the barrel.

We are cowboys; we ride the frontier; we chase bank robbers and we chase Indians and they chase us as we slap our thighs, and chase each other yelling as loud as we can. Most of all we have great imagination... riding new frontiers in the wild, wild west...

"There's a little cowboy in all of us, a little frontier."
Louis L' Amour

Rubber Gun Wars and Snuff

As we get older, we make rubber guns and have what we call rubber gun wars. With a handsaw, we cut a piece of wood into a long barrel about a foot and half-feet long, and sometimes longer. One end of the wood we carve into a hand-held stock the shape of a pistol. To that, we affix a strong wooden clothespin. Next, we tie one side of the clothespin with a strip of rubber to the stock. All cars have rubber inner tubes in the tires and a lot of available ones are lying around which we cut into thin rubber strips. We tie a thin strip of rubber into a knot making a long ring that we stretch from the end of the barrel back to the stock at the clothespin. When the clothespin is squeezed, it will release the rubber band and shoot quite a distance, and land often hard enough to put a welt on a body.

Rubber gun wars are exciting and daring to be sure, and we chase each other hoping to get a good shot at the "enemy". I sneak up on my friend Bobby Beggs and release the clothes pin- my rubber goes high and hits him right on the back of his neck. Yelling his head off, because it must have hurt like the dickens, Bobby chases me all the way back to my house. I climb up in the peach tree. This gives me a good advantage to shoot him again. He goes home howling. That ends the rubber gun war . . . for the day

Our brother Buddy chews Red Mule chewing tobaccer. Buddy drives his car with the window down. From time to time, Buddy spits his tobaccer' juice out the window; I learn fast that if you are ah sittin' in the back seat behind Buddy, you had better not have your car window down!

Unknown Destinations

As we get older, making our own wagons is not so difficult, although a little hazardous; sometimes when riding, the result can be a bruised elbow, skinned knee or worse.

The body of the wagon is sawed from a single piece of 4x4 lumber about four feet long. The rear axle is of 2x4 wood and bolted solid to the 4x4. On top of the rear axle, we nail a small board for a seat. The front axle is a 2x4 wood with a single bolt through the center of the 2x4. This swivels on the 4x4 for turning.

Our wheels are cut from small tree trunks that we cut about the same size in circumference. We drill holes in the center of the wheels for the axels. The axels are metal rods, which are attached with large horseshoe nails under the 2x4's. Bicycle tires are cut and nailed on the bottom of the wheels with roofing tacks. A rope is tied to the ends of the front axle for pulling and to guide the wagon left or right.

As we sit on the wood seat of our wagon, we pull tightly on the rope at the same time we brace our feet strongly forward on the front axle. This gives us some stability as the wagon races down the hill with dare devil excitement for the ride of our life. We are on our thrilling journey to our unknown destination- our wagon has no brakes. **NO Brakes!! . . . .**

We make it through most of the day without any incident. On the last trip of the day we daringly give ourselves a running start and jump into the wagon heading down the hill. We make it past the first little curve, but on the second twist of the road we lose control and go tumbling over the hillside into the bushes. All bruised and scratched up, we lay there on the side of the hill. I stand up and feel this pain in my elbow and I can't move it. Hugh and I hobble back home.

Mama looks worried as she takes me to the hospital and says,

"Now you have broken another arm; this is the second time-what are you going to do next?"

The doctor puts my arm in a cast. We return home and I say to myself, "What a day!"

I look over at Hugh, shake my head, point to my arm and say to him,

"Hugh, I'm ah gonna give you my share of the wagon. I don't want that wagon no more!"

Looking at my arm he says,

"Are you crazy? I ain't gonna ride that wagon no more either!"

The next morning, I take my wagon over to Willie J's and say to him,

"Willie J, I'm sorry about those banties. I'm ah' gonna give you and Joel Rakestraw my nice wagon. It will give you the thrill of your life!"

"Life is a journey of thrills where the destination is unknown."
Joshiki

We like to make our own wagons and have fun; however, some of us do take time to attend church on Sundays. At least I do, and I attend a lot of churches on Sundays . . .

I Done Got Religion

In Tupelo, I done got religion, I go to church every Sunday. I go to all the churches on a Sunday, well almost all, but not anymore to that there Catholic Church.

I don't think anybody goes to church any more than I do. I am the fastest kid in town when it comes to going to church. Timing is important. First, I go to the Methodist church near my home and then the other churches, one after the other. Like I say, timing is important. I grab small food items, stuff my pockets, stuff my mouth, take long drinks and lickety-split I'm off and running to the next church.

At the churches, Sunday school classes end about the same time. I cannot be late at any church. As the classes end, if I am late, I will miss out, as those greedy kids will have done ate them all and there is nothing left to drink in the pitchers.

Usually, I am never late, and you can hear those kids' folks ah yelling, "There comes that kid again!"

Like I done said, those Catholics don't have to worry none, 'cause I ain't ever going back to that church. At that church, I had to stand in line with other kids. They weren't smiling; I don't know why they weren't looking happy, as it is Sunday and I am always happy on a Sunday, going to church.

The kid ahead of me gulps and walks away. It is my turn. It looks like the man gives us only one cookie at a time and he is so stingy, because that one is so small and the drink is tiny. He says, "Open your mouth, son."

Now, for what I think I am about to get, opening my mouth is not difficult at all. He puts a dry wafer in my mouth, mumbles in some foreign language, and then tells me to drink from a silver cup and . . . I do.

I gulp, with open mouth, blink three times and wobble away. Like I say, I will never go back again to that there church . . . for cookies and kool-aid. What have I done wrong? . . . I must remember to ask God in my prayers.

As I lie in bed this Sunday night, I look up and ask God,
"What have I done wrong?"
Then a voice out of the night says to me,
"This is going to take more than one night!"
Joshiki

Oh my goodness gracious . . . does he know about my school days?

Slow Learners

June, July and August are my favorite months. The end of May is always the happiest time of my life. School is out! I will have the next three months to have fun and make money. What a wonderful time of year!

There is lots to do, fishing, frog gigging, rabbit hunting, swimming in the creeks, and my favorite past time . . . making money!

I love selling flowers from the cow pastures and picking blackberries to sell to the ladies in our little town. They make those wonderful southern blackberry cobblers.

I also make money-collecting bottles. Soft drink bottles are worth two cents each, milk bottles five cents, and my least favorite way to earn money- picking cotton in that hot Mississippi sun. *In the 30's and early 40's in rural Lee County, Mississippi, my days in Tupelo alongside of Kings Creek are much like the scenes from Tom Sawyer and Huckleberry Finn. The tranquil setting is pretty much the same- the times a little different.*

As the long days of summer shorten into fall, my mood begins to change. I go into a depression, dreading the first day of school. The terror I feel is overwhelming. I am horrified that I will not be able to keep up with the other kids in school. I am not looking forward to the scolding I will get for looking out the window daydreaming. My punishment will be to stay after school to write, "I will pay attention in school." one hundred times. The school bell rings, and Charlie McCarty yells,

"Come on, Ray! Let's go down to the creek and catch us some fish." Bobby Beggs says,

"I got me a new cane fishing pole."

"Let's go!" yells Ed Dickerson.

They can see the unhappiness on my face as I reply,

"I can't go. That teacher done told me I gotta' stay after school."

This is a terrible punishment for me. While my friends are hurrying down to Kings Creek for some fishing before dark, I have to stay after school and write one hundred times, 'I will pay attention in school'. After a few times of having to write, "I will pay attention in school", I get smart; I pull some fishing string out of my pocket, tie three slanted pencils together and write three lines at one time.

The teacher did not say I could not write three lines at a time. Everyone-*should* try it! It looks as if I have written one line at a time. I did not cheat; I merely increased the production time by two thirds. Later, I asked my daddy if he thought that it was all right and my daddy said,

"That man, Henry Ford, would be mighty proud of your production line, son."

My teacher must have thought,

"That kid may be a slow learner, but he sure is fast with a pencil."

My teacher does not know about my production line. I hurry down to Kings Creek to do some fishing with my friends before the sun sets. "Hey, y'all wait for me!"

Is it A.D.D. (Attention Deficit Disorder) that handicaps me from getting an education, *or is it the enchanting mysteries of Kings Creek?*

Sometimes in the midst of talking with my friends, a friend would touch the elbow of another and say, "He's not listening." My mind was somewhere else. At the time, I did not know I had A.D.D. All I knew was that I was considered a slow learner and a dreamer. I never felt like I was slow, instead, I was innovative. I learned to compensate for my lack of ability and to rely on my common sense.

"Sometimes it is more important to discover what one cannot do than what one can do."
Lin Yutang

Miss McKinley
Annabel Lee

I cannot remember the highest grade I completed. My younger sister, Geri thinks I finished the seventh grade. If I remember correctly, I was in second grade for two years, another two years in the fourth grade and held back in the seventh grade to go to summer school. Summer school was like a prison sentence to me. I left that school and never went back!

"I have never let my schooling interfere with my education."
Mark Twain

I remember the only year of schooling that I ever liked was my year in the fifth grade. Miss McKinley is my teacher. I like Miss McKinley, as she teaches me prose and poetry. I like poetry and I recite for her poems by Henry Wadsworth Longfellow, Walt Whitman, Edgar Allan Poe and others.

Miss McKinley's eyes look as if they are filling with tears; she has a distant look on her face. She is far, far away from this classroom. *I wonder what she is thinking about* . . . as I recite "Annabel Lee" by Edgar Allan Poe.

It was many and many a year ago,
In a kingdom by the sea,
That a maiden there lived whom you may know
By the name of Annabel Lee;
And this maiden she lived with no other thought
Than to love and be loved by me.
I was a child and she was a child
in this kingdom by the sea;
but we loved with a love that was more than love -
I and my Annabel Lee;
With a love that the winged seraphs of heaven

coveted her and me and this was the reason that, long ago,
in this kingdom by the sea.
A wind blew out of a cloud, chilling my beautiful Annabel Lee;
So that her highborn kinsman came
And bore her away from me,
To shut her up in a sepulcher
In this kingdom by the sea.
The angels not half so happy in heaven,
went envying her and me.
Yes! That was the reason.
That the wind came out of the cloud by night,
Chilling and killing my Annabel Lee.
But our love was stronger by far than the love
of those who were older than we
of many far wiser than we
And neither the angels in heaven above.
Nor the demons down under the sea
can ever dissever my soul from the soul
of the beautiful Annabel Lee.
For the moon never beams without bringing me dreams
of the beautiful Annabel Lee;
and the stars never rise but I feel the bright eyes
of the beautiful Annabel Lee;
And so, all the night-tide, I lie down by the side
of my darling, my darling, my life and my bride
in the sepulcher there by the sea,
in her tomb by the sounding sea.
Edgar Allan Poe

I write some poems of my own, and for that, Miss McKinley praises me. She gives me great encouragement when she tells me how much she likes my poems. For a wonderful brief time in a schoolroom, Miss McKinley brings to me much happiness, and an eagerness to learn that I had not previously encountered in school.

"Poems relax the mind; they are like daydreams filled with happiness."
Joshiki

I did not know much about reading until Miss McKinley's 5th grade; with much patience, Miss McKinley has taught me to read. Now, I read everything I can get my hands on. Often at night Mama calls out,

"Ray, its two o'clock in the morning- you have to go to school in the morning!"

Learning to read has opened up a whole new world of opportunities to seize, and in this world of opportunities, I find many exciting things.

God Bless You Miss McKinley!

"The Gods cannot help those who do not seize opportunities."
Chinese Proverb

Nanny

A whole new world is open for me since I've learned to enjoy books, and in this world I find many new and wonderful things. I like to read about animals. I love animals! I read about horses, snakes, pigeons, chickens, and goats. I am learning about and enjoying my new found friends. I am now beginning to think about Willie J's crossed-eyed nanny goat that I like so much

Nobody in all of Lee County, Mississippi has a pretty cross-eyed goat like Willie J's nanny goat. She is the nicest goat I ever did see. Willie J done told me- his goat is easy to take care of, as she will eat just about anything. I think to myself, *"Mama will like this goat."* More so, I want that nanny goat, so this morning I go over to Willie J's house and say,

"Willie J, y'all ah been ah wantin' real bad some of my banties. I will trade you six of my banty chickens for that one goat- that's three pairs of young pretty colored banties for one ugly old goat. With three pairs of banties, you will have a lot of pretty banties . . . just like me!"

"Well, Ray since you keep ah hankering for my nanny goat and my mama done told me that my goat has gotta' go! You gotta' deal! I wanna' have a lot of banties-just like you!"

"Willie J, I'll be back this afternoon with three nice colored pairs of my banties."

After leaving Willie J's house, I am scratching my head about this trade. Everybody likes my banties; I don't want nobody raising banties in competition to my banties. Lemme' think; I gotta' do something.

"Here you are Willie J, just like I promised; here's three pairs of pretty banties, a pair of black, a pair of white and a pair of red; now, you have some good little banties! Three pairs is more than enough. You won't need no more. Now, let me have my nanny goat before my mama comes ah looking for me; it's gettin' near supper time!"

Later, my friend Pete Goosman done told me that my friend Willie J ain't my friend no more, "Willie J says, He don't like you no more, and neither does he like those three pairs of colored banty roosters. He said, three of them has their tail feathers cut off! He says, the three that have their tail feathers cut off look like hens, but they ain't hens, because they keep on ah crowing and they don't lay no eggs!"

I name my new goat, Nanny. I think that her real name is a nice name . . . Nanny! Nanny is a little old and she don't give no milk; her left ear won't stand up; she don't have much teeth and like I say, she's a little cross-eyed. She is an awful pretty goat!

Mama don't seem to mind my goat. Mama says Nanny is like an automatic grass cutter as she eats the grass and weeds around the house. But, all that changes the day my nanny goat rises up on her hind legs and eats mama's favorite go-to-town yeller' dress hanging on the clothesline. That dress is mama's good dress. It has green frills; so, I'm ah thinking those frills, they kinda' looked like grass, *you know what I mean*; anyway mama doesn't like my goat anymore. She yells . . . "That goat has gotta' go!"

I trade my nanny goat to Joel Rakestraw for a bicycle. Joel is also my friend; well he was, until I traded him that nanny goat!

Feeling sorry for my sister Geri because I had done gone and sold her little red sports car, I give her my nice bicycle that was only missing one small part.

Geri is still mad at me, as she yells at me,

"How do you expect me to ride this bicycle? It don't have no handle bars!"

I yell back,

"That was a fair trade with Joel Rakestraw; that nanny goat don't have no horns neither! Just wait till' that goat eats one of Joel's mama's dresses! That nanny goat will be ah coming back and that goat is all yourn'!" *Willie J and Joel Rakestraw will soon be ah gettin' their revenge.*

Miss McKinley's Band

There is a lot going on in our little city of Tupelo, Mississippi; at least I think so- *y'all know what I mean*... everybody knows what's happening in Tupelo; well most everybody does. Aside from the usual chatter about the football team, there is a lot of talk about the coming school play. The whole town is buzzing with excitement, and the talk turns to the students of our school . . . Milam Junior High. People are telling one another about us puttin' on a school play titled ... *"STRIKE UP THE BAND!"*

The whole town will be coming to see it! They say the Mayor is coming and guess what... I'm ah gonna' be in the band! Miss McKinley's fifth grade class will be the musical band in the play. Miss McKinley tells us that over the weekend we are to make our own band instruments.

Miss McKinley makes suggestions as to who is to make what instrument to play. Miss McKinley asks me if I could make a xylophone. I ask her,

"Would y'all kindly say that again!"

Miss McKinley explains the xylophone to me and suggests ways for me as to make a nice one that will surprise everyone and bring enjoyment to our audience. Now, y*'all know what she means, 'cause, I sure don't!* But I'm soon gonna' find out!

Monday we bring our band instruments to school for practice. Earl Moody- empty handed, cocks his head and gives Miss McKinley that quizzical look. Miss McKinley gestures with her hand outstretched and softly says,

"Earl, you may ring the cowbell."

Billie Jo Stoker is supposed to be the star of the show with her flute act ... but Joel Rakestraw done gone and stole the show with his drum set.

Joel got one of his mamas' galvanized washtubs, two water buckets and his grandpa's bedpan. He has turned them all upside down on a plank across a cane chair. He has cut himself two sticks, with knots on the ends, out of small tree branches. Joel is a big show off, drumming away.

He must be thinking that he is Gene Krupa. For cymbals, he takes two of his mama's cooking pot lids that he bangs together. Joel sure knows how to make music!

Ed's got a washboard that he rubs up and down keeping time with Joel's drums. Bobby brings his juice harp. (Jew's harp) Charlie is good on his harmonica as he rings out the melody, and Miss McKinley gives Earl a cowbell to ring. Mary Bell Stoker's younger sister, Billie Jo, plays a flute that she herself has made out of a short length of bamboo cane.

Billie Jo taught by her big sister is real good at playing the flute.

We all are in our places on the stage of Milam Jr. High school . . . the night of the great performance is finally here! *"STRIKE UP THE BAND," Miss McKinley's Band!*

I'm not so envious any more of Joel's drums as a lot of people in the audience are looking at my nice xylophone that I have made. I am mighty proud of my xylophone. It was kind of easy to find different sizes of glass bottles, a gallon jug, a quart milk bottle, some small vinegar bottles and two empty bottles of Old Crow Whiskey from the widow Hawkins' garbage can. I look out into the audience; I know they like what they see. I am ready to play for them.

I have arranged my bottles side by side with a cord across a pole that I have erected. The bottles I filled with different levels of water.

During practice, my xylophone lets out some nice musical mellow sounds, as I ever so gently tap them with my sawed-off broom handle.

Here's what happened last week. Willie J wanted to trade me an old pair of roller skates that he done lost the key to, some of his marbles and would you believe it, his nice store- bought spinning top, for three pairs of my banty chickens. I had looked him straight in the eye and told him that I ain't gonna' do it! I told him I would trade him six of my pretty banties for his old one-eyed goat- and I did. Willie, J. ain't happy about this!

Now guess what? Would you believe it . . . Miss McKinley has done gone and made Willie J our orchestra leader! He proudly walks to the center of the stage, bows to the audience, and turns to face us.

As we stand on the stage, someone dims the house lights, and turns the spotlight on us, Miss McKinley's Band. I look out to see six hundred pairs of eyes looking at us. This makes me a little nervous and . . . what if Earl rings the cowbell at the wrong time? With Earl, anything is possible!

Our conductor, the great Willie J, slowly raises his arms high over his head, with wand in hand-his right arm is rising higher and higher. He points the baton at me.

This movement sets Earl off. Earl vigorously+ rings the cowbell! The great conductor, Willie J is looking straight at me. He gives me a hard look, coming down fast with his wand as he glances at Joel Rakestraw, nods and yells . . . "Now!" At this signal, Joel loudly bangs his washtub.

I jump and nervously come down hard with my broom handle on my xylophone's biggest water bottle, the gallon jug. Water explodes from the jug and floods the stage; I lower my head and stare at the water with my mouth wide open.

There is silence from the audience, which seems like an eternity. You could hear a church mouse tiptoeing. In the front row, the fat lady wearing a large purple hat, starts laughing! The rest of the audience joins her, laughing and loudly applauding.

Earl has a big grin on his face as he is joyously ringing the cowbell! I raise my head and look out over the audience. I am happily smiling and throwing a kiss to the fat lady as I begin to tap lightly on my remaining xylophone . . . Our band-Miss McKinley's Band . . . plays on!

On the Warpath

David Nash lives in the south side of Tupelo down from Reed's shirt factory, on the north side of Kings Creek, down where the creek runs under Highway 45. His family is kinda rich, as his daddy is ah plumber.

We don't have toilet problems down on our end of Kings Creek, 'cause we have an outhouse. We don't mind the fragrant smell of our outhouse as it is kinda like the dogwood blossoms along the creek. During the summer though, when things begin to heat up, it is best to bring a clothespin. I guess our outhouse don't make David's daddy no money.

Now, David's daddy has done gone and built David an Indian teepee. It has bears, buffaloes and an eagle painted on the sides. We want to play Indian in that teepee, but David won't let us play in his teepee. We decide to hold our tribal war council and we Chickasaw Indians come to the decision- its war!

"Bobby, you run over to Mr. Moore's and get some of them turkey tail feathers lying around."

Bobby says,

"Well, what if there ain't none lying around?"

I yell back,

"Well, there is' turkeys there, ain't there? And those turkeys have tail feathers, don't they? Bobby, why do you think God gave you those big feet and yo' cotton pickin' hands for? Now, go get those turkey feathers! Charlie, you bring some of yo' mama's red lipstick."

"Ray, are you outta' yo' cotton pickin' mind? My mama's gonna' kill me if she thinks I'm gonna' wear her red lipstick!"

"Don't be crazy, Charlie; you're gonna be an Indian, not Snow White! Charlie, bring some of yo' daddy's black shoe polish. Earl, you bring one of yo' daddy's corncob pipes.

I'll go out into the field along the creek and fetch us some rabbit *tobaccer*."

And just like that, we are now brave Chickasaw Indians on the warpath!

We sit around cross-legged and apply our war paint. For me, it is a red circle around my left eye and a black circle around my right eye. I paint a red X on my forehead and a black one on each cheek. We all look ferocious until we begin to pass around the rabbit tobaccer' war pipe. We gag and turn pale- we don't want to be Pale Faces . . . we are now Chickasaw Indian Braves and we are on the warpath.

The sun is sinking low through the willows as us Indians on the warpath sneak up on the south bank of Kings Creek. As Indians, we have our own hand-made bows and arrows. We have soaked the tips of our arrows in coal oil, *what them Yankee's call kerosene.* We strike a match, pull back our bows, and slice the air with flaming arrows. David Nash's teepee goes up in flames. We are dancing up and down yelling like real Chickasaw Indians on the warpath, until Mr. Nash's front door bursts wide open. A shotgun sound splits the air, fired up into the sky. We Indians quickly make our retreat through the cornfield. That burning teepee and Mr. Nash's shotgun . . . ends the Chickasaw Indian War!! *A few years back, Geri and I visited the Nashes. I apologized for leading an Indian attack on their father's teepee. Mr. Nash had recently passed away. The family was happy to hear the story of the Indians' attack on David's teepee.*

It is exciting to wear our war paint and shoot our flaming arrows; yet, we have more exciting days coming to our little town.

Guess what-the fair is coming to Tupelo! This is an exciting time for all of us kids. Even my little sister, Geri, is jumpin' up and down yelling,

"I'm gonna' ride the merry-go-round!" She is asking,

"Are y'all gonna' ride the rocket? I think that's scary!"

The Mississippi Alabama Fair and Dairy Show

This is what Geri remembers about the Fair and the Picture Show

Geri says, "When the Fair comes to our town it is bigger than Christmas. We wait for it all year and the nearer the time comes, we are all busy, trying to make some money so we can go. On Children's Day, we can get in free. Otherwise it is not free.

The Ringling Brothers Circus comes in by train Sunday night. They set everything up Monday. Today is Tuesday, Children's Day. We meet at the school and walk to the Fair Grounds. Our Tupelo High School Band leads the way as we walk down Main Street. It is a great day!

The sideshows and rides come in by truck, but what is most exciting is watching the circus unload on Monday!

Bright and early, on Monday morning, Daddy takes us to see the Ringling Brothers Circus unloading. The circus people come along with the train and we can see them getting off the train and walking down to the Fair Grounds leading the ponies and elephants. We are in awe as we see ferocious tigers, lions, bears and other wild animals unloaded in cages and boxes and then pulled to the fair- grounds by local farm tractors.

In the morning and afternoon, the circus people practice their shows down at the grand stand. We can see the acrobats swing on the high-up swings throwing and catching each other. As they practice, they use nets. Later, for the show, there are no nets. The show is truly exciting as they walk way up on the high wire with no nets below. It is fun to see the girls ride the ponies and elephants around; the lions and tigers when they roar scare us, but we like it. Watching them practice is like seeing the circus and it is free to watch!

The Midway is where the rides and sideshows are. In addition, there is the freak show and the midget show where the little people sing and dance-it is great entertainment!

I am not old enough to go to the fair on Children's Day because I am not yet in school. Daddy takes me to the fair. The smell of cotton candy, hot dogs, and hamburgers is in the air. The Merry Go Round . . . such beautiful music as I have ever heard. Daddy let me ride one of the horses and it is wonderful as I go round and round with the wind in my face.

As we walk down the midway, I see some amazing rides that I am too little to ride. People are playing games."

"Step right up", the man says.

"We walk the midway passing sideshows where people come out on the stage in front of the big tent and give a preview of the show. Crowds gather for the preview, some go in to see the show, some walk on to the next show.

Daddy and I are standing in front of a show tent. I am watching the pretty ladies in their beautiful evening dresses dancing and a man saying,"

"Step right up folks; this is the famous Sally Rand Show."

"The beautiful, vivacious, dazzling Sally Rand is out front; a crowd is gathering. I see daddy is talking to some of his cousins, all men. I am busy looking at the pretty ladies in their swirling long dresses on the outside front stage. All of a sudden, the outside preview show ends. At that moment the crowd starts moving; daddy holds my hand as we and his cousins walk inside the show tent.

Inside, daddy and I sit down in seats alongside his cousins. All I can think is- I am again going to see the pretty ladies in their beautiful silk and satin dresses dancing. The men start hollering and whistling. It is then that I hear daddy holler,

"Gal, drop that fan!"

"When we get home mother says,

'What did you and your daddy do at the fair today?'

All I can say is, 'Mama, daddy was ah yelling **'Gal, drop that fan!'"**
"To show her how daddy yelled, I ran around yelling over

and over **Gal, drop that fan!** Mama did not get mad at daddy. I never ever heard our mother and daddy having a cross word with each other.

I do not think watching this show of pretty girls was planned as daddy just met up with his male cousins and they got caught up in a spur of the moment thing. But, they did seem to have fun. At the time, little did I know that this show was the very famous Burlesque Queen Sally Rand Show!

The Fun House with scary things jumping out at us and laughing at ourselves in those crazy mirrors is so much fun for us. We act silly inside, but to get out of the fun house, there is only one way. As we leave, we step on something hidden, and air blows up our dresses as we scream and laugh trying to hold them down. There is no getting around the big blast of air if you want to get out of the fun house.

The Motorcycle Show where men are riding at high speed around and around on a big round wooden wall is mighty exciting. We think they might fall riding around the side of the wall at those high speeds, but they never do.

Besides the Merry Go Round, are other fun rides: the Caterpillar, the Whip and the Ferris wheel keep us laughing and ah yelling. There are crazy Bumper Cars and . . . The Rocket! I am always afraid to ride the Rocket until I say to myself.

"Ain't nothing gonna scare me!"

I ride it, screaming and yelling like everybody else. I get off and walk away laughing.

Many, many games to play to try and win something align the fairway; toss a penny in a dish, or pick a floating plastic fish for a prize. In a booth is a funny man with a mustache who can guess your age and weight. Stopping at his booth, I hit a pad with a large wooden hammer to make a metal ball go up a wire cable towards a bell.

The man says that if I ring the bell, I will get a prize and I say to him,

'Mister, how do you expect a little girl like me to ring that bell!'

There are places where we can buy souvenirs like Mexican hats, walking sticks, umbrellas, twirling batons and small china dogs and cats. We have saved our money for a long time to enjoy this fair with all the exciting sights and sounds- this wonderful fair and its many thrilling attractions!

All along the midway are lots and lots of eating places with good things to eat: Ice Cream on a stick that they roll around in melted chocolate; next, they roll it around in a dish of nuts covering the chocolate- it is one of our favorites. Cotton candy, hot dogs, corn dogs, hamburgers, roasted peanuts and popcorn in colorful stands dot the midway walk. I like hearing the men in the hamburger stands sing out their song:"

"Hamburgers, hamburgers
Get em' already and they are all red hot
Onion in the middle an' pickle on the top
Hamburgers, hamburgers!"

Geri adds, "When I run out of money, I go to the exhibit buildings made out of brick from our Tupelo brick factory. Many Tupelo houses are made out of Tupelo brick.

In the exhibit buildings are many different things to see from collections of all types to flower arrangements. Judges are nearby to look over all of the exhibits. They give out ribbons for 1st, 2nd, and 3rd place. The Blue Ribbon is 1st Place. Farmers and their wives bring in their livestock and homemade goods from all over the surrounding Mississippi and Alabama counties. I am sure that this is why they call the fair, the Mississippi Alabama Fair and Dairy Show.

In one of the buildings, we see prize-winning cattle. Judging the milk cows must not be easy as Mississippians are well known for their good milk cows. On exhibition in the next building are calves, goats, sheep and pigs raised by 4-H young people. Some stalls are decorated with shiny blue ribbons- the proud owners standing nearby.

We walk along to the next building where chickens, ducks, geese, turkeys and other fowl are sounding off in a farmyard chorus. They even have some pretty banties. Ray likes this exhibit.

I like the building where the farm wives bring in lots of home canned foods. Jars and jars of colorful fruits and vegetables and all kinds of tempting pickles. The wives can most everything that their families eat throughout the winter.

They show their handmade quilts, tablecloths, many pieces of lovely hand embroidery, and crocheted dresses, etc. As at home, most farmers' wives hand make their own clothes that they wear. Their handiwork is truly beautiful as we linger along the rows inside the buildings.

The tables display fresh vegetables in season. The women display interesting arrangements of fresh flowers that grow in their gardens. I will always remember the variety of these attractive exhibits for the rest of my life."

Geri tells me about the day that her sister Betty wanted to go to the fair . . .

The Picture Show

"One of my older sisters, Betty is a teen-ager and like all teen-agers, she and our cousins are excited about the fair. I think the fair must be a good place to meet boys. Mama believes that if you don't have a job, you have to have some kind of responsibility. Mama works at night at the hospital; so, she has Betty baby-sitting me and it is Saturday night-the last night of the fair. Betty has to come up with a plan to baby sit me and not miss out on all her fun at the fair. What a plan it is! Betty and our first cousins, Francis Ruth Hall and Beatrice Bates, most likely have made arrangements to go to the fair early so they put me in the picture show. I am as happy as any little girl can be.

The Strand Picture Show is on Main Street, not too far from the fairgrounds. The Strand is showing a Porky Pig Cartoon, World News, the serial Flash Gordon and two full-length cowboy pictures, The Yellow Rose of Texas starring Roy Rogers and Carolina Moon starring Gene Autry. They are two of my most favorite movie stars. Roy Roger's horse is Trigger and Gene Autry's horse is Champion. The picture show makes me content as my sister and my cousins knew I would be. They even bought me some popcorn-anything to make me happy!

Well, I sit through both picture shows and fall asleep during the last one. When I wake up, it is all dark inside the theater and I am scared, because I have heard that there are big rats running around after the picture show closes looking for popcorn. I slowly walk up the aisle; it is pitch dark. I make it to the front door and it is locked! Now, I look around and I am really scared!

The Strand has French doors with small glass panes. I peer through with my nose pressed on the glass, and I can see people walking up and down on the sidewalk. They are coming and going to the fair. I start to bang on the door and no one hears me; feeling trapped, I start to cry.

Through my tears, I see Betty and our cousins walking up and down the sidewalk. They have this worried look on their faces. Again,

I start crying and ah hollering really loud and I'm banging on the glass panes. Oh my goodness gracious, they finally hear and see me and run to the door. Betty stays outside near the door; our cousins leave and come back with a policeman and the manager of the picture show. They unlock the door and let me out. I am one happy little girl again. I run up to them and say,

"Did y'all ride the Rocket? '"

Buttercups

"Ma'am, please buy my flowers; they are the prettiest buttercups. I picked them fresh early this morning and they are only five cents a bunch. They are so pretty, and Ma'am, you are mighty pretty yourself this morning! Especially for you . . . two bunches for only nine cents!"

"Why, of course darling, I will buy two bouquets of your pretty flowers." I get a big hug.

I learn early in life that ladies like pretty flowers. I also learned early in life our Southern ladies like pretty compliments and lots of hugs. *Ma'am, you sure are mighty pretty this morning!*

During the spring, buttercups grow wild out in the cow pastures west of Kings Creek. Buttercups are what Yankees call daffodils. I tie my buttercups into little bunches that I sell to the office ladies in Tupelo. To hold my flowers, I have cut a cardboard box down and tied each end with a cord that I put around my neck. This places the box of flowers in front of my belly. This leaves my arms free to hand the flowers to the ladies, to hug them and of course . . . to collect the money.

"Sorry, darling, I would just love to buy your pretty flowers, but I don't have nothing to put em in." *The loss of that sale taught me a lesson in marketing!*

In town, we have a little five and dime store, *Kuhn's*. I decide to go to Kuhn's for flower vases. Kuhn's has exactly what I need- some pretty little flower vases for five cents each. From then on, I have a few vases in my flower box. I buy them for five cents each. How much money do you think I charge for my flower vases? Ten cents? Fifteen cents? No, I sell them for five cents. Yes, I sell them at cost and that makes them affordable for my customers.

Unbeknownst to me at this young age, it is a precious lesson for those exciting business years to come in East Asia.

The Lyric Theater

The Lyric Theater that we call the "picture show" is right up the street from our home on the corner of Court and Broadway. George Douglas' pretty aunt is the ticket seller at the picture show.

After school, I race to the picture show to ask Miss Douglas if I can get her something, as she cannot leave the ticket window to go to the store. With a twinkle in her eyes and a soft smile, as sweet as Tupelo honey, she says to me,

"Oh, Ray, you are so nice to me. You are always thinking of me."

When Miss Douglas talks to me that way, it makes me wish I was grown up.

"Thank you ma'am, Miss Douglas, whatever I can do, I will always be here for you."

"Darling, you can take this nickel and run down to the store
and get me a Moon Pie."

"Yes ma'am, I will be right back!

Miss Douglas, my friends tell me that in the picture show Pinocchio is so funny, that his nose just keeps right on ah growing when he is ah telling ah lie!" *I gulp as I say this.*

When there is something, I want . . . there is no kid in Tupelo as fast as I am.

Here you are, Miss Douglass; I ran as fast as I can go.
I almost ran out of breath; but for you, here I am!"

"Well, thank you darling; you are fast. You can go on in the picture show now to see Pinocchio."

Sometimes good things just don't last forever. Would you believe it! Some of the other boys caught on as to why I left the school door on the run, lickety-split racing across the school grounds; no longer interested in shootin' marbles or spinning tops.

They now know that my secret is no secret anymore; it is a race as to who will get to the Lyric first to offer Miss Douglas their services in return for a free show. On the afternoons that I miss out, it is because I had to stay after school and write on my tablet one hundred times, *I will pay attention in class.*

It is time for a new plan.

1941 The Year of the Snake

As I run from school to the Lyric picture show, I grab a few flowers out of some lady's front yard. The ladies' beautiful yards have lots of pretty flowers of every color. I hide my pretty flowers in a paper poke so as those copycat boys won't discover my secret.

"Here you are, Miss Douglas; these flowers are all for you!"

"Oh, thank you, darling! These flowers are so pretty; would you please go get me a Moon Pie?"

"Yes ma'am, Miss Douglas . . . I sure will, Miss Douglas, I will be right back!" *Lickety-split and I am back!*

"Oh, darling, thank you. This is my favorite Moon Pie, Banana! You may go in to see the picture show. I will wait for you tomorrow . . . only for you!"

"Yes ma'am, Miss Douglas; sometimes I may be a little late from school, but I'll be here!" *I am again in control. I will keep my good service a secret! . . .*

"The secret to success is good service!"
Joshiki

Peanuts, Ten Cents!

The one and only time I ever went to a baseball game in my whole life, was to sell peanuts.

In our little town of Tupelo, on the corner of Main and Front Street an old crippled man sells peanuts and candy from a small wood stake-bodied red wagon. Someone in the early morning pulls the old man in his wagon to the street corner where he sells his goods. Late in the afternoon, he asks any of us kids if we can pull him to his home and we do.

His peanut bags are five cents each and packed tightly. So tight they are as round as softballs. One day he says to me,

"There's a baseball game down at the fairgrounds. You and your two little friends take these peanuts to that there ball game and sell them for five cents. I will give you two cents a bag, and you give me three cents."

And, I say, "Yes sir, Mister!"

These bags of peanuts are packed so tight, I think they are gonna' burst. I take one and unravel the ears that are twisted on both sides of the bag at the top and flatten the bag out. Now it looks twice as big as before.

I say to my friends Bobby Beggs and Earl Moody,

"Let's go sell peanuts!" And sell peanuts we did! We sell them all! "PEANUTS TEN CENTS! PEANUTS TEN CENTS!"

I learn early in life: "S*ell for whatever the market will bear!"*

East Tupelo, Mississippi

Mayor Martin and City Government

Life is not easy in East Tupelo during the war. Mama buys for breakfast what she can afford, one day at a time. It is usually a can of salmon . . . it is expensive, nine cents a can! She makes salmon patties and mixes them with flour. Some days it seems as if there is more flour than salmon. After breakfast, we go to our East Tupelo School.

Sometimes, we kids get a free lunch at school. Today, they place rice on my plate, but I refuse to eat it- we never eat that stuff at home.

"Teacher, I ain't gonna' eat that there rice!" I push my plate back a ways. I can be starving, but I will not eat this rice.

Finally, to get me to eat rice, they make some brown gravy, pour it over the rice and sprinkle a little salt and pepper on top- just like we do at home, when we have mashed potatoes with gravy on top.

"The secret is in the sauce!"
Joshiki

Our school has kids of many different ages-first grade through twelfth grade. East Tupelo is not a part of Tupelo. We are a separate little town. As one drives east out of Tupelo and enters East Tupelo, a sign reads:

EAST TUPELO MISSISSIPPI
Unincorporated Town

Our Mayor is Mr. Martin and he owns the grocery store; he appreciates my hard work of going around East Tupelo picking up empty Coca-Cola bottles and other soft drink bottles wherever I can find them; for that, I get two cents a bottle refund. Mayor Martin also pays me well for my position in city government-he pays me five cents for removing the dead dogs that get killed on the road by a car.

This pays more than finding Coca-Cola bottles, but Coca-Cola bottles are easier to find. *You know what I mean.* When I see a dog on the side of the road, I stand on the other side of the road and wait for a fast car ah coming and then on my side of the road I hold out a bone and call *"Here doggie, here doggie. Naw'! You know I would not do that! I am only joking."*

My city government position is to tie a rope to the dead dog, drag it off down to the creek, and bury it. I am a political appointee. Sometimes, Mayor Martin, as a special bonus gives me my favorite, a Moon Pie, for my dedication to work in our city government. I guess I can proudly say, "I am officially East Tupelo's Dead Dog Catcher!"

The money I make collecting Coca-Cola bottles or pulling dead dogs off of the road helps me to buy a little extra food as I am usually always hungry. When I am not working, I am usually in school, except for the days that I cannot resist the warm summer sunshine and the urge to go fishin' down at Kings Creek.

At our school, my little sister, Geri, has got a new friend. She says his name is Elvis Presley.

A Shy Boy Named Elvis

Miss Camp and Blue Moon over Kentucky

In our school, there is a shy boy named Elvis Presley. He likes my sister, Geri, as a friend. Geri and Elvis are in the same schoolroom. I do not see a lot of Elvis, except now and then playing or walking with my sister Geri, as I am older than he is. In their sixth-grade school picture at Milam Junior High in Tupelo, Elvis is the only boy wearing overalls.

In later years, Geri told me,

"No one knew we were going to have our picture taken that day. It was not a picture taken by the school. Our teacher, Miss Camp, took our picture with her Brownie Camera." *I ask Geri to tell me more about Elvis. Geri says,*

"The first time I remember seeing Elvis was at East Tupelo School (known later as Lawhorn School). I was in the second grade. One afternoon, the school bell rang and I was just poking along the hallway.

When I went outside, all the kids had left the school ground. One kid who I didn't really know was on the swings, looking at me. He said,

'I'm a monkey'; at the same time, he popped a yellow pencil in his mouth and started to swing. I laughed as he did look like a monkey with a banana between his teeth. He slid off the swings and started walking along with me. It was as though he was waiting for me.

As I learned later, Elvis was very shy and other kids sometimes picked on him. He surely picked me out to walk home with every afternoon, because on the school ground I would never let anyone pick on another kid. Something my older brothers had taught me- never take anything from anyone. Elvis really needed an older brother like the ones I had.

Now, I never start a fight on the playground, but I settle a few. So every afternoon after last bell, Elvis is usually there and we walk home together. When we get to a certain place, he turns and walks in one direction, and I another. I really never knew where he lived. Didn't know until later years that Elvis's daddy was in prison and he and his mother were living with family further down on Canal Street from where we lived"

Geri continues her story; "I meet people through the years who say they know Elvis and after I ask them a couple of questions, I know that they never knew Elvis. Once, I met a man who said he was his cousin. I asked him, 'What was Elvis' mother's name?' He could not tell me. One Sunday morning, I was watching a special on T.V. and I saw a woman who says she goes to the same church as Elvis. I know this is not true. I was friends with her when we were young girls and I know she did not go to the same church as Elvis. We lived next door to our Uncle Gus's store on Canal Street. We moved back to Tupelo when I was in the middle of second grade. I was so glad to be back at Church Street Primary School, and soon forgot about the boy I had walked home from school with. Until, one day at Milam Junior High School, on the first day of school, I saw a familiar face on the playground, and it was Elvis. His hair was combed and parted, not a hair out of place, not like most boys. We were in sixth grade by then and in Miss Dewey Camp's class, a teacher every one dreaded. She turned out to be my favorite teacher. She showed no favoritism to any child- rich or poor. She made us answer roll call by reciting a Bible verse and that did not hurt us one little bit. Miss Camp was the first teacher to start calling me Geri instead of Geraldine, as I really hated my name, Geraldine. She was the only teacher who made me stay in after school. A boy behind me had poked me in the back trying to tell me something; I turned around, and although I never spoke a word, Miss Camp said I was talking in class. So after school I had to write: I will not talk in class ever again one hundred times on the blackboard. It was a pleasure to write I will not talk in class ever again, trying to be neat and use very good penmanship, because that is the day Miss Camp and I bonded. I do not know how Miss Camp got the reputation of being a mean teacher- but it must have been some country club kid, because she treated everyone alike and she did not have a teacher's pet. Little class programs are always fun in Miss Camp's class. I can still hear her say,

"Elvis is going to bring his guitar and sing for us."

And, I can hear myself saying, *"Oh no, not that kid again!"*

I did not like 'hillbilly' music- that is what we called it; now they call it 'country music'. I like the big band sound, something my big sisters were always jitterbugging to while listening to the radio. On the playground, when we are playing dodge ball or some other game,

I turn around and there is Elvis standing as close to me as he could. Kids would come and go in school; Elvis was one of them. Little did I know his family had moved to Memphis, as some people did in those days, because there were more jobs in Memphis. I guess his daddy had gotten out of prison by that time. As before, I see his mother picking him up from school as we walk out of the schoolyard. I once asked Johnny Tillotson if he ever knew Elvis and he said he didn't. I told Johnny that I never thought Elvis would die so young and that someday I thought I'd look him up and we would sit down and talk about old times. Elvis touched so many lives. He was a dear sweet boy and really very shy until he got on stage and did what he loved most.

I didn't see or hear from Elvis for many years until one morning I was listening to a Memphis radio station, and the announcer says,

"Here from Tupelo, Mississippi is Elvis Presley with "*Blue Moon over Kentucky*."

That afternoon I stopped by a friend's house and she said,

"Did you hear that song this morning by Elvis Presley?""

"Yes, I did."

"Is that the same Elvis Presley we know?" I said,

"I think that it is."

After that, it was just Elvis. I didn't run after Elvis, nor did I follow him that much, but I did go to the premier of his movie "Love Me Tender" at Lowe's theater in Memphis with friends, as I was living in Memphis at that time. The last time I saw him in person was at the Memphis airport when he was on his way back to Hollywood to start filming "Love Me Tender." He walked right up to me and called me by my name, the name I have always hated, 'Geraldine'.

I replied to Geri, "Elvis was a good down home Tupelo, Mississippi boy, one of the nicest people that one could ever hope to meet. He loved to sing and play his guitar. From humble beginnings, Elvis created a life of his own that touched the lives of many people worldwide. He was a very compassionate, generous and caring man."

"All that Adam had, all that Caesar could, you have and can do.
Build, therefore, your own world."
Ralph Waldo Emerson

Praise the Lord and Pass the Ammunition

There's a War Going On

We move back to Tupelo from East Tupelo; I am glad as there is not much I can do to make money around East Tupelo. Some kids mow lawns but everybody knows, I ain't gonna' do that . . . I hate work! Anyway, in East Tupelo, I didn't look at pulling dead dogs off the road as work. I guess you could just say that I was in business for myself . . . the *disposal business.*

In Tupelo, I have more good chances to make money. In East Tupelo, like I said, pulling Mayor Martin's dead dogs down to the creek is not work. It is business . . . although it is a stinking business! I would much rather be selling buttercups- they smell better.

During the winter, when flowers and blackberries are not available for picking, I sell hardware. Now, what I mean by that is soft drink bottles, milk bottles, wire coat hangers and the best of all . . . scrap iron.

My goodness gracious, would you believe it someone had dumped a red Radio Flyer wagon in the trash? My "new" Radio Flyer put me in the business of transporting and selling scrap iron. A new Radio Flyer costs almost three dollars and I ain't rich like them kids in Highland Circle. All this Radio Flyer is missing . . . is the left rear wheel.

I soon take care of this problem by simply cutting a piece of wood and tying it on the left axel with bailing wire. This evens out the level of my wagon to support the load, and as I pull my wagon, people can hear me coming.

"Mister, can I have that old iron lying beside yo' house; it ain't doing you no good. I can help you take it away. It ain't worth nothing!"

I do not mind the cold winter air; the thought of making money keeps me warm. I learn quickly that copper brings in the most money.

Then it happened!

My scrap iron moneymaking business done come to an end. All my great collection is now a donation for the war effort.

My little sister, Geri yells at me,

"Shame on you, Razor Blade! All of us kids are bringing scrap iron to the school ground to help win this war that our brothers are fightin' in. Look at you! You are trying to line your pockets with cash like you always do. For the love of making money, you are out selling that scrap iron! Don't you know that they use scrap iron to make ammunition? She scolds me real good with her hands on her hips and her legs spread apart in a defiant stance . . .

"Don't you know that those Japs bombed Pearl Harbor?"

I listen to Geri; she has a lot of common sense for a little kid. Now, Geri knows just as much about my moneymaking ways as I do. She often tags along when I am looking for things to sell, and is often helping me to make money. From now on, I take my scrap iron to school and pile it on with the scrap iron that the other kids bring. Praise the Lord- we are doing our part for the war effort.

Firmly fixed in my mind by Geri, we are gonna' fight our enemies-the Germans and the Japanese. We all need to help in every way that we can . . . We are gonna' win this war!

"Better to fight for something than live for nothing."
General George S. Patton

What Time is it?

One morning, while pawing in the pile of scrap iron on the school grounds, I find an old alarm clock. The hands still run when the clock is wound up. I also find a large, short chain that I attach to the clock. I attach the clock and chain to my waist. Now, I have a jumbo pocket watch! I am the clown for the day. All the other kids think that I am so funny and so do I . . . until the alarm goes off in the middle of class. *Ring! Ring! Ring!*

Here I am again after school is out, while my friends go outside to shoot marbles and spin tops, staying in the classroom to write a hundred times, *"It is time to be good in school."*

After school, many times in the evenings we played Monopoly.

Monopoly

This is what my little sister Geri has to say about Monopoly:

"When we were kids, we had a Monopoly game and we played it for hours on end. This game taught us a lot about handling money, buying property, going to jail, getting out of jail, and about community giving.

Ray, being the oldest of the group of kids still at home, is always the banker. It is my desire to be the banker, as Ray always wins. But later, I learn that it is not because he is the banker, but the mathematical and calculatoring way he plays the game."

I thought about what Geri said . . . Caculatoring? Now, I think my little sister just invented a new word, but it sure makes sense to me! If mathematics can be mathematical, then why is it that calculating, cannot be calculatoring or even *caculatorical*? This is common sense!

"Are you listening, Mr. Webster? When are you gonna' get with it in your dictionary? Like the way we talk. I ain't gonna' stop using ain't, just because you say' *ain't'* . . . ain't proper!

No doubt, we down in Mississippi that speak good English have been using 'ain't' forever. So, put ain't in yo' cotton-pickin' dictionary. Just because you don't like it, I ain't gonna' stop using a word that we grew up with and so did our daddies and our granddaddies. Ask my brothers and sisters and all of my cousins if that ain't so!"

Some people like Mr. Webster just don't know how to properly talk southern English. *Now, back to what Geri had to say.*

"Ray taught me never to rent if I could buy, but if you don't have money, you cannot buy. If you have money, buy up property like utilities, railroads, high rent properties and quickly put houses on them. Once they are landed on, you will get paid! Then you will have more money to buy more properties. Ray likes money and knows the ways and means to get it. I will see a lot of his money-making adventures as he travels down the road of life.

Every Christmas I donate a Monopoly game to Toys for Tots, hoping there is a Ray Payne out there somewhere."

"The first step towards getting somewhere is to decide that you are not going to stay where you are."

J.P. Morgan

Geri's Roastneers

'Roastneers' is what we call young plump corn down south. It is tender and has a sweet taste when picked young, then roasted. When just out of the oven, it is best to smear roastneers with freshly churned butter. Now that is livin'!

For you Yankees that don't understand our way of life . . . it is not roasting ears- it's *roastneers*.

Now, this is what Geri has to say about what was her roastneers:

"There was a cornfield across from Kings Creek when we lived on West Main Street.

One day Mother said, 'Geri, why don't you go across the creek and get us a mess of *roastneers*?' I looked at the creek and decided that I could never get down the creek-bank and then cross the creek and come back up the other side, and then back down and back up with an arm full of *roastneers*. I decided to go across the bridge and then down a small bank by the highway. It was a pretty good climb with an arm load of *roastneers*.

Now, our Mother was most likely looking at that cornfield all summer and knew the time was right for *roastneers*. She said, □Now, be sure to get the younger ears, and make certain they□re plump; so, I went across the bridge and down the bank and into the corn field. As I had never picked an ear of corn in my life, I remember how the corn stung my fingers as I was picking it and I thought, I hope I□m getting it right. It was quite a load for ten-year-old arms. As I was climbing back up the bank to the highway with the armload of corn, a car came by. Just my luck for a car to come along as in those days there wasn't a lot of traffic. The car pulled over to the side of the highway. The man inside the car opened the car door leaned out and said,

'Little girl, that is my corn!'

He commanded me in a gruff mean voice,

'Put that corn on the floorboard of my car.'

I did what he told me to do. He scared me to death. I put the corn in his car. Quickly, I turned and ran for home. I arrived home fairly out of breath, and told Mother what the man did. I was really shook up about the ordeal and Mother did not make too much out of it. But, we did not have *roastneers* for supper that night.

All of my life, I thought about those *roastneers* and that mean old man in that car. Many years later, I came to the conclusion that the corn field did not belong to him and he was playing a dirty trick on a little girl. He got the roastneers away from me, and probably laughed all day about intimidating a little girl and taking her *roastneers*. Guess his kids had *roastneers* for supper that night."

If I had been older, I would have watched out for cars coming down the road. Didn't think I was doing anything wrong going after some *roastneers*. I thought Mother knew the man who owned the corn and knew it would be okay with him. I think about that afternoon every time I see a cornfield.

Ray is now calling me, "Hurry up, come with me and let's go collect Pepsi-Cola bottle caps . . . come on let's hurry!" And I think to myself,

"What's next?"

Geri's Red Sports Car

"Razor Blade," now this is my sister talking. *She still calls me Razor Blade, as some of my friends did, because I was so thin.* This is what she had to say about her little red sports car that she remembers so well and will never let me forget!

"Razor Blade, I remember you would say to me,

'Geri, let's go over here to this gas station; they have a cold

drink box. Put your hand in and take out the Pepsi caps.

We only want the Pepsi caps. Hurry, we have to go to another place and get all the caps there before somebody else does.

Now, come on, Geri, run!'"

Stores, gas stations, and corner grocery stores had drink boxes or as they are called today, soda machines. My hands were smaller than Ray's. My six-year-old hands fit right into the box that caught the caps.

"Ray, what are you going to do with all these Pepsi caps?"

"Never mind- we have to hurry and get more . . .

Come on, Geri"

Geri continues:

"Little did I know that there was a contest going on for collecting Pepsi-Cola bottle caps. There was a prize for the top collection turned in. The prize was a red sports pedal car. Buckets full Pepsi caps were collected by Ray and me all around our little town of Tupelo."

"He won it! He won it!"

I shouted as I danced around the room. Ray brought the little red sports pedal car home and set it in the middle of the living room floor. He said,

"Look, Geri, this car is too small for me. I'm gonna 'give it to you." I was so thrilled and could not wait to ride in it.

It was a wonderful car. I got in the car and peddled it across the room. I was enjoying my little red sports car. I suddenly hear the noise of a real car driving up to the house and I look out the window and see a big black car in front of the house.

A tall man gets out of the car walks up to our door and knocks. I had never seen this man before, but his name was Mr. Douglas; the same man that I hear people around town whisper about being so rich. People say he lights his cigars with a five-dollar bill.

He says to Ray,

"How much do you want for that car?" *And right then and there, Ray, you sold my first sports car right out from under me. I think you sold it for twenty dollars. That was the most money I had ever seen. Mr. Douglas said that he wanted to buy the car for his children. I was happy that his children were going to get the car; after all, I got to ride in it once!*

What made me so happy and proud was that you had won the car, with my help. Over the years, I think about the Douglas children and wonder how they liked their red pedal car that they did not have to earn in any way. I think some children are just spoiled and don't have to work for very much at all."

I said to Geri,

"If I remember correctly, the car was a sports car; the pedal car was red with whitewall tires and was larger than the normal pedal car.

You are right in calling the car a *sports car*, as it had curved fenders and looked different. It was a sports car with a fancy dashboard. Every kid in town wanted to win that sports car. It was given away at the Lyric picture show as a Pepsi-Cola promotion. I remember you and I ran all over town for days collecting those Pepsi-Cola caps. Geri you collected more than anyone in town did and you gave them to me. Many people were at the picture show for the drawing including George Douglas, the rich boy who was my age, and he wanted that sports car in the worst way!

Geri, as you know the Douglas' children were all adopted. George and June were a little closer in age, Michael, a little younger. When George turned sixteen, his father gave him a brand new Plymouth convertible for his birthday. George ran away from home with the car! He said he wanted to travel. The police found him over in Arkansas out of gas and out of money. George told me that his daddy sent him just enough money to buy gas to get back home.

The Douglas' lived in a big colonial home over on Jackson Street- you know, where the rich people live. When we were in our early teens, George's older sister, Joan dyed her hair red and she was so proud of her hair as she walked in front of George and me. I was so impressed with the color change and innocently asked,

'My goodness is it red all over?'

She quickly pulled up her dress- my eyes almost popped out of my head!

In later years, I think the Douglas' fell on hard times. George went with me to New Orleans to join the Navy. He was accepted and I was turned down because my arm was crooked at that time. In the early sixties, George passed through Okinawa during his tour in the navy. It was some time in the late sixties when I last saw George; he was a bartender over on Gloster Street in Tupelo.

"Geri, it is good to know that you enjoyed your nice new red convertible car ride across the living room floor at least once before the arrival of Mr. Douglas and his twenty dollars."

The question I hesitate to ask,

"Geri, when I sold that little red sports car for twenty dollars, did I give you any of that money or did I just pat you on the head and say, '*You are a good little sister.*'

"Razor Blade, you didn't give a dime! You had me help you carry that red sports car out to Mr. Douglas' car!"

I watched you carry my shiny little red sports car out to Mr. Douglas' waiting car, and then you took me to the corner drug store and bought me a Hershey's Chocolate Bar to make me happy."

"Geri, you're lucky I didn't charge you a nickel for the ride!"

Geri is good about remembering stories from our childhood days that I just don't remember. She also remembers stories that our daddy told us that I find quit amusing . . .

The Fortune Teller

Geri said, "Daddy had a large one-eyed black and white bulldog that had lost one eye in a fight with a big ol' yeller tomcat. One day, someone stole the dog. Daddy went to see a fortuneteller, a colored woman who lived in Palmetto. She told him who had it and where he could expect to find it.

He got in the car and drove to the house where she said it was, and sure enough, the bulldog was chained- sitting on the front porch. Daddy stopped the car in front of the house, whistled and called his name. The bulldog's ears stood straight up. He was so excited to see daddy that he strained against the chain until he broke free. He ran straight to daddy and jumped into the car. Daddy calmly drove off with his bulldog. Do you remember this story? Daddy used to tell us some really good stories.

Here is another story that I remember daddy told me. A young man visiting our older brothers stole mother's wedding ring. He took it downtown to a jewelry store in Tupelo and sold it. Daddy went to the same fortuneteller, and after asking daddy some questions, she told him who had taken it and where it was in Tupelo. Sure enough, when daddy went to the jewelry store, he found mamma's ring and got it back. I remember he came home carrying a box of plums and mama's ring." *Geri reminds me of more of daddy's stories,*

"Razor Blade, do you remember when all of us kids were in the car going down a dirt road when daddy points off in the distance to a round silo?" He says,

"See that round silo over there-that's where a man ran himself to death." We are immediately curious and say,

"He did? Daddy, why did he do that for?"

Daddy, with a twinkle in his eyes replies,

"He was running around and around trying to find a corner to pee in!"

As Geri recollects some of her favorite childhood memories she says,

"Do you remember eating plums from the many plum thickets in and around Tupelo? All of us kids knew where every plum thicket was. In the early spring, we like to pick green plums and eat them with salt. In the summer we sell the ripe plums in lard pails. People would buy quite a few and make plum jelly!"

"Yes, Geri, I do remember that plum jelly. Mama would spread it thinly over some bread for us- what a treat!"

Geri's memories make these past times so clear in my mind. She says,

"I picked blackberries straight from the bushes, and only once do I remember selling them. Most of the time mother would say,

'Geri, why don't you go pick some blackberries and I will make us a blackberry cobbler.'

And boy, I ran to the blackberry patch nearby our house on West Main Street and filled my little pail. Nothing smelled more heavenly than a fresh pie from mama's oven.

At other times we took canned carnation milk and whipped it, added sugar and had whipped cream on the ripened blackberries. Delicious!

For another treat, we had an old molasses can. We put carnation milk, sugar, and flavoring in it and then set it into a pan of ice and with the bail of the can we would switch it back and forth and make ice cream.

The other night, I was thinking about how we took crackers and placed marshmallows on top of the crackers, and put them under the broiler of the gas stove. The broiler toasted the marshmallows to a golden brown. I make some of these occasionally now, and I still like the good taste."

Thank you, Geri for the memories!

Frog Giggin' an' Yankees

The sun is sinking low over the hills to the west- casting streaks of orange colored light through the cottonwood trees alongside Kings Creek. The moon is slowly rising from the east. Off in the distance, we can hear the call of the bullfrog: *Belly deep, belly deep, belly deep!*

"Y'all come on," yells out Ed Dickerson,

"Let's hurry on down to Kings Creek. It'll be dark soon. I got the carbide lights and Bobby's got the tow sack to put the frogs in. Y'all got yo' gigs?" *Now, I'm ah thinking'. You can bet yo bottom dollar that big city Yankee boys don't even know what a frog gig is. I am ah guessing that they don't know that the gig is on the end of a wooden pole . . . you know, kinda' like a broom handle about six foot long. The gig has three to four sharp prongs, with a notch cut near the end into one side of each prong. When we gig a bullfrog, the frog cannot pull off the gig. I'm ah wondering if Yankees know what a tow sack is.*

I say,

"Wait a minute Ed, I'll run into the house and get my sixteen gauge double barrel shot gun. I'll load it with bird shot for close range; those cottonmouths are gonna' be out, too. You know this time of year they get mighty cantankerous.

They're out looking for those frogs, too!"

Mama yells out the back kitchen door!

"Now, you boys be careful of those snakes . . . you hea'!"

"Listen at that frog, *belly deep*, *belly deep*.

That bullfrog is a dead giveaway with that loud belly deep.

You would think that if he learned to keep his mouth shut, he wouldn't be in the frying pan!" says Bobby.

Ed says,

"Listen at 'em. There he is! He's a big one, sittin' there on that flat rock at the edge of the bank. That's a big ol' frog . . . I got the light on 'em.

Ray, gig 'em before he jumps!

That's it! The light's on 'em. Now, we got 'em!"

We fill that tow sack with bullfrogs in no time. They are jumping around in that there tow sack like two pigs in a poke.

We go back to the house where mama throws some lard into her cast iron frying pan- and heats it up. She sprinkles on some cornmeal- salt and pepper – and commences to fry up our frog legs for some good down home eatin'. She sets down a large platter of hush-puppies with a plate of fried green *tomaters* . . . and a big pitcher of sweet tea

"You boys come and get 'em and don't you forget to wash your hands!"

As we fill our plates from mama's platters in the center of the table, I see on the counter mama's coconut-bananer' puddin'. We dive in, smacking our lips, eating our fill until we think we will croak. Mama is passionate about her southern cooking. That fact makes me a very happy southern boy.

"Find something you're passionate about
and keep tremendously interested in it."
Julia Child

Now, I want to stop right here and now, before there is a big problem. We need to let Yankees know- if you are gonna' try this good southern food; you don't eat the whole frog!

Before we sit down to enjoy our southern finest, let me tell you something and especially for you Yankees: Mama cuts the legs off below the back of those frogs and then she cuts off the feet. The bodies and feet of the frogs, she throws out the back door for the cats. If you Yankees don't have a cat, give them to your mother in-law as a gift.

Now, sumpin' Yankees should know, "Don't get scared when those frog legs are jumping around in the fryin' pan! They ain't gonna' bite y'all. It's just natural when they mix with that hot lard. Y'all Yankees would jump too, if you mess with that there hot lard! Now, I'm ah thinking . . . Yankees don't know what they is ah missing! There's nothing better tasting . . . than a mess of fried frog legs and some of mama's coconut- bananer' puddin'!

Now, sometimes our talk around the table leads to Yankees. We never forget 'em! Our daddies talk about 'em; our big daddies talk about 'em and their daddies talked about 'em. There's just some things down south that we'uns just don't fergit! Yes sir, we never stop talking about those damn

Yankees. It's not just because they talk funny. There is another reason; my daddy said it was a war of northern aggression; it was them there Yankee soldiers marching all across our land, stealin' our crops, and ah burnin' our homes. They caused a terrible war and we ain't likely to fergit it. That's right! We southerners know South Carolina did fire the first shot at Fort. Sumter like it says in our schoolbook, but it was in self-defense!

"You know, Ed; I don't think them Yankees would like frog legs!"

Ed laughs and says,

"You know, Ray, when that frog is a croaking *belly deep*, don't you just picture that a Yankee would be ah thinking that that frog was a telling him that he outta' be standing in the creek *belly deep*."

We all laugh at that. We like laughing at Yankees!

We like telling funny jokes 'bout Yankees. We never git' tired of it.

Sompin' else about Kings Creek, we have a lot of cottonmouths . . .

Cottonmouths
All Shook Up

Down south, we call water moccasins, cottonmouths. *Now, let me tell you*, they are mean and deadly snakes. They can kill you! You had better not go poking at one. When they are mad, they coil back and raise their heads and open their mouths real wide and show there crooked fangs. Inside their mouths, they are as white as cotton around a Christmas tree.

When you see a cottonmouth, you had better back up and get out of that snake's way. The snick cottonmouth is more aggressive than the snook cottonmouth. Cottonmouths would rather be left alone, but they are not cowards. They don't want you to go pestering them. If you are in the wrong place, at the right time, a cottonmouth will strike. It has strong deadly venom. Don't let anyone tell you that these snakes are not aggressive. When they become defensive, they get very aggressive. Just mess with one and you will find out.

Down in the shallows of Kings Creek where the creek slightly bends and the stream runs slow, there is a large snook cottonmouth lying on the sand on the opposite distant side of the creek happily sunning itself.

I have brought my sixteen-gauge double barrel shot gun loaded with birdshot for hunting doves. As I stand on my side of the creek, that snake does not seem to pay any attention to me. The creek is quite wide in the shallows at this point and a little distant for sixteen-gauge birdshot. I think I can wake him up with birdshot. And, wake up that snook cottonmouth, I did!

At that distance, the birdshot spreads out and patters the snake with stinging shot. That snakes is mad now, and guess who is standing on the opposite side of the creek?

You are right; it's me!

That cottonmouth speeds across the shallows at a mean pace. I thought it was just going for the water, but he kept on comin'. That snake is coming fast and straight for me. I cut loose and let it have the other barrel from the sixteen-gauge right in the head, only a few feet away! That stopped that snook in his tracks! Like I said, don't let anyone tell you that cottonmouths are not aggressive. Just try messing with one! Another word of advice: don't any of y'all get between a snick cottonmouth and her home. The snick's home is water.

One late afternoon in Palmetto on Uncle Thomas and Aunt Grace's farm, I am out in the pasture picking blackberries. There is good profit in blackberries. The labor is free! I can pick a gallon lard pail of blackberries in about an hour. I can sell them to the housewives in Tupelo for fifteen cents a gallon. You know, southern ladies make those delicious blackberry cobblers. I am selling blackberries and gettin' rich!

I am on my way back to the house with my pail full of berries. Off to the right is the pool where the cows and horses water. Off to my left in front of me is a large snick cottonmouth. This time I did not have a gun. This snick is very upset. I am coming between this snake and her home-the water.

The snick rises up with two thirds of her body up off the ground. She stands her ground. She is swinging her body from side to side. I am all shook up, thinkin' *I am gonna' lose those beans that I had eaten for dinner. Now for the Yankees let me explain again; in the south we eat breakfast, dinner, and supper!*

Do you Yankees know a male cottonmouth from a female cottonmouth? Well, we southern boys do! Don't you Yankees try to tell me that you think it's because a female cottonmouth hisses more! Now, you northern boys know that a male deer is called a buck, and you know that a female deer is called a doe. But, I'll bet that you don't know, that down home in the south, a male snake is called a snook and a female snake is called a snick.

I slowly back up. Her eyes are right on me. I very cautiously and slowly move back and around, to the far left. The snick keeps two thirds of her body up in the air, ready to go on the attack. As I move further away, keeping an eye on me, she slowly moves to the pool. I know that by slowly backing up and going around, I am doing the right thing-knowing never to get between a snick cottonmouth and her home.

A week later, Geri is yelling, she is madder than a wet hen,

"Razor Blade, what do you mean you want me to go down into that creek again! I am not goin'. Do you think I'm crazy? The last time you took me and my friends down into that creek you had us scared half to death. You said we were goin' exploring. You took us exploring all right, some exploring! You took us to a wide place in the creek; don't you remember you had us jumping from stone to stone and every time we jumped on a stone a cottonmouth came slitherin' out. There must have been a dozen of them. I am not gonna' go no more; do you hear me? I am not gonna' go! There is just too many of those cottonmouths. Don't you know they can kill you! So there, I am not goin'!"

So as Geri, I hope, will go down to the creek again with me, I'll go to war to thin out the cottonmouths, so the creek won't be such a threat to her...

"It is not the knowing that is difficult, but the doing."
Chinese Proverb

The Truce

"When we remember we are all mad, the mysteries disappear and life stands explained."
Mark Twain

It is a hot Lee County summer day when nothing seems to move along Kings Creek, not even the cottonwood leaves. I have my .22 rifle and bullets with me; I have.22 longs for doves at a distance, and some .22 lead hollow point shorts for cottonmouths. On this hot summer day with nothing to do, I go insane or was it my sister that made me go insane *(it must have been the heat.)* I declare war on the cottonmouths of Kings Creek. There is just too many of them.

I am at a section of the creek down in the slews where the water stands still, a place that I have never gone to before-not even for fishing. I know that still slew water has only mudcats. You gotta' be pretty darn hungry to eat them mudcats. Mudcat catfish taste like mud. The slew is a dangerous place in Kings Creek; it is over grown with small trees. There are dead branches lying around and no doubt a lot of cottonmouths! To go down into that slew is not too smart of a thing to do. However, this hot summer day I must have gone mad and left my brains at home.

Carefully, I look around making my way slowly down the bank between the trees towards the water of the slew. As I near the water, across the creek on the opposite bank sunning itself on a rock, I see a snick cottonmouth. I raise my .22 to get the snake lined up in the sights of my rifle. It is then I spot another snick lying directly ahead of me on my side of the creek, not too far from my feet. I slowly lower my .22 to get the one on my side of the creek before bringing the rifle back up to get the one on the other side. Off to my right, I hear a soft rustling sound like a gentle wind caressing a cotton wood leaf.

Out of the corner of my eye, I see a large snook cottonmouth lying on a dead trim limb. This snook is the largest snook cottonmouth I have ever seen in my life and he is less than three feet away level with my neck. He slowly coils back, going into his strike position. There is not much time to spare; he is getting ready to strike . . . ever so slowly and cautiously, I turn my.22 towards the cottonmouth and as I do, he coils a little more back for the strike.

His tongue is flickering; he is measuring the distance. In direct line with my neck, only a lightning strike away, it is a deadly confrontation- the cottonmouth's life or mine! Lining up the barrel of the rifle, not more than a foot away, simultaneously with the strike- the hollow point tears into the snake's open mouth.

I'm all shook up; I turn back to my left, lower the .22 and straight to the head, hit the snick cottonmouth in front of me. I raise my rifle sighting in on the cottonmouth across the creek. Because of the distance, I go for the body knowing that the hollow point will do its job. The lead hollow point blasts a large hole in the snake's body.

She somersaults into the water. I lower my rifle, look around and cautiously make my way back up the bank. From that day on, for peace of mind, I have made a truce with the cottonmouths; I have found happiness ever after. *I just don't wanna' talk anymore about them there cottonmouths, as there is some exciting news goin' round in the county. Mr. McCarty's State Champion purebred coon dog Howler has done gone givin' birth to a litter of blue-blooded coon dogs!*

Cottonmouths of Kings Creek, snicks and snooks, do not hunt for me and I will not hunt for thee!

"Hunt for peace of mind and thou shall find happiness."
Joshiki

I enjoy all summer long . . . swimmin', fishin' and frog gigging in Kings Creek; however, it does not give me the spending money I need for clothing, cheese and crackers, Moon Pies, R C colas, and spinning tops and marbles. I enjoy picking plums and blackberries that I can sell to the ladies in town, but what I need is a real job.

Sure enough, I land a real job down at the Liberty Taxi Company. They like my go gettem' style and say I was just what they is ah lookin' for!

I think they don't know . . . I was not exactly what they had in mind. They didn't know what they was ah gettin'!

Taxi Drivers Shouldn't Smoke

"Hey Mister, I see y'all got ah sign up; y'all want somebody to answer the telephone for ya'll taxi drivers . . . I am real good at answering telephones."

I get a job answering the phone at a taxi stand down near the Greyhound bus station. I don't keep the job very long though. By the time I get off the phone with the customers and have to relay the address to the drivers, I have already forgotten the house number. My A.D.D. never does bother me much, although it does bother some people . . . like taxi drivers.

One day, while working at the taxi stand, I get real hungry and go down the street to a grocery store and buy a Moon Pie, an RC Cola, a five-cent box of crackers and what I think is a little five-cent bottle of catsup *–which it ain't!* I have never seen or tasted Tabasco Sauce before. I am so hungry that I eat that whole box of crackers, emptying that bottle of Tabasco hot sauce; smoke is comin' out of my ears and tears are ah comin' from my eyes. Thank goodness for my Moon Pie and RC Cola- cools me right down.

I ain't never smoked a cigarette. Well, I can't really say I ain't never smoked, 'cause if I said that I would be telling a lie and I ain't good at telling lies. Just ask my former friends, Willie J and Pete Goosman. When I was a little kid, my friends and I go out into the fields and get some small brown leaves that we call rabbit *tobaccer. We* crumble it and roll it up in some small pieces of brown paper sack just like we seen our daddies do when they roll their cigarettes.

After smoking that rabbit *tobaccer* just once, it was enough. No more of that! So, next we make ourselves some corncob pipes and smoke corn silk. That weren't no good neither; we felt woozy just like that rabbit *tobaccer* made us feel. George Douglas' daddy smokes cigars and he seems to like them. We don't have no cigar, but a dried grapevine . . . kinda looks like a cigar. After a few blisters on our lips, we swear off smoking forever and I ain't never smoked since, and taxi drivers shouldn't smoke, neither.

Those taxi drivers are sitting and smoking up a storm, which ain't good for their health; so, I decide to put a big firecracker under the bench with the fuse on the end of a cigarette. When the cigarette burns down to the fuse, that big firecracker goes off with a loud bang! I am smart enough not to stick around to see it happen.

Later, my daddy hears from someone that, that there firecracker went off like a shot gun and those taxi drivers jumped three feet up in the air. You can bet your bottom dollar, without a second thought I will not be going back to collect my twenty-five cents in pay.

We are growing up together around Kings Creek- Ed Dickerson, Bobby Beggs, Charlie McCarty, Earl Moody and we all need jobs to earn spending money. With this thought in mind, we are all soon employed at our little local café **. . .** a café that will have an effect on the future of our lives **. . .** Whit's Café.

"All that we are is the result of what we have thought."
Buddha

WHIT'S CAFÉ and Mayor Ballard

Up from Kings Creek on West Main going east is Cross Town, where Mr. Whitworth's ... Whit's Café is located. It's cattywompus on Hwy 45. Cross Town is in Tupelo, but it is called Cross Town 'cause that's where Hwy 78 and Hwy 45 cross over. Everybody in Tupelo knows this.

As a carhop at Whit's Café is where I learn the restaurant business. Mr. James Ballard is the manager of Whit's Café and he ups and marries Mr. Whit's young daughter, Vassar.

The large, flat grill is a marvelous thing. As I get older, Mr. Ballard sometimes lets me come in and cook on the grill. We cook a variety of good food- you name it on our big grill: steaks, burgers, grilled cheese sandwiches, bacon, ham, sausages, eggs, and pancakes. This busy grill gives off wonderful simmering sounds and smells as we turn the food. It sure cooks everything good! I say that the best steaks and other food cooked on the flat steel grill come off tasting delicious, as the good tasty juices do not run out, but stay mingling in the current food that we are cooking!

Yes, sir, under the tutelage of Mr. James Ballard, I become a restaurateur at Mr. Whitworth's *Cordon Blu-* Whit's Café in Tupelo, Mississippi. *In later years, James Ballard became the Mayor of Tupelo, Mississippi. It seems that he knew many things about life besides cooking on a grill.*

Later, in Japan thousands of miles away from Kings Creek, I become one of the American soldiers that introduce to Japan the art of cooking on a grill . . . Teppanyaki

"A journey of a thousand miles must begin with a single step."
Chinese Proverb

Kings Creek
Whit's Café

We are all working at Whit's Café, car hopping and cooking on that big flat steel grill that constantly turns out such wonderful food. Whit's Café carhops stay outside the restaurant waiting for those big old cars to drive up for carhop service. We carhops wait for customers on the south side of the restaurant, as it is a little warmer against those cold winter winds that come south down out of that there Yankee country.

There is a small hole in the brick wall on the south side of the restaurant. Sometimes we bet a penny to see who can throw a penny through that small hole. It is not that easy to do.

One slow afternoon, I am car hopping alone. In my pocket is a silver half- dollar (*in those days they were all solid silver).* I take the silver half-dollar out of my pocket and rub it; sometimes I flip it. I like the nice rich feel of it. It is more than a day's pay and I will be going to Tupelo Hardware store in the morning to make another payment on the new Schwinn bicycle that I have on layaway. I often walk to Tupelo Hardware just to touch the bicycle that will someday be mine.

Now, one of the faults of my nature is that there are times when I get a little crazy. Sometimes, I do things spontaneously in the urge of the moment, not thinking of the realities or consequences of **. . .** *what if?*

Rubbing my silver half-dollar, day's pay, between my fingers an uncontrollable urge comes over me. I spin around like one of them baseball players and put that silver half-dollar right across home plate, straight through that hole, without a hair to spare on either side. I stand there with mouth open and eyes bulging; it must have been a whole minute. Not believing what I was not seeing and what I was not seeing was my silver half-dollar- it had disappeared through that hole. With the faults of my impulsive nature, my hard-earned silver half-dollar was gone.

Working at Whit's café gives my friends and I a regular job with a steady income. Our strong friendship is the best of all. *As we all grew older and went our separate ways, I am sure we have often thought of each other, School Principal Paddington's paddle, Kings Creek and Mr. Whitworth's Whit's Café.*

Wham!

Mr. Paddington's Paddle

I love our little shotgun house on the side of Kings Creek where I raise my pigeons and banties. Living here in this little house gives me much happiness. There's fishing, frog gigging, rabbit hunting, dove hunting, and . . . working at Whit's Café and

yes- playing hooky from school!

Well, let me tell you something; the first day of playing hooky from school is wonderful and exciting. The next day ain't wonderful; it is sheer panic, just thinking about going back to school and knowing that the principal, Mr. Paddington is just waiting to spank my butt with his spanking paddle and it does hurt.

"Bend over, boy! Your teacher sent you to my office, because you have been ah playing hooky again!" says Mister Paddington.

"Bend over, boy!" *Wham!* And that paddle hits my butt!

"Ow! That hurts'!"

"Boy, are you going to play hooky again?" He raises his hand higher . . . *Wham!*

"Ow! No, Suh, I ain't gonna' play hooky no more, Mr. Paddington!"

I never did like school, except for Miss McKinley's fifth grade and I sure did not like going to Mr. Paddington's office.

Our home is full of love and good times. Kings Creek is a happy place, but school . . . is a different story.

My friend, Earl Moody is bigger in size than the rest of us, and looks like he can whup' any boy around. He gives those real mean looks, yet I know that Earl just wants to be in our group. Earl knows he is my friend! He just wants to be one of us . . .

Blaming your faults on your nature does not change the nature of your faults."

Indian Proverb

The Voice of Authority

Most of the time at Whit's Café, we are carhops, but sometimes Mr. Whitworth lets Earl work inside making sandwiches. Earl is a little slow in making sandwiches, but he is well-known for making good sandwiches. Earl becomes a famous sandwich maker at Whit's Café. Sometimes customers tell us carhops,

"I want a barbeque sandwich and I want Earl to make it."

Mr. Whitworth knows a good thing when he sees it. He makes famous Earl . . . a full-time sandwich maker. Famous Earl is all smiles! I think to myself, *It sure must be nice, to be famous!*

Earl seems to like me and will do anything I ask him to do. Some folks say Earl is slow . . . maybe just a little slow; well, that is just fine with me-Earl is a friend.

I find out about the Boy Scouts and I really want to be a Boy Scout Patrol Leader. I don't want to take time to get to become a Patrol Leader; I need Earl in my plan to become a leader of other scouts. I don't want to explain to Earl too much about my promotion plan to be an instant Patrol Leader. *I don't want to confuse him!*

I tell the Scoutmaster of the troop near Kings Creek that I want to join his troop; I want to be a Patrol Leader. With an amazed look, he says,

"*Ah, Patrol Leader?* Boy, you will be joining the troop as a Tenderfoot and that is the lowest rank there is in scouting, and besides, you don't even have a patrol to become a Patrol Leader!" *I did some serious thinking about what he said!*

I am not in the army, but I am already beginning to think like one of those army privates; which is a little cunning when it comes to being in authority.

"Hey, Earl, how would like to be a Boy Scout Assistant Patrol Leader?"

"What's that?"

"You know Earl, you boss other guys around, just like army

sergeants."

"Who, me?"

"Yeah, Earl, you! You can boss 'em around and you can march 'em up and down just like those army sergeants do that you see at the picture show."

Earl straightens up, nodding his head up and down with a big grin on his face, as if he already is one of them there army sergeants.

"Yea', Earl, I'm gonna' be a Patrol Leader in the Boy Scouts, and I choose *you* to be my Assistant Patrol Leader.

I'm gonna' let *you* be the one to boss the other boys around!"

Earl stands a little taller.

"You mean that I can be the boss; I can march 'em around? I'm ah gonna' stand 'em at attention; march 'em up

and down, *hup-two-three-four*, just like them sergeants

do in the picture show?"

Earl is delightedly hopping from one foot to the other. He is gettin' real excited about all this marching up and down-yelling,

"Hup-two-three-four ... hup-two-three-four!"

"Yes sir, Earl, you can bet your bobtail that I'm gonna let you boss 'em and march 'em around up and down.

Now, Earl this is what you gotta' do; you gotta 'go out and get eight more boys and you tell em' they are gonna' join the Boy Scouts ... OR ELSE!"

My Boy Scout uniform is given to me by a lady that I used to sell buttercups to. She lives over on the side of Town Creek going east out of Tupelo. Her only son was killed in France during World War I. It is his Boy Scout uniform she is parting with. She hands the clean pressed uniform to me and with moist eyes says. "This is the way he would have wanted it."

I am so proud and happy to wear her son's uniform. I am ready to find my patrol.

The 'Flaming Arrow Patrol' is the scout troop's newest patrol. I choose that patrol name from a list of patrol names, because my friends and I were in the Chickasaw tribe- on the warpath –complete with war paint and flaming arrows.

In the history of scouting, I am probably the only Tenderfoot that is a Boy Scout Patrol Leader. On the first day of joining the scouts, I have my very own handpicked Assistant Patrol Leader and a new patrol, the Flaming Arrow Patrol. Earl is happy with the authority he is given. Earl is mighty proud as he marches the patrol up and down . . . *hup-two-three-four* . . . with the voice of authority.

The Troop Scout Master scratches his head. He, too, is happy with the authority of having a larger troop. *I am quickly learning how to work with people to get what I want.*

"Give people the authority they want, to get what you want!"
Joshiki

Golf Anyone?

It is early morning; Earl Moody and me are at Ed Dickerson's house. Ed's daddy is grumbling about playing golf at the Tupelo Country Club. He is telling Ed that he didn't break a hundred and I said,

"Mr. Dickerson, why do you want to break a hundred?"

"Because, I normally shoot in the low nineties-that's why!"

"Mr. Dickerson, ain't one hundred better than ninety?"

"Not in golf, it ain't; the lower the number, the better the score."

To me this don't make sense. *Do you know what I mean?* This is not what Miss McKinley taught me. Ed's daddy went on to say,

"I paid that caddy twenty-five cents for eighteen holes of golf and he could not even find my ball."

And, I thought to myself, "T*wenty-five cents for being a caddy and finding golf balls, wow!"*

"Come on Earl, we gotta' go."

I head for the door with Earl trailing behind me.

"Ray, where are we going?"

"Earl, we are going to the Tupelo Country Club; hop on your bicycle and let's go make some money."

"Mister would you and your friend like ah caddy? Me and my friend Earl here are real good at finding balls."

"Well, ok boy; we pay caddies twenty-five cents for eighteen holes of golf."

"That's fine mister; we will help you, don't you worry none about breaking a hundred and don't you worry none about me finding your ball!" *Little did I know that* **. . .** *that first hole . . . would be our first and last hole* **. . .** *to be a caddy.*

The mister steps up and asks me for the driver. *Well, I had to think about that*, and I said," Mister, we ain't got no driver; we ain't even got a car.

With a bewildered look, he points to the golf club that he is gonna' hit that ball with. I took the club out and handed it to him. I'm ah thinking- I sure hope he knows what he is doing!

He puts a golf ball on a little wooden peg he stuck in the grass and swings close to it a couple of times, and I think to myself: *He is ah missing that ball every time he tries to hit it; no wonder Mr. Dickerson didn't break a hundred.*

The mister steps a little closer to the ball, raises that driver back high over his head and comes down sompin 'fierce.

I *Suwannee*, he knocks that ball a country mile straight down into the middle of the fairway and over the hill out of sight.

I take off ah running down the fairway and over the hill. I come back running as fast as I can, with a big smile on my face.

"Here it is, mister; I found your ball . . . now you can hit it again!" *I'm ah thinking to myself . . . "Jesus Christ, must also be a caddy at the Tupelo Country Club, because the man keeps on ah yelling' out his name!"*

Model T Ford

It is a Fine Car

It is an open car. *It is a fine car!* The car has a folding collapsible canvas top that we pull up and close when it rains. The patched holes in the canvas are hardly noticeable. There are a couple of broken leaves on the left rear springs. With every bump, the broken springs let out a little musical squeak. We tie the front rod steering ball with bailing wire. This keeps the front wheels of the car from wobbling, but more importantly, it keeps the car on the road. *It is a fine car!*

We are about fifteen years old, my friends and I; we all work at Whit's Café. I have decided that we should get us *a fine car. Why should we get us a fine car?* The answer is simple. Girls! I have been taking notice of the girls . . . they seem to be growing up. They don't like riding on the handlebars of our bicycles no more. They now like to go for a drive . . . *in a fine car.*

Mr. Holloway, who lives over on Church Street has done gone and bought himself a brand new Studebaker Coupe. This is a surprise to me, as Mr. Holloway has driven his Model T Ford ever since his ol' bulldog Hector, was a pup. Now that Mr. Holloway has a nice brand new Studebaker Coupe, the Model T Ford just sits in his driveway. The tires have gone as flat as Mr. Holloway's feet.

My friends and I have been eyeing the Model T. Today is the day! The girls ain't gonna' wait for us no longer- no more bicycles. They want to ride *in a fine car.* I run as fast as I can over to Charlie's house, knowing that Ed and Earl will be there. Howler, Mr. McCarty's state champion prize winning blue ribbon coon dog, has done gone an' given' birth to a litter of coon dog puppies.

Ed and Earl will be wantin' to see them puppies. So I hurry and I can see that Mr. McCarty ain't in no good mood about Howler's coon dog puppies; he is ah yelling something like,

"I paid that ol' man Ebenezer Treadwell over yonder in Alabama one hundred dollars for his Alabama State Champion coon dog, Thunder, to mate with my champion coon dog, Howler!"

Mr. McCarty just won't stop yelling,

"One hundred dollars for each puppy; I could've sold eight little coon dogs for eight hundred dollars. Now look what Mr. Holloway's ol' bulldog, Hector, has done gone an'done!

Nine hundred dollars down the drain! Gone, gone, gone! Someday I'm ah gonna' shoot that ol' bulldog Hector!" I nod my head and grin at Mr. McCarty!

"Hey, y'all, come on, put down those puppies and let them sleep. Let's run over to Mr. Holloway's house and talk to him about selling us his Model T Ford. *It is a fine car.*

Hey look, this is our lucky day; Mister Holloway is home in his driveway polishing his brand-new bright red Studebaker Coupe. Mr. Holloway sure is mighty proud of his new car.

"Mr. Holloway, how much do you want for that ol'Model T?" I ask.

"It sure don't look like it's worth much," Ed puts in his two cents.

"Do you still have the crank handle?" asks Charlie, a little too eager. I shoot him a look.

"Who would want that ol' car?" says Earl pretending to be disinterested.

"My friends and I can help you get rid of it real cheap... so how much do you want for that ol' car?" I ask him again.

Mr. Holloway amused at all the questioning, squints his eyes ever so slightly and cocks his head to the side,

"Boy, I'll have you know all that car needs is a little hay bailing wire to keep the steering rod ball tied down to the front axle and oh yes, you need to pump up the tires. *It is a fine car!"* He pauses, his face softening,

"Son, I reckon this nice car is worth more than twenty dollars," he pauses again,

"But, since you boys work for Mr. Whitworth at Whit's Café, I will let you have *this fine car* for say ... only twenty dollars."

"Twenty dollars!" Charlie shouts as he glances over at Ol' Hector. I shoot Charlie another look. Seeing Charlie, Ol' Hector with a guilty look on his face, hides under Mister Holloway's new Studebaker Coupe.

Head down, slowly looking up and hoping for a little sympathy, I say,

"Mr. Holloway, we ain't got no twenty dollars. We only got eighteen dollars. We don't make much money carhopping at Whit's Café; only

Earl takes a little more because he works inside. Mr. Whitworth says Earl makes the best sandwiches."

Earl straightens up with the air of importance!

"Well, if you boys mow my front lawn, mow out back, and cut the grass on the side of the house, you can have that there *fine car* for only eighteen dollars."

Now that almost stops the deal right then and there.

Mr. Holloway's lawnmower is hand pushed and pulled and as y'all know, I hate any kind of manual labor, especially when it's *me* doing the labor!

"Will you excuse us, Mr. Holloway?" I ask. Mr. Holloway's eyebrows rise in amusement.

Earl, Ed, Charlie, and I huddle. We come to a quick agreement.

"Mr. Holloway, we gotta' go now. We gotta' go work at Whit's Café. We will bring you the other two dollars tomorrow. Mr. Holloway, do you have any spare bailing wire lying around to tie down the front rod steering ball, also it will be must kindly of you to pump up the tires after you cut the grass."

We shake hands all around, we have just bought our first car, a Model T Ford. *It is a fine car!* The next day we go to pick up our nice shiny black car.

"Here we are Mr. Holloway. Here are the other two dollars," I say, handing him the money.

He says,

"Thank you, boys- this here *fine car* is all yours. By the way boys, do you have a driver's license?" he asks, looking at me.

"A driver's license?" repeats Charlie with a look of bewilderment on his freckled face.

"Mr. Holloway, what's that?" I ask.

"That's right boys; the state government done made it the law in the state of Mississippi; you now gotta' have a driver's license to drive a car."

Not too happy about this news, I ask,

"Where do we get that?"

"Over at the courthouse. You pay one dollar and you have bought yourself a driver's license. With that license, you can drive a car. You don't need nothing more!" *I thought to myself, I sure don't like having to pay one whole dollar just to drive a car. I have driven mules and wagons and I didn't have to buy no driver's license!*

"Earl, how much money you got?"

"I got fifteen cents!"

"Ed, how much you got?"

"I only got a nickel!"

Charlie pipes up,

"I got thirty five cents!"

"All right y'all, that's good. I got the rest with enough left over for us to split a big ol' Moon Pie!"

Earl nods his head up and down, looks at me and says,

"I guess we had better put that there driver's license in my name. You know that Mr. Whitworth says, I am the best."

"Whoa . . . whoa wait a minute Earl!" I yell back,

"Mr. Whit might have said you are the best sandwich maker, but he weren't talking about the best driver to drive *ah fine car;* besides, Earl you don't know how to drive and I do!

"When I was ten years old, my uncle Thomas let me drive his mules and wagon to Palmetto from the cotton gin in Verona. He said it was good for me to get the experience to know how to drive. So, you see Earl, you ain't got no driving experience like I do! That there driver's license is gonna be in my name, because with my driving experience . . . I can keep the wheels on the road!"

The driver's license owner is settled; we run over to the courthouse to buy my first driver's license. Excitedly, we all run back over to Mr. Holloway's house. Mr. Holloway has pumped up the tires- we all happily jump into our own *fine car*. I am behind the wheel; I lift the spark lever up, slip the throttle lever down a few notches and turn the switch key. Earl jumps out of our *fine* Model T, runs to the front and turns the hand crank to start the engine. It sputters to life, Earl runs and jumps back in . . . and away we go! Off to Whit's Café.

It is a fine car!

Late in the day, I drive our Model T Ford home to show my daddy. I go in the house and tell daddy and Geri about my friends' and our *fine car*. I proudly announce to them- it is *a fine car*! Geri runs to the window, looks out and gasps at the sight of the Model T.

"Oh, I have never seen such a strange funny-looking car in all my life," she giggles.

Daddy goes outside and walks around looking at our *fine car.* He smiles and slightly nods his head up and down with amusement. No doubt, it takes him back to his younger years. He remembers the Model T car so well. Daddy sets the spark, goes to the front and inserts the crank handle. With big eyes and much curiosity, Geri follows him out. She has never seen nor heard of a car crank handle.

Daddy looks at Geri out of the corner of his eyes and warns,

"Geri, do you see that I have placed my hand over the crank handle with my thumb alongside my fingers? When the engine starts, it may kick the crank out of my hand; if it does, this way it won't break my thumb. Geri, stand further back as we don't know which way this crank handle may fly."

Geri stands back and excitedly says,

"I *Suwannee*! I have never seen such a funny looking car in all my whole life. Why does it not have a starter like other cars? I have never seen a car that you can only start with a funny shaped iron rod."

She squats at the side of road, intently watching daddy.

Daddy turns the crank handle over and over, the engine sputters, comes to life, putt.. putt.. putt.. putt with an increasingly vibrating clanging noise. Geri yells, "I *Suwannee* . . . look at it! It's shaking around, jumping up and down!"

"Oh my goodness gracious . . . it's doing the jitterbug!" as she jumps around to the rhythm of the purring motor.

Happy days are here again! My friends and I thought they would never end, until one day we take some girls for a drive in our *fine car* to the Private John Allen National Fish Hatchery in Tupelo. In the sunny afternoon with the top down, the girls are laughing and singing in tune with the squeaking of the broken rear spring.

"Happy days are here again
The skies above are clear again
So let's sing a song of cheer again
Happy days are here again
Altogether shout it now
There's no one who can doubt it now.
So let's tell the world about it now
Happy days are here again!"
Milton Ager Jack Yellen

As I drive around one of the large fishponds, the bailing wire we used to tie the front axle with . . . to keep the wheels on the road . . . breaks! The two front wheels roll free with a mind of their own. The churning of the back wheels propels the front wheels guiding the Model T Ford right out into the deep of that big ol' fishpond and down we go . . . Model T, girls and all! Swimming furiously to the surface, we watch the gurgling waters swallow our Model T Ford. It is never to be seen again, and neither are the girls after they scramble back up the bank and run screaming down the road! What an experience. It *was a fine car!*

"Life is a series of experiences, each one of which makes us bigger, even though sometimes it is hard to realize this."
Henry Ford

I Wanna' Be a Sailor!

If it had not been for Pulliam Bell, I would have been in the Navy!

It is one of those hot, *donwanndonothin'* days, I'm sittin' out back of the house under a cottonwood tree eatin' some cornbread, enjoying a cool glass of buttermilk- reading the Sunday funny papers. My favorite is Popeye the Sailor Man. Around the corner of the house comes George Douglas.

"Hey, how y'all doin'? I see you are reading tha' funny papers? Did you see where Alley Oop done killed that dinosaur attacking Moo? You wanna' go fishin'?"

George and I have been good friends for a long time now. We do a lot of fishing and frog gigging together along Kings Creek. We often play hooky from school together and we both know the hurting end of our school principal's paddle. But, that paddle is not big enough to keep us away from the call of Kings Creek on a beautiful day.

George is a little different from my other friends, as he comes from a rich family. His family is in high cotton. *You know what I mean*. They live high on the hog. George says that his daddy belongs to the Tupelo Country Club. George's daddy is a Mississippi business gambler- you know, with pool halls and things like that. George is the oldest of three children-all adopted. The Douglas' live in a big colonial home on Jackson Street. George don't act like he is rich, as we all do the same things together. Except he don't have to work for his spending money; his mama and daddy give it to him.

I take a long drink of buttermilk and look up from my Sunday funny papers.

"George, I'm gonna' join the navy!" I declare with a wide grin.

"You gonna' join the navy?" his mouth wide open in astonishment.

"That's right George. I'm gonna' see the world on those big navy boats! Mama wouldn't sign for me at seventeen and now tomorrow I'm gonna' be eighteen, so I'm gonna' join the navy and be a sailor just like them sailors in picture shows.

I'm gonna' go to all those foreign countries- you know like that there Hawaii. I seen two of them sailor boys yesterday at Whit's Cafe; they was ah passing through and I said to them,

'I wanna' be a sailor just like y'all'

They told me that there was this recruiting office over yonder across the Mississippi River in Louisiana in that there city they call, *Nu Awleans.* I'm gonna' hitchhike down there and go over that river and be a sailor just like those sailor boys I seen yesterday. I ain't gonna' tell my mama that I'm gonna' go. I am packin' my bags up in my room. I'm gonna' be a sailor; I am gonna' see the world way away from Lee County, Mississippi . . . so, good-bye, George!"

"Hey Ray, wait a minute, if that's what you're gonna' do, me too! I'm gonna' go with you and join the navy! I have always wanted to ride on one of them big boats and go see those foreign places. I want to go with you to that there Hawaii."

"George, you can't do that; you is rich; yo' mama and daddy will skin you alive."

"Ray, I'm eighteen! I'm a man now. I can do anything I want to and they cannot stop me. Besides Ray, how much money you got?"

"I don't have a lot of money George, but if I hitchhike I got enough to eat on. I got enough money for some Moon Pies and RC Cola. Besides, at home, I'm gonna' make some of mama's peanut butter banana sandwiches, so I won't be hungry on the road to *Nu Awleans*. That's all the eatins I'll ever need!"

"George, I just can't wait to join the navy. Those sailor boys say I can eat three meals a day, get paid fifty-three dollars a month and every year I'll get a thirty-day vacation. George, that sure beats the heck out of working at Whit's Café!"

"Ray, you don't have to hitchhike. Do you know that I've got enough money for bus fare for the two of us?"

I gasp. "All the way to *Nu Awleans'*?" I blurt out- with a bewildered smile at the very thought- maybe I won't have to hitchhike after all.

"That's right, all the way to *Nu Awleans*," George replies.

I don't have to think much about this good news. Things are looking a lot better already!

"George, to tell you the truth, I don't have much money. I'm pretty much broke."

"Well, Ray, the reality is, I'm not broke. So, don't you worry none about being broke. I got money from my generous allowance. I've been savin'some in case I want to run away from home again . . . but, after the last time, my daddy done gone and sold my car. So, see? You being broke don't matter no how! I got money," he says to me with a grin on his face.

"You know, George, the reality is, I think you will like being in the navy. You'll look real good in that there sailor uniform, with that smart little Dixie ice-cream cup-looking hat and those bell bottom pants . . . just like those sailor boys you see in the picture shows. You know, they kinda look like those bell-hops that we see at the Jefferson Davis Hotel right here in Tupelo."

"A theory must be tempered with reality."
Jawaharlal Nehru

Off in the west, the sun is settling over the hills, casting shadows along Kings Creek as I say to George,

"It's gettin' late- tomorrow is a big day. Let's go down yonder to *Nu Awleans*, Louisiana first thing in the morning. I'll go home and make us some peanut butter banana sandwiches. You pick up some Moon Pies and RC Colas on the way. We'uns will take off early in the morning on the first bus ah headin' for *Nu Awleans*. I'll meet you down at the bus station. Now, don't go forgettin' them Moon Pies!"

"Nu Awleans"

The early morning sun races the shadow of our Greyhound bus as we roll through the Mississippi countryside- acres and acres of cotton fields- cornfields waving in the morning breeze as we ride past lush farmlands with white painted houses. Through the little towns, we keep on rolling. People are waving from the streets; with our southern manners we wave back politely until they are lost to sight. As the Greyhound moves through the lowlands of the delta country, the sun is settling into the lateness of the day.

George and I are having a good time dining on peanut butter banana sandwiches, RC Colas, and Moon Pies. *George sure knows how to travel first class!*

Going to Nu Awleans' is a big trip for me. My bicycle had never taken me much more than ten miles from Tupelo, except for two bus trips to Memphis, Tennessee where I got a crick in my neck from looking up at those tall buildings. Would you believe it, some of them buildings in Memphis are ten stories tall and I didn't see any stairs. They have something that we don't have in Tupelo; they are called elevators. We rode them elevators up and we rode them down. Just for fun, we rode up and we rode down some more. I remember it was as much fun as . . . riding a flying jenny!

As the bus pulls into the *Nu Awleans'* bus station, it is kinda' late in the evening.

"George, I don't know nothing about this hea' *Nu Awleans'* and I'm sleepy. There are some benches in that little park under that there streetlight. I guess we can lay down for a while." We sleep well.

The sun is rising in the east, casting a picture of colors over the city, chasing away the shadows of the night, bringing to George and me a new day in this great city of *Nu Awleans'*.

This is our day- we wake up to the chattering of hungry squirrels looking for their breakfast.

"Come on, George, get up! Today is the big day! Whoopee! We are gonna' be in the navy. Let's go, George,-I'm hungry!"

George sits up, rubs his eyes and points across the park.

"You see that sign over there? That's a doughnut shop. Look, there are girls!"

"Girls?" My day has just gotten better. Across the street, I see a sign that reads, "*Krispy Cream Doughnut Shop-get them while they're hot!*" I see girls behind the counter.

"George, get them while they're hot? Do you think they're talking about those gals?"

George laughs as we make our way across the street and then he becomes a little somber. George glances out of the corner of his eye at my right arm. *Is George thinking of something . . . that I had not thought of?*

Feeling mighty good about joining the navy, we swagger through the Krispy Cream doughnut shop doors like we is something important. I say to the brunette waitress,

"Hi, honey; how y'all ah doin'? We'uns is from Missippi'. I betcha' y'all don't know that- do you? We're gonna' join the navy to be sailors!" I give her a little wink and smile.

"Coffee, doughnuts, and a little kiss,"

George says with a big grin, as he looks at the menu hung behind the girls.

"Not again! Another two Mississippi country hicks!" whispers the cute blonde to the brunette with the red lips. The tall brunette does not reply; she is smiling at me as she says,

"Y'all come on in. What would you like to have this mornin'?

George and me are having a good time eating our doughnuts, drinking coffee, and flirting with the girls behind the counter . . . I think they kinda' like us after we tell them we'uns are from *Missippi.* They think we are sumpin' special- as we are ah gonna' join the navy. George pays and leaves two nickels for a tip. I yell back over my shoulder,

"We'll be back, you hea'! We are gonna look for that there navy recruitin' office! Don't y'all forget us now!"

The little blonde mumbles under her breath as she picks up the telephone,

"Don't let the door hit you in the butt!"

A mailman on the corner of the street is taking letters out of a big blue mailbox.

"Mister Mailman, how do you get to that there navy recruitin' office?"

"Do you see that streetcar down the street?"

"No suh."

"Look straight ahead; the recruiting office is across the street."

"Do you mean that there train?"

The mailman says, "No son, in New Orleans we call that a streetcar."

Again, I guess there are some more things that we just don't have back home in Lee County, Mississippi. I know it don't look like no car, but it does have wheels and it's on the street so I guess that make sense to me.

"When you reach the end of what you should know, you will be at the beginning of what you should sense."
Khalil Gibran

Mississippi, now that's the way it's spelled, but that ain't the way *we* say it. If someone tells you they is from Mississippi and they say it the way it's spelled, then let me tell you right here and now, they weren't born and raised in the state of Mississippi. We that are born and raised down home always say, "*Missippi'.*" That's the way it is and that's the way it has always been **. . .** "*I'm from Missippi'!*"

George and I see that navy recruiting office from across the street; how could anyone miss it with big posters on the windows that read:

WE WANT YOU!
JOIN THE NAVY AND SEE THE WORLD

As we are crossing the street to the Navy recruiting office, I say,

"Let's hurry, George! Come on, George, let's go- we are gonna' join the navy. We are gonna' see the world!"

George and I open the navy recruiting office door. We walk right in as if we are home and with a friendly smile I say,

"How y'all ah doin'-'? It's good to see y'all. Here we are! We are here to join the navy! We'uns is from over yonder in *Missippi'*. We betcha' didn't know that!"

My goodness gracious, these navy recruiters are not smiling. I guess it is too early in the morning for government people to smile. They were enjoying their Krispy Cream doughnuts and coffee **. . .** until we walked in.

The navy folks look up and at each other when I say again in a loud, positive voice that jolts them out of their seats,

"We are here to join the navy!"

I kinda' straighten up when I say that. After all, they are lucky to get George and me, because we could have joined the army.

A big fat sailor, rubs the sleep out of his eyes, squints and says,

"Sit down . . . !

We will be with you in a minute . . . after we finish our doughnuts and coffee."

George and I sit there watching them enjoy their doughnuts. The fat one is ah lickin' his fingers after the last bite. I sure am hoping he ain't gonna' shake my hand after that.

"And now . . . what can we do for you?" says the fat one.

These navy recruiters ask us a bunch of questions and look us over like they is examining mules at a livestock show or sompin' like that. Finally, one of the recruiters, the one with a bunch of stripes on his arms, looks out of the corner of his eyes, begins to shuffle papers and says to George,

"Sign here, boy. You are going to be in the navy."

The skinny one with red hair turns to me with a sly grin and says,

"Boy, you can go home now."

"Go home!!!"

Now, I am just struck dumb, like I had been kicked by an ol' cow!

"I don't want ah go home. I want ah be a sailor! I want ah be in the navy! Just like my friend here, George Douglas! I want to see the world!"

"Hey, look at that arm! You are handicapped. That arm of yours is crooked."

"Mister, it don't bother me none. It has been that away most of my life. Look, Mister Recruiter, I can pick cotton, ride a bicycle, climb trees, ride horses," and with a friendly smile I say,

"I can swim real good!" *I said that with a sincere face, as it is clear that I am trying hard to get into their navy. I was ah guessin' they don't want nobody in the navy that can't swim!*

The red head yells at me,

"Boy, you have to go on back to Mississippi."

Hearing this, I look over at his friends for sympathy- the red head smiles again, moving his head from side to side, and says,

"I see you met the girls at the Krispy Cream doughnut shop, the little blonde . . . now ain't she cute? Now, you go on back to Mississippi- it must be clear to you it's almost time for our break."

For the long road back to Tupelo, I will need something to eat. I go back to the doughnut shop, with what little money I have, buy two doughnuts in a poke- not the happy person I was in the early morning. On the way out of the door . . . the little blonde makes a frown, hanging up the telephone- she shouts at me,

"I see you met my boyfriend . . . he is the one with red hair!"

"When the character of a man is not clear to you,
look at his friends."
Japanese Proverb

I'm Gonna' See the World

I leave *Nu Awleans* feeling mighty sad and lonesome. George is going to see the world and I am ah goin' back to Lee County. I hitchhike some and walk some, head low, just shuffling along, kicking at the dust in the road. Nothing seems to matter much anymore. Life is passing me by.

As the moon begins to rise to occupy the night, the disappearing sun spreads faint traces of gloomy colors over the cotton fields; I know that I need to get some sleep for an early morning start, besides, timber rattlers will be out on this road tonight.

Off on the side of the road I see a cotton wagon. I climb up over the side of the wagon and plop down in the comfort of the cotton. I fall fast asleep under a blanket of stars. The early morning sun is spreading its light over the cotton fields when the owner of the wagon wakes me up.

"Boy, are you here to pick cotton?"

Now, picking cotton is something I know a whole lot about but I say,

"No suh! I would be most happy to oblige you Mister, but I gotta' get on home to Tupelo. I need to fix this arm, 'cause I'm gonna' join the navy. I 'm gonna' see the world, just like my friend George Douglas did yesterday in *Nu Awleans.* I thank you suh' for letting me sleep in yo' cotton wagon."

I tell the man good-bye. Not happy and feeling mighty miserable about my situation, I start walking again hoping of some miracle to straighten my arm.

"Every human being has the potential to create
a happy or a miserable life."
Dalai Lama

As I walk along, I straighten up and tell myself miracles do happen. I remember one day I went home from school hoping to find something to eat, but there was no one home and no food, not even a piece of bread in the house. I was so hungry, my stomach ached. I slowly started my way back to school when suddenly; there it was as I stepped off the curb, lying in the gutter-a dollar bill. Yes, a whole dollar bill! I ran fast down the street to a grocery store and bought me some cheese and crackers, a Moon Pie, and an RC Cola. I ate like a king before going back to school. *Miracles do happen.*

As I walk along the side of the road, I also remember on the way out of that recruiting office, the old navy guy with a southern accent, the one with a lot of stripes on his arm, had seen how sad I was. With a friendly touch on my shoulder, he had said to me just as I was fixin' to leave,

"Son, if you straighten out that right arm, you come on back down to New Orleans and I'll see to it that you can join the navy." I walked out of his office, feeling a little better, he gave me hope.

I catch my last ride into Tupelo sitting on top of the big milk cans in the back of a truck. Drivers pick up cans full of milk from farmers and deliver the milk to the milk plant for bottling. The milk cans rattle and shake with every bump in the road. Nothing comfortable about this ride. I must keep my legs from getting pinned between the large cans, but I am happy for the free ride home.

I hop off the milk truck near our little shotgun house on Kings Creek. I kindly thank the driver and his helper. I walk through the front door; mama sees me and says,

"Lo and behold, I *Suwannee* to my name . . . look who is home from the navy already! Baby Ray, you must be hungry."

"Yes Mama, I am powerful hungry."

Mama sits me down at the kitchen table and gives me some fried green tomaters', cornbread, black-eyed peas, collard greens and some bananer' puddin' to eat along with a big glass of sweet milk.

I like milk and drink a lot of sweet milk when I can afford it; sweet milk is kinda' costly though at ten cents a quart. Sometimes, I drink buttermilk because it is only five cents a quart. In the South, there are two kinds of milk and we drink both all the time. Mama says Yankees don't like buttermilk? My daddy once said, "Yankees don't like anything about the south, except our wimmen'."

Awleans, she can see the sadness in me.

"Baby Ray, you go see Doctor Feemster at his office on Main Street and you tell him that you are the youngest son of Nell Payne. If there is any way possible for Doctor Feemster to help you fix that arm, he will!"

As mama is now a practical nurse at the hospital, she knows all the doctors. It doesn't take me long to find the doctor. I see a sign that reads, Doctor Benjamin Feemster. I walk right in and his nurse says to me,

"Darlin', what can I do to help you with?"

I reply,

"Ma'am, I need to see the doctor right away because I want him to straighten out this here arm so I can join the Navy." I hold my arm up for her to see.

Doctor Feemster must have heard all of this. He came right out of his office to see for himself who wants to be in the Navy. He asks me,

"You are a Payne?"

"Yes, suh!"

"I know your three elder brothers were in the war. James was in the Marines, Buddy was in the Army Air Corps, and Hugh was in the Army. So why do you want to be in the navy, Ray?"

"So I can see the world!"

Now that makes sense to Doctor Feemster, so I say,

"Doctor Feemster, suh', can you straighten out my arm?

I want ah join the navy real bad and they said if I could get a doctor to straighten out my arm, they will let me in the navy."

"Do you have money to get to Memphis?"

"Memphis? No suh', Doctor Feemster. I don't have no money. I spent what little money I had gettin' back to Tupelo from *Nu Awleans.* I know that if I work hard at Whit's Café car hopping, I can save enough money to get to Memphis and have a little money for food. I want to be a sailor real bad! I reckon all this is gonna to take some time, and the Navy is ah waitin'!

To my surprise, Doctor Feemster says he can arrange for Campbell Clinic in Memphis, Tennessee to operate on my arm. They will straighten it out and that he can arrange to have it done and it won't cost me nothin'.

"Ray, you will have to make some money to get yourself up to Memphis and get yourself back down here. Here is the address." *Doctor Feemster is a good man.*

"Look for the good in people, and you will find it!"
Joshiki

As I leave the doctor's office on Main Street, I think to myself, "Oh, my goodness gracious, what am I gonna' do? I don't have no money. What I need is a miracle."

The Miracle of the Ring and Cousin Bert

Now, I don't know why another miracle happened, but it did. Stepping off the sidewalk looking down at the curb it happened like it was just waitin' for me; I see lying at my feet- a man's gold ring. It is a real gold ring with a little diamond sparkling in the center.

It is late in the afternoon as I sit on the courthouse steps across from the Lyric picture show wishing I had a dime so I could go in see that there serial, *The Dead End Kids.*

The Dead End Kids is about kids in that big northern city of New York. It surprises me as to how those dead end kids grow up. You know what I mean . . . like playing pinball machines, robbing candy stores and other crazy stuff like that!

Some of my older cousins are sitting around whittling wood, talking about the wild goin' ons' of Mary Bell Stoker at last Saturday night's school dance. I am all ears; this is so exciting- everybody knows Mary Bell, well, the older boys do!

As they talk, I hold up my gold diamond ring to the sun, so as I can see the pretty diamond sparkle in the sunlight. One of my older cousins, Bert, also sees that diamond sparkle in the sunlight. He says to me,

"My goodness gracious boy . . . where in the world did you get that there diamond ring?"

"Cousin Bert, I found it over on Green Street by the curb, just lyin' there . . . like it was ah waitin' for me. Now, it is mine! It sure is pretty, ain't it? Look at it sparkle!"

I can see that cousin Bert wants my gold ring with the sparkly diamond in the center real bad. He always dresses up real sharp for the girls. Cousin Bert is a ladies' man- he shore' looks mighty handsome in his white ruffled shirt, pink bow tie, gray striped pants just touching his well-polished high top shoes.

His pants are held up for all to see by wide purple suspenders. Sitting at a jaunty angle upon Cousin Bert's head is a little straw hat. The hat has a purple band that holds a toothpick. The purple hatband matches his purple suspenders with style. Cousin Bert is a sight to see! He sure knows how to get the attention of the ladies! *I am mighty proud that cousin Bert, a real fine ladies' man, is my cousin!*

Cousin Bert says,

"Boy, look, do you see this?"

My eyes get as big as Cousin Bert's hoot-owl eyes as he holds up a twenty-dollar bill. Cousin Bert just can't be satisfied without my gold diamond ring, so he says,

"Cousin, I will give you twenty dollars for that ring!"

With the look of hunger in my eyes, I say,

"You will? Ah whole twenty-dollars? Memphis, here I come! I'm gonna' fix this arm. I am gonna' be in the Navy!"

"The satiated man and the hungry one do not see the same thing, when they look upon a loaf of bread."

Rumi

No more hitchhiking for me, I am taking the bus- I got money! I am gonna' straighten out my arm and I'm gonna' be a sailor. I'm gonna' see the world just like my friend, George Douglas. Today, I got a post card from George. He says he is ah gonna' go to a place called San Diego. I guess that place San Diego is one of those foreign countries that George is ah gonna' see.

The next day I'm on the Greyhound bus heading for Memphis. I'm ah goin' to Campbell Clinic to get this arm fixed- I'm ah gonna' see the world!

May Not Be Able to See You Again

Before I go into the hospital to get my arm fixed, I want to see our daddy. Jobs are scarce in our little town of Tupelo. So, daddy finds a job parking cars in Memphis. He lives in a small room downtown, up on the third floor of an old brick building. I see a neon sign outside his window that just keeps flashin' on and off throughout the night. I don't know how daddy ever gets any sleep with that neon sign flashin' off and on like that.

The next day, I see the parking lot where daddy parks cars. All day long daddy guides 'em in and backs 'em out, guides 'em in, and backs 'em out. A job is a job! Daddy has had many jobs since losing the farm. Losing the farm breaks his wild hill country spirit. Now, he is doing whatever he can to help support his family- the little ones still at home.

The doctors and nurses at the Campbell Clinic in Memphis are mighty nice. They cut my arm open at the elbow and take out little bits of shattered bone and whatever else had been in there from the time that I broke it when I was about four years old. When I wake up (they had put me to sleep for the operation) one of the nurses says,

"Son, it's going to hurt for a while."

"That's all right with me, ma'am. I do not mind if it hurts. I am gonna' be a sailor. I'm going to see the world!"

The next day they let me out of the hospital and my daddy comes to see me. I sure am glad to see my daddy and grateful for his company. I don't get to see him near as much now that he works in Memphis.

As we stand on the sidewalk outside the hospital; daddy takes out his old well-worn billfold, and opens it. Inside is one five-dollar bill. He hands me the five dollars (this is a lot of money). He says,

"I have not been able to do much for you. This is all I have and I want you to have it. You take care of yourself, you hea'!" He puts his hand on my shoulder, looks into my eyes,

"Remember your upbringing. Take care of family. Help others when you can. I may not be able to see you again." He turns and walks away, back to his job at the parking lot.

I walk in the opposite direction down the street that leads to Mississippi. The thought hit me- *what did he mean?*

"I may not be able to see you again."

I stop and turn to look back at my father. Hugh Payne is slowly walking up the street, his head lowered, not the dashing young man that he once was when he rode down out of those hills, kidnapped our mother, threw her on the back of his horse and rode away with her-back into those hills from whence he had come. Losing the farm, the Great Depression of the thirties, the years of hoeing and picking cotton for a dollar a day have taken their toll on our father.

In the summer of 1946, Henry Hugh Payne, our beloved father, leaves our world at the age of fifty-two. Two years later in the summer of 1948, our beautiful mother, Nell High Payne joins our father at the age of fifty-two. The children they raised so lovingly in Lee County Mississippi love them deeply. Life is not fair for us to have lost them so early in life.

"Being deeply loved by someone gives you strength, while loving someone deeply gives you courage."

Lao-Tzu

Pulliam Bell

The summer of 1946 . . . Year of the Dog
If it had not been for Pulliam Bell, I would have been in the navy.

After the operation in Memphis, my right arm is healed; it is still a little crooked, but not as much as it was. I am gonna' hitchhike back down to that *Nu Awleans* recruiting office and I'm gonna' tell them navy folks that I am ready to join their navy. *I am ready to see the world!*

I bet some of them navy boys cannot even swim or even paddle like a dog, but I know if I tell them that, they will sink the ship right out from under me. They will say,

"Boy, look at that arm!"

And they won't let me in their navy. I do not know why in the world my crooked arm bothers some people. It never bothers me none. I never did think much about it. Later on, I will find out that I need to be a little more cautious about my crooked arm.

"We are what we think. All that we are arises with our thoughts.
With our thoughts, we make our world."
Buddha

It is in the early hours of the morning that Pulliam Bell stops by our house on Kings Creek. *This morning, Pulliam Bell will change the course of my life forever.*

Pulliam stands tall and proud- his head held high in his airborne uniform. On the left shoulder of his jacket is the patch of the 11th Airborne Division. On the left side of his chest are the jump wings of an Army Paratrooper. Behind these wings is the blue patch of the infantry. His paratrooper jump boots shine with high polish, laced with white parachute shroud lines. High upon his head, proudly displayed on his service cap, the paratrooper emblem stands out; issued to only the best . . . America's elite all-volunteer Army Paratroopers.

"Infinite striving to be the best is man's duty, and its own reward."
Mahatma Gandhi

Pulliam says,

"*Howsyomamanem*'- would you like to do some fishin' this afternoon?"

I reply,

"*Mamanem'* they is fine. Doin' some fishin' sounds good to me." Pulliam smiles and says, "As I walked across Kings Creek Bridge on 45 on the way over here, I saw some sun perch swimming in the shallows. I can come back a little later in the afternoon- lets go catch us some of them sun perch. They'll taste mighty good with a little cornmeal sprinkled on 'em."

In the middle of the afternoon, while digging for some fishing worms, Pulliam says,

"Man, you outta' see 'em. Those Jap gals sho' are pretty and they ain't got yeller skin neither!"

"Oh, yea', no yeller skin?"

"You know, we paratroopers get good pay- almost double other private's pay," Pulliam says while he digs out another worm for his bait can.

"We get fifty dollars more a month, because we jump out of airplanes . . . and we have fun!"

Now, I don't quite like hearing that part.

"Pulliam, I don't think jumping out of airplanes sounds like
fun to me! Besides, I'm gonna' join the navy and see the
world!"

Pulliam hangs his head to one side, looks at me with a little smirk on his face as if he knows something exciting *that I don't know.*

"Do you wanna' look at some pictures of them Jap gals?"

And I did. I looked at them again and again, carefully handling each one.

"Pulliam, they sho' is mighty pretty, just like picture girls in a Sears and Roebuck catalog. I like them slant eyes- they got that exciting mysterious look, as if they know something

. . . that we don't know. Pulliam, maybe jumping out of airplanes ain't so bad after all. Later on can I see more pictures of them pretty Jap gals?

Right now before it gets dark, let's go on down to the creek and catch us some sun perch and maybe some catfish, too. At home we got some cold buttermilk and mama will make us some hushpuppies. We got some good ol' watermelon that I traded a banty rooster for. Best of all, this morning, mama made a blackberry cobbler! *In one minute, Pulliam Bell with pictures of them Japanese gals- done changed the course of my life forever.*

Goodbye navy . . . hello Airborne, and just like that, the navy lost a good man!

PRIVATE PAYNE

Army Serial Number: RA14236468

"What is your name?" said the army recruiter.

"My name is Payne and I want to be a paratrooper!

I want to volunteer for the 11th Airborne Division. My friend, Pulliam Bell is in that division and I want to go to Japan right away."

This army recruiter looks at me and raises his eyebrow as he gives me the once over. He looks as if he has some important questions for me. I guess he never saw Pulliam Bell's pictures of them Japanese gals. Again, he says,

"What's your name, son?"

"Payne."

"Payne what?"

"Well, my mama calls me Noel and my daddy calls me Allen, but all my brothers and sisters call me Baby Ray."

He looks at the ceiling, shakes his head and says,

"Sign here!"

And sign I did, with wild anticipation of seeing if those Japanese gals have yeller' skin.

I'm gonna' be in the army. I'm gonna' to be a paratrooper and I'm gonna' jump out of airplanes. As a private, I'm gonna' get army pay of fifty-three dollars a month, plus another fifty dollars a month for paratrooper jump pay. I'm gonna' be rich! I'm gonna' go to Japan and see all them pretty Japanese gals Pulliam was ah talking about! *Little did I know that later on in life I would find out I did not have a name. I will have a problem in proving that I am me. I am ready to buy a house in Hawaii under the G.I. Bill. They asked me for a birth certificate, so I wrote to the state capital of Mississippi. Jackson.*

What I got was, 'Boy born August 8, 1928 to Hugh and Nell Payne, unnamed'! Now would you believe that? I don't have a name! I thought of

naming myself Clark Gable, but I changed my mind. Mr. Gable wouldn't like that . . . I figured he wouldn't like the competition. My brothers and sisters call me Ray. My mama would be pleased with Noel. My daddy got his way with Allen. So, I named myself, Ray Noel Allen Payne.

I'm not really in the army yet, I have to hitchhike all the way down to Biloxi, Mississippi. That is where that there Keesler Army Airfield is. When I get there, I will take my physical and get sworn into this here army. My arm is still a little crooked, but it don't bother me none. Those navy sailor boys had already taught me something about the military; the Army medics is ah gonna' strip me. They is ah gonna' look me over real good. They want to see if I have any of them there handicaps. My right arm is a little crooked, though not as much as before, but it is crooked!

I have a plan.

There is an old Japanese saying, "*The nail that sticks up, gets hammered down.*" Well, this nail ain't gonna' stick up and get hammered! I stay behind everybody as much as possible. When they say put your arms up over your head, I am a little slower to put 'em up. When they say take 'em down, I am fast to take 'em down. That crooked right arm went unnoticed. Thank you, navy for the learning!

I am sworn into the United States Army. I am a Private in the Regular Army: Serial Number: RA14236468. Ahead of me, just being myself, I will have a long and colorful history as the longest serving Private in the United States Army! Today, that record may still be standing.

"The snow goose need not bathe to make its self-white. Neither need you do anything, but be yourself."

Chinese Proverb

You Are in the Army Now!
I'm in Charge

I do not know why some things just happen . . . they put me in charge of eight other Mississippians. These Mississippians are from the Delta and they do talk different. We are about to board a train. Of course, I have seen trains before, but I have never been on one. This will be a new experience for me, and I am excited. The army is sending us to Fort Bragg, North Carolina. We are to get our uniforms and equipment issue from the Quartermaster upon our arrival.

Now, let me tell you about us Mississippians. We are southerners and we like our way of talking, because we understand each other. Not like those Yankees with their many different accents and funny ways of talking to each other; but, I must say our Mississippi Delta boys do talk mighty slow. It takes them forever to say something. You could go to sleep just waiting for them Delta boys to finish a sentence and that must have been just about what that Yankee sergeant did, but before he went to sleep, he put me in charge. *It is my first command.*

"Hey, Reb!"

"Me, sergeant?

"Yes, you! Are you the one that actually volunteered for the Airborne?"

"Yes sir, sergeant!"

"Well, you are in charge. At least I can somewhat understand what you are saying. I hope you can understand them country yokels better than I can! Here are their orders and every one of these soldiers' records. Get em' on that train, move 'em out and . . . good-bye!"

"Yes sir, sergeant!"

"Now, y'all come on! It's time for us to go! You heard what the sergeant said-cotton-picking time is over. You are in the Army now!"

I round up the Delta boys and get 'em on the train. I see the Yankee sergeant let out a long sigh of relief. The whistle blows and with a puff of steam, we are on our way to Fort Bragg- home of the 82nd Airborne Division! Being from Northeast Mississippi, I can understand these slow talkin' Mississippi Delta boys at least better than this Yankee can. *The Germans will never forget the 82nd Airborne Division.*

The Army issues us our uniforms and what they call underwear. I had never worn underwear in my life. It is yet another new experience I can write home about. These things are like shorts tied with draw strings that you see boxers wear in the picture shows. We got some socks and two pair of boots. I never did have two pair of shoes in all my life. *This is gettin' to be too good!*

We are issued our gear- two fatigues and one Class A uniform for Saturday morning inspections, going on parade and looking good when we get liberty to see the girls. We are bound for Fort McClellan, Alabama for basic training on yet another long train ride. Why didn't they just send us to Fort McClellan, Alabama in the first place? I am beginning to learn about these officers and their way of planning. They make things look complicated. I am noticing that officers mostly stand around and talk to each other. They let the sergeants run the Army. I guess this is the smart thing to do.

The train stops at some little country town. Just before the whistle blows to move on, some guy gets out of a little white truck. Big red letters are stenciled on the door: *Nick Russo's Quick in and out Service*

Russo brings on board little paper box lunches. He quickly passes them out for our lunch. Nick Russo is in a big hurry to get off this train. He knows why, and after we open the boxes, we also know why. This is my first experience with *GOVERNMENT CORRUPTION!* Our lunch consists of a thin cold cheese sandwich, a small apple, and a little cookie. *In the years to come I learn a lot about characters with ulterior motives like Nick Russo-characters involved with government corruption, receiving large illegal profits from any and everything from pencils to B-29 Bombers!*

"There is no greater injury to one's character than practicing virtue with ulterior motivation."
Chuang-Tzu

Fort McClellan
Letter to Mama

Arriving at Fort McClellan, we move into wooden barracks. The roofs look like tarpaper. I often write home to mama. She sends me boxes of homemade teacakes and lots of my favorite Moon Pies. She had done the same for my three older brothers during the war. With my southern upbringing, I share my teacakes not only with southern boys, but also with the Yankee boys and even sometimes give them one of my Moon Pies, never forgetting my duty of southern hospitality. In my first letter home, I tell mama how good it is to be in the Army!

August 28, 1946

Dear Mama,

You don't have to worry about me getting wet when I go to the outhouse, because there ain't none! Would you believe it? The outhouse toilet is inside our barracks and we don't need no Sears Roebuck catalog neither!

And mama, they gave me two pair of shoes and you know I have never had two pair of shoes in my life! They sure are good to me. They give me new clothes and believe it or not they feed us three times a day-breakfast, dinner, and supper- now, what more could I ask for? I am never hungry; I have learned to sit next to some of them Yankee city boys. They don't eat much. They mostly drink coffee and smoke cigarettes, so I eat their food for them.

Would you believe it, we get off Saturday afternoons and the whole day off on Sunday. Tell Cousin Archie that if he wants some of this good life, some new shoes and lots of time off, he had better join this here army right away before many others learn about it!

Mama, this here Army sure beats the heck out of working
at Whit's Café!

Your loving son,
Ray

We are at McClellan for basic training. We are here for them sergeants to *learn us* how to fight wars and this they do well. On the firing range, I fire well enough to earn the badge of expert. The target don't run around to the other side like a squirrel in a tree. Hitting that bull's eye and firing expert was an easy thing to do. It was like shooting a squirrel out of a tree and the squirrel don't even move. If there are some things for sure that southern country boys know how to do, it is to ride and shoot.

At McClellan, the young boys out of the cotton fields of Mississippi and other parts of the country become men. In basic, we are all privates. I am now a Squad Leader. It is my second command after being in charge of the Delta boys, *and my last command,* of my three years as the longest serving private in the United States Army.

After basic training, I say good-bye to my fellow Mississippians, the Delta boys. I also say goodbye to a few Yankees that I had gotten to like . . . somewhat.

I am now on a train bound for Fort Benning, Georgia. Fort Benning is America's premier jump school for America's elite Parachute Infantry Regiments and I am gonna' be a paratrooper. Upon our arrival at Benning, we go right into training to be glider troopers.

Fort Benning

Gliders Are For the Birds

During WWII, America's Airborne Divisions consist of one Parachute Infantry Regiment and two Glider Infantry Regiments. Shortly after the war, the Airborne began to combine all regiments, becoming paratroopers as well as glider troopers, now trained for both. Previously glider troopers wore a glider on their hats and paratroopers wore the parachute. After training, we wear a parachute over a glider. I am among some of the last in the Airborne being trained for gliders.

I want to tell you this right here and now, I would rather be a paratrooper any day than a glider trooper. To some extent, I can control my parachute. I can slip wind to help control the direction of my fall by pulling my risers left, right, front, or back. I can control the direction of my descent somewhat before hitting the ground. But not in a glider! We are at the mercy of the pilot and the co-pilot and *they are at the mercy of the glider.* We have twelve glider troopers on board, plus equipment. This is a lot of weight and there are no motors! NO MOTORS!

Gliders, after being cut loose from the plane have no choice but to go down. In combat, if they are not shot out of the sky, they do not know what lies ahead: anti-glider poles, open ditches, trees, or whatever. If they miss, the landing zone there is no way out, but to land and hope that the glider can clear the obstacles. Those gliders are put together with a steel frame and fabric. I can hear them flapping in the wind- it sure gets on your nerves. Sometimes, they break apart on landing.

My cousin Buddy Anderson, who graduated from Benning, and went on to the 82nd Airborne Division, and I are on the field training in gliders when one of the C-47's in our training class B-13, lost one of its engines right after take-off.

The C-47's tow two gliders (*like a goose formation*). That C-47 with only one engine did not have the power to gain elevation with those two heavily loaded gliders dragging it down. They cut our gliders free. With no power, and with a prayer, the gliders had no choice but to go into the trees. *Those gliders kill seven of our buddies this day. I never want to see another glider for the rest of my life.*

We lost seven friends in death, not knowing that another one of us will be joining them soon. There is now the uncertainty of strength for the future. With the skepticism of what the future may bring, there will be many jump school quitters.

"Banish uncertainty. Affirm strength. Hold resolve.
Expect death."
Tao

Who Wants to Be a Quitter?

Run, Ray, run! My brothers and sisters call me *Baby Ray*. They had read in school about a little boy named Baby Ray.

"*See Ray play. See Ray run. Run, baby Ray, run!*"

When I arrive at Ft. Benning for jump school, there is no play and it seems that all I do is run! *Run, Ray, run!* We run to each training session. We run to breakfast; we run to dinner; we run to supper; we run and run and run and then, we run some more!

I am pretty slim from being hungry most of my life, so it doesn't bother me none. I like running. I can run for miles. Some of the Yankees from those big northern cities just can't take all the running, and quit jump school early. A lot of Yankees and a few southerners quit because of the hard training. What we all dread most are the 34-foot towers we have heard so much about. When one jumps from the towers, the feeling is as if he is being jerked half in two. Just looking at those tall towers ensures that some will be quitting before that first tower jump!

Note: *The 11th Airborne Division composed on formation of the 511th Parachute Infantry Regiment, the 187th Glider Infantry Regiment and the 188th Glider Infantry Regiment, the division mustered 8,321 men—about half the usual strength of a regular American World War II infantry division. Once activated, the division remained in the United States for training and exercises at several locations. As the division, like all airborne units, was intended to be an elite formation, the training regime was extremely arduous. There were 250 feet (76 m) and 34 feet (10 m) towers from which prospective airborne troops would jump off of to simulate landing by parachute, lengthy forced marches and practice jumps from transport aircraft; to pause in the doorway of an aircraft during a practice jump resulted in an automatic failure for the candidate. The resultant failure rate was accordingly high, but there was never a shortage of candidates, as the rate of pay was much higher than that of an ordinary infantryman.*

Now, for some of us, we just cannot be brave enough to quit. We *know* what they do to *quitters*! Quitters have to clean all of the latrine toilets at Benning. I have had some experience cleaning toilets back in basic training at Fort McClellan, but it wasn't punishment for quitting, it was punishment for just about everything else in the book! Cleaning toilets is a dirty job. *I know a lot about cleaning toilets! Would you believe you could get in trouble cleaning toilets?*

They don't ship quitters out of Benning right away. Quitters are held over to make sure they are punished real good. The cadre makes sure that all at Benning know that they are yellow quitters. Quitters wear a yellow helmet stenciled in big red letters: QUITTER. Troops at Benning can hear quitters shouting a mile away,

"I am a quitter!" as they run down the road.

"I am a quitter! I am a quitter!"

The two hundred and fifty foot towers that drop us while we are strapped in a chute are not so bad, nothing like the jolt of those notorious thirty-four foot towers. Big wind machines inflate our chutes on the ground. The force of the wind drags us across the ground. We pull on our risers and pull ourselves to our feet. This is to teach us, that when we hit the ground in high wind and are being dragged along, how to bring us to our feet and collapse our chute. Some of us are scratched up and get a little bloody being dragged across the ground. A little blood dries up in a few minutes. In our souls, some of us have the will not to quit. No, Sir! I ain't gonna' be a quitter!

Quitters with feeble souls wished they had never quit. Cleaning toilets, washing pots and pans can go on for a long time.

"Great souls have wills, feeble souls have only wishes."
Chinese Proverb

Cleaning toilets is something I definitely know a lot about; back when I am in basic training at McClellan, our lieutenant is the officer to inspect the toilets that I have just cleaned. He is a nosey lieutenant. Maybe that is why he wants to inspect the toilets . . .

Attention!

Today is the day! Our lieutenant is coming to inspect the toilets that I have just cleaned. I tied a cord through the long row of toilet seats and then wait. As the lieutenant comes through the door with a tech sergeant, the sergeant yells,

"Attention!" I yank that cord real hard! All the toilet seats jump straight up to attention! The lieutenant's mouth flies open in surprise. I am laughing so hard even the sergeant has a little grin on his face, until he sees out of the corner of his eye the look on that lieutenant's face. I too, see that look . . . I am not laughing anymore. The lieutenant grits his teeth, makes an ugly frown and says,

"Well, Private Payne, if you get so excited about making toilets going up and down and stand at attention, when an officer is around, then you can just keep these toilets company for the weekend. You will make sure that these toilets are real clean and ready for my inspection Monday morning, and they will go up and down and stand at . . . attention! Have a good weekend, Private Payne."

"Yes sir, lieutenant! Yes, sir!" *Like I said, I know something about cleaning toilets!*

"It's best not to get too excited or too depressed
by the ups and downs of life."
Dalai Lama

The Kiss of Death

It is in the early morning. I am at one of the thirty-four foot towers waiting for my first jump from that dreaded tower-the tower we have heard so much about. I am uneasily looking at the tower, when a sneering voice next to me says,

"Boy, how did you get into this jump school?"

That sure takes my mind off the tower. With bated breath, I look around and I see Sergeant Swartz for the first time in my life.

"I'm gonna' be a paratrooper, Sergeant."

"Boy, you can't be a paratrooper! You are handicapped. Look at that arm. It is crooked!" *Now, I look at that arm as if I am seeing it for the first time in my life.*

Sergeant Albert Swartz is my new Cadre Sergeant. He has short blonde hair, steel blue eyes, and a thin-lipped grin that curls into a sneer out of the corner of his mouth. His hands are on his hips, feet spread far apart. At this moment, Staff Sergeant Albert Swartz with his sneering grin holds my life in his hands! He is the kiss of death. *He looks just like that movie star Richard Widmark, in the movie- Kiss of Death, when Richard Widmark with a long snickering laugh shoves that old lady in a wheelchair down a long flight of stairs.* Sergeant Swartz looks at me out of the corner of one eye, curls one side of his mouth and snarls,

"Boy, you are out of this jump school! The Airborne ain't no benevolent society for handicaps!"

Things have gotten real *serce'*! In Mississippi, we know what serious is, but when things get real bad then it becomes real *serce'!*

Sergeant Albert Swartz is now . . . *the kiss of death.*

I plead,

"Please, sergeant! I can run all day. I can do push-ups. I can do chin ups."

I was gonna' tell him that I can swim real good, but I didn't say that, 'cause I know that only those navy people would like to hear that. Besides,

I don't like those sailors no more. Forcing the words from my mouth,

"I can do anything, please, sergeant. I can play baseball . . . please, sergeant; I want to be a paratrooper."

He drops his jaw, squints his eyes, tilts his head to one side and gives me that sneering laugh. *He must like baseball.*

"Without knowing the force of words,
it is impossible to know men."
Confucius

Sergeant Swartz sneers,

"So, you want to be a paratrooper?"

"Yes sir, Sergeant."

"Where are you from boy?"

"*Missippi'*, sir."

"Mississippi? Well, ok . . . Reb." *I am proud to be called a Rebel, but I ain't gonna' let on, and let that damn Yankee know that, 'cause he holds my life in his hands; he is the kiss of death!*

"Boy, when you get up on that tower and jump, you sing 'Dixie' and you better sing it loud and clear! Do you hear me?"

"Yes sir, sergeant! Yes sir!"

Sergeant Swartz yells,

"And soldier, don't you call me, sir. That's for those officers standing around over there."

"Yes sir! I mean, ah yes, Sergeant Swartz! *"I know he is a damn Yankee, but I don't care, I am gonna' be a paratrooper!*

Nobody likes those thirty-four foot towers. The towers are to train jumpers for the opening shock of the parachute as you exit the plane. When you jump the tower, it is one hell of a shock! After the shock, you slide down a long slanting cable for a rough PLF (*parachute landing fall*). But, I don't care; no thirty-four foot tower is gonna' stop me from being a paratrooper.

I climb up to the top of the tower, putting all dread behind me. I jump, singing "Dixie" as loud as I can. I probably woke up General Robert E. Lee. *For all y'all Yankees that don't know . . . General Robert E. Lee was our Commanding General in our glorious American Confederate States of America during our war against northern aggression.*

My daddy had said, "Those Yankees liked our wimmen! My Granddaddy had said, "That war ain't over yet!"

I get yanked hard and go sliding down that steel cable to land at the feet of my sergeant.

"Good going boy; you are gonna' get through this jump school and every time you jump, I want to hear you sing 'Dixie'. Do you hear me?"

"Yes sir, Sergeant Swartz!"

"Private Payne, don't call me sir!" *Sergeant Swartz is a Master Jumper. He is a veteran of the 503rd Parachute Infantry Regiment. The 503rd was engaged in many battles in the Pacific during WWII. The most notable of their jumps is Corregidor Island in the Philippines where they engaged in intense combat. The 503rd was awarded the Presidential Unit Citation. Two paratroopers of the 503rd were awarded America's highest award, The Congressional Medal of Honor.*

During the war, the 503rd Parachute Infantry Regiment killed 10,000 Japanese soldiers and also the 503rd lost a good many of their paratroopers.

It is indeed an honor for me to be one of Sergeant Swartz' students as he is pushing me hard to make sure that I get through jump school. He senses how much this means to me- being a paratrooper. *My head is a little mixed up . . . I am beginning think of Sergeant Swartz, this Yankee, as my friend.*

I pay attention to what Sergeant Swartz tells me. Every time I jump that dreaded thirty-four foot tower, I sing as loud as I can. I hear Master Jumper Sergeant Swartz yelling, "Louder! Louder!" So, I sing:

"I wish I was in the land of cotton,
ol' times there are not forgotten,
look a way, look away, look away,
Dixie Land."

My Granddaddy would've been mighty proud of me.

"When the student is ready, the master appears."
Buddhist Proverb

The Five, Five, M- - - - - F- - - - - -' Five

I do not know why it is this way in the south. It is not mine to reason. It is the way it has always been. In the Deep South, Fort Benning, Georgia is no different. I had never thought much about it.

We go to the airfield for training sitting in the back of a six-by . . . a six-by-six is a truck with six wheels. *Now, don't that just make sense?*

Across the field from another direction, comes another six-by with three colored boys in it. They came from another part of Fort Benning. From where in Benning, I do not know, as they are never seen in our all white PX snack bars or picture shows. They train with us, but always a little off to the side. I can see the look of determination on their faces. *Georgia is no different from Mississippi or any of our other southern states of the Confederacy; we just do things different down south.*

Each day after training, the colored boys get back on their truck and go back to where they came from. At graduation, I am happy to see that with their dedicated determination and their vision of tomorrow, all three make it through jump school. They accomplished their dream. They are now United States Army Paratroopers.

"Without a dream, there is no vision
and without a vision people perish"
Joshiki

They have a dream. They go on to join the all-volunteer elite 555 Parachute Infantry Battalion, the only colored paratroopers in our segregated Army.

On parade, they are proud magnificent paratroopers. They call themselves, "The Triple Nickel". They also jokingly like to call themselves the, "Five, Five, M - - - - F - - - - - -' Five."

I salute the 555 Parachute Infantry Battalion.

"I have a dream!"
Martin Luther King

Now, sometimes with my A.D.D., I do not pay attention as well as I should. This can get a little dangerous. I am determined to be a paratrooper. I am soon to learn that if I am going to be a paratrooper, I had better take good care of my parachute.

Twist and Shout

As I board the C-47 for my first jump, Sergeant Swartz pulls on my sleeve and says,

"As the stick shuffles along and you reach the door to jump, look straight out; don't look down. Remember, now!

When you get to the door, do not look down, jump- yell out, 'Geronimo . . . one thousand . . . two thousand . . . three thousand . . . Your chute will open . . . and if it does not open," He gives me that snickering Richard Widmark laugh . . .

"Trade it in for a new one!"

Our World War II T-7 chutes are designed to get us down fast and as safely as possible. One of the first things that Sergeant Swartz had told me was,

"Pay attention and pack a good chute. Your chute is your best friend."

It is a beautiful day. As I leave the door of the plane, the blast of air hits my face. I yell Geronimo one thousand . . . two thousand . . . three thousand . . . I wait for the jolting shock of the opening chute. This time it is different as there is no shock. I am falling rapidly. I hear the whirr of the chute. I look up to see my chute fluttering wildly. It is not fully open. I shake my risers, praying this may help. I am ready for a miracle; with my fast descent, the wind catches my chute with a twist, and my chute pops fully open, descending rapidly joining others as they fill the sky, getting ready for our PLF

(parachute landing fall).

I have learned the dangerous way - my chute is my best friend. From now on, I will treat my best friend with all due respect. Unfortunately, I did not do that for this jump. I thought I knew it all. I just kinda' lackadaisically threw that chute together.

Later, Sergeant Swartz says,

"Boy, you could have broken your neck. Next time you pack that chute the way those parachute riggers taught you or you are going to look mighty funny walking around like a chicken without a head."

"Yes sir, Sergeant Swartz."

Sergeant Swartz is right. That chute had not opened too well. The chute did some jerking and twisting . . . and I did some shouting. One of those risers crossed where my neck connects with my shoulders. I could have broken my neck. Instead, the riser wrapped across my neck and gave me a bad burn. Little beads of blood popped up where my neck joins my shoulder. *After that, who do you think had the best packed chute at Benning?*

"Sergeant Swartz is Private Payne going to get the Purple Heart?" asks my Chickasaw Indian friend, Running Horse.

Sergeant Swartz laughs and says, "No, you don't get the Purple Heart over a little blood. Your parachute is not the enemy. Stay out of danger! That chute is your best friend. If you want to be paratroopers and live to tell about it, you had better learn this: At twelve hundred feet there are just eight seconds to death!

"He who learns, but does not think, is lost! He who thinks, but does not learn is in great danger!"

Confucius

Pull It! Pull It!

"It has been ah raining hard all night. Those clouds over on the Alabama side don't look so good. They'd' have been ah plowing up those fields. It's gonna' be mighty muddy." says Running Horse.

Being a Native American, maybe Running Horse could smell those fields over yonder in Alabama. Horse is a Chickasaw Indian from Oklahoma, and that is why I like Horse. We Mississippians know that the Chickasaw Indians are originally from northern Mississippi. I have picked up many of their arrowheads along Kings Creek.

Running Horse is in my stick. *A stick is a line of paratroopers, hooked up to a static line ready to go out the door.* We have made our jump and are on the ground. Like we have done before, we look up to see a stick coming out of one of the other C-47s. Parachutes are blossoming in the sky. We count **. . .** one, two, three, four (we see a space **. . .**) here comes *six*, seven, and eight **. . .** five's chute didn't open in the stick coming out of the door of the C- 47. He must not have snapped proper on the static line. He needs to pull his reserve now!! ! We on the ground are yelling, "Pull it! Pull it!"

Holding our breath, waiting for him to pull his reserve chute, we increase our tension-filled voices, calling loudly to him as a group. . .

"Pull it! **Pull it!** "As we look up to see him rapidly falling, Horse, with his hands held high towards the sky, is chanting to the Great Spirit.

"O Spirit teach me to pray and pray with deep concentration. O Spirit, balance my meditation with devotion. Purify my devotion with all- surrendering love unto thee."

Swami Yogananda

We lose another buddy on this dark day. We are all feeling the sadness of today's jump **. . .** I am about ready to wish that someone would say something about my crooked arm, so I can leave this field forever, and go home to have some of Mama's banana puddin'- never to see this place again.

Sergeant Swartz comes walking over from the other side of the field to where we are standing and says,

"Come on son, let's go! There's nothing you can do here.

In a few days, you will be a paratrooper. You will be going to Japan-seeing all those pretty Jap gals. *"I am beginning to feel better already!*

The next morning on our five-mile run, as the ground flies beneath us, we sing one of our airborne songs:

"He was just a rookie trooper and
He surely shook with fright,
He checked off his equipment and
Made sure his pack was tight;
He had to sit and listen to those
Awful engines roar,
You ain't gonna' jump no more!
Gory, gory, what a hell of a way to die,
Gory, gory, what a hell of a way to die,
Gory, gory, what a hell of a way to die,
He ain't gonna' jump no more!

'Is everybody happy?' cried
The sergeant looking up,
Our Hero feebly answered "Yes,"
And then they stood him up.
He jumped into the icy blast,
His static line unhooked,
And he ain't gonna' jump no more.

He counted long, he counted loud,
He waited for the shock,
He felt the wind, he felt the cold,
He felt the awful drop,
The silk from his reserve spilled out and
Wrapped around his legs,
And he ain't gonna' jump no more.

The risers wrapped around his neck,

Connectors cracked his dome,
Suspension lines were tied in knots around
His skinny bones;
The canopy became his shroud;
He hurtled to the ground.
And he ain't gonna' jump no more.

The days he'd lived and loved and
Laughed kept running through his mind,
He thought about the girl back home,
The one he'd left behind;
He thought about the medics, and
Wondered what they'd find,
And he ain't gonna' jump no more.

The ambulance was on the spot,
The jeeps were running wild,
The medics jumped and screamed with glee,
Rolled up their sleeves and smiled,
For it had been a week or more
Since last a 'chute had failed,
And he ain't gonna' jump no more.

He hit the ground; the sound was
'SPLAT' his blood went spurting high,
His comrades were all heard to say 'A hell of a way to die!'
He lay there rolling round in the
Welter of his gore,
And he ain't gonna'
Jump no more."

As we ran with solemn reverence, we began to sing slowly.

"There was blood upon the risers;
There were brains upon the chute,
Intestines were a 'dangling from
His Paratrooper suit,
He was a mess; they picked him
Up and poured him from his boots,

And he ain't gonna' jump no more
Gory, gory, what a hell of a way to die,
Gory, gory, what a hell of a way to die,
Gory, gory, what a hell of a way to die,
And he ain't gonna' jump no more!"

"When the character of a man is not clear to you, look at his friends."
Japanese Proverb

Some years later, the airborne develops a cotter pin that is inserted after you hook up on the static line . . .

The Cotter Pin

I hate to think, over the years how many paratroopers lost their lives for the lack of a cotter pin. As the stick lines up inside the aircraft, ready to jump-they click on the line. At this point a cotter pin is inserted. It would guarantee that a paratrooper's static line was connected to the cable. Before the cotter pin was used, a paratrooper when getting ready to jump, would think he was hooked up to the cable, when in fact, he was not. The cotter pin prevented this kind of error and ultimately saved lives.

"For the lack of a nail, a shoe is lost,
For the lack of a shoe, a horse is lost,
for the lack of a horse, a battle is lost.
My kingdom for a horse, cried the King."
Shakespeare

We all know that black cats and the number thirteen are unlucky and we don't walk under no ladders neither!

Many have quit in our class, B-13. Furthermore, eight of our buddies are dead. We are now down to less than half of our class that we started with. I can feel it coming, there will be more of us quitting before sun down . . . I haven't seen any black cats.

Airborne All The Way
Author Unknown

These men with silver wings
Troopers from the sky above
In whom devotion springs
What spirit so unites them
In brotherhood they say
Their answer loud and clear,
"Airborne All The Way"

These are the men of danger
As in open door they stand
With static line above them
And ripcord in their hand
While earthbound they are falling
A silent prayer they say
"Lord be with us forever,
Airborne All The Way"
One day they'll make their final jump
Saint Mike will tap them out
The good Lord will be waiting
He knows what they are about
And answering in cadence,
He'll hear the troopers say
"We're glad to be aboard, Sir,
Airborne All The Way

I look at Running Horse and say,

"Horse, we ain't quittin'. I don't care what! We are gonna' be paratroopers. We are going to that there 11th Airborne Division in Japan. We are gonna' go see those pretty Jap gals."

"You know Horse, Pulliam said them Jap girls don't have yeller skin!"

Running Horse speaks up,

"Ok, paleface, me go too, but tell me . . . what's wrong with yellow skin?"

Most Americans have not the faintest clue of just how fragile life is, what it means to live life to its fullest, to "Walk The Walk" along the razor's edge! Stare fear and death in the face and tell 'em to piss off". The Paratrooper

Ten-Foot Pole

In Atlanta, on a weekend pass from Benning, I meet a sweet-as-honey little Georgia gal. Her name is Betsy Hokum. She is a mighty pretty little girl, big blue eyes, freckled faced, with slightly buck teeth resting between her sweet red lips. Her blond pigtails are tied with little red satin ribbons. She wears a pleated yellow polka-dotted short skirt, white socks with shiny black sandals. Betsy is the cutest thing . . . you ever did see!

I can't believe it myself . . . I am hooked and now . . . engaged to get married.

The army pays us privates fifty-three dollars a month, once a month. I am not a paratrooper yet, so I do not receive the additional fifty-dollar jump pay. My new love takes much of my pay; *she is in love.* I buy my new love a sparkling cat's eye engagement ring. That ring cost me a whole nineteen dollars and ninety-nine cents. But, you know, nothing is too good when you are in love!

My new love, charming Betsy, says to me,

"Darlin', now don't you go fool around with none of them Jap gals when you get over to that there Japan."

"Honey, don't you worry yo' pretty little head none; I wouldn't touch those yeller' skin slant-eyed Japanese gals with a ten-foot pole!" *At the time, little do I know the liar that I will become!*

After two days of holding hands and kissing, she says to me in a serious tone of voice,

"*Sugar Pie*, do you love me?"

I gulp, blink and reply,

"Well, yea', I recon' I do."

She narrows her eyes, looks me straight in the face and says,

"Well, soldier if you love me . . . you need to fish or cut bait! Will you marry me?"

I gulp again; stammer as I hesitantly reply,

"Well, ah . . . ah yes, I recon' so,

I say, *"Howyoumomanem'?"*

She relaxes as she says,

"They's' fine."

My new fiancé proudly takes her catch home to meet her mama and daddy. At the supper table, her daddy looks at me and says,

"Son, my daughter tells me that you are going to that there country of Japan. You will be gone almost three years. I guess that it will be mighty lonesome over there for you."

"Yes suh, mighty lonesome, but I will find something to do to help make the time go by faster." *I was thinking of Pulliam Bell's pictures.*

"What are you gonna' do after you come back to the states?"

"Well, I recon' I will go back to work at Whit's Café in Tupelo, in Missippi'. After all I do have lots of experience.

His daughter is looking at me with those big blue eyes full of pride and there is love in her heart.

I make the best peanut butter banana sandwiches you ever did eat. I got my mama's secret recipe!" *Little did I know Mama's secret peanut butter banana sandwich recipe in the months to come in Hachinohe, Japan, will get me one of the best jobs that I will ever have in my whole life! Well, it was . . . until Buck Sergeant Johnny Jardine done done me in!*

I had not been in love since I was in love with Dorothy Ann Brown back in the fourth grade. It was a powerful love back in Tupelo, Lee County, Mississippi. Dorothy Ann would let me carry her schoolbooks. She liked it that way and so did I. I was the only boy to carry Dorothy Ann's books and no other boy had better even think about it!

Dorothy Ann's daddy was a preacher man; he got a better preaching job way down in tha' Delta country. When he moved . . . he took my first love with him!

The Delta, as we all know, is where those Mississippi boys talk real slow. I think about Dorothy Ann often and the happiness we had being together. I am sure that she thinks about me, too. Now, we have taken new destinations in our lives. I bet those slow talking Delta boys would take forever and a day to say, "I love you, Dorothy Ann."

"I can't change the direction of the wind, but I can adjust my sails to always reach my destination."
Jimmy Dean

Dorothy Ann didn't get no engagement ring. My new love, Betsy, my fiancée, looks at my brand new expensive engagement ring and says,

"Darlin', precious . . . I'll wait for you forever. Now, don't you go messing around with none of them Jap gals! . . . You hea'!

"Honey, you know I won't! Like I said, I won't touch
those yellow-skin slant-eyed Jap gals with a ten-foot pole.
Darlin', sweet thing, sugar bun, don't y'all worry yo'
little head none. I will soon be shipping out after
graduation from jump school, but darlin', again, don't you worry . . . I will write you every day!"

When the U.S.S.Breckenridge troop transport ship docks in Yokohama, I never write back. Pretty Japanese gals sure make a liar out of me!

Graduation

The Paratrooper Creed

I volunteer as a paratrooper, fully realizing the hazards of my chosen service. By my thoughts and my actions, I will always uphold the prestige, honor and rich esprit-de-corps of the only volunteer branch of the United States Army.

Graduation is a great day for all of us. We stand tall with pride as our coveted and much- prized paratrooper jump wings are pinned on.

Now, I will say this: *"I strongly detest and resent those that wear our jump wings when they are not United States Army Paratroopers! Our jump wings were designed prior to WWII for America's elite all-volunteer Army Paratroopers, ONLY! Others that have made five parachute jumps out of an airplane should not wear our jump wings. You are not America's Army Paratroopers!*

To these people, let them issue plastic toy wings. They should not wear United States Army Paratrooper wings! You become one of America's elite Army Paratroopers when you jump out of a plane in the darkness of the night. You are heavily equipped with a main chute, reserve chute, trenching shovel, belts of ammo, your own weapon, the barrel of a .30 caliber machine gun, or a mortar plate and your trench knife, in case you make it down and find yourself in a difficult situation like hung up in the top of a tree. Then . . . you are an Army paratrooper!"

"Man becomes the master of difficult situations. By refusing the assistance of weak men, he relies on his own strength of character."

I Ching

Good-Bye Benning

Running Horse and I are destined for one of America's WWII elite and much combat decorated parachute infantry regiments, the 511th Parachute Infantry Regiment of the 11th Airborne Division.

We are now paratroopers; we are on parade, good-bye to the towers, good-bye to the gliders, good-bye to our friends that are off to other airborne units and good-bye, Benning.

It is not easy to say good-bye to Sergeant Swartz.

As we shake hands, my eyes get a little misty. Sergeant Swartz made that fateful decision not to see my crooked arm. He definitely sees me through some of the darker days in jump school and develops my confidence to become a paratrooper.

Sergeant Swartz puts his hand on my shoulder, and with these profound words of kindness says,

"Godspeed, stand tall, take care of yourself and remember . . . never look down!"

"Kindness in words creates confidence. Kindness in thinking creates profoundness."
Joshiki

Sergeant Swartz will always be remembered as a cornerstone in my life. He is a true friend. He helped to channel the direction my life is soon to take. I will always be grateful for his dedication to the U.S. military and his compassion towards me. *Little did I know that day, that Sergeant Swartz and I will meet once again on a hot dark night in the summer of 1948 . . . The Year of the Rat on the outskirts of Tokyo when Private Perkins and I, are facing four very drunk 1st Cavalry soldiers.*

Tattoos

Four or five of us pretty much stick together among the ones destined for the 11th Airborne Division. We arrive in Stockton, California waiting for the U.S.S. Breckenridge troop transport to take us to Japan.

I say to my buddies,

"Hey, y'all let's go downtown this weekend! It's payday!

Let's go see the girls and have some fun- we got our jump pay!"

No one thought about having K.P. until it was posted on the bulletin board. *K. P. - Kitchen Police means washing dishes, pots and pans.*

Running Horse, Floyd Perkins and Ray Payne are the lucky ones. Our names are posted for K.P. duty. Normally, we would say we are unlucky, but not tonight! Our other two friends went downtown, got drunk and tattooed. After seeing those tattoos that they have to live with for the rest of their lives, I will wash pots and pans on K.P. anytime!

"Remember that not getting what you want
is sometimes a wonderful stroke of luck."
Dalai Lama

When I see people proudly showing their many tattoos, I tell them, as they get older it may be difficult for some to find work, but they, with their tattoos should not worry, as they can always find work . . . *as a freak in a circus sideshow!*

"You are . . . who you are."
Joshiki

Private Floyd H. Perkins

I met Private Perkins for the first time in Stockton, California. He is a volunteer for the 11th Airborne Division. He is also is ah wantin' to see those Japanese gals to see if they have yeller' skin. Perkins is from Texas. We think a lot

alike . . . pretty girls!

Now, from watching cowboy movies at the picture show,

I always reckon that all Texans are tall, but Perk with his big feet is not so tall. He says they are good for dancing. Perk is one of the happiest folks I know, but I have seen him get fighting mean and then he looks about ten feet tall!

Perk had gone through an earlier class at Benning. He had been locked up in the stockade for a while; because of a bar fight in Phoenix City . . . "Sin City".

Perk will fight to get what he wants. He likes cigarettes, whisky, and wild women! Perk's favorite song is,

Cigarettes and Whiskey and Wild, Wild Wimmen'- They'll "drive you crazy; they'll drive you insane!"

They kept Perk in the Airborne. I guess the army didn't want to waste their money after puttin' him through jump school.

Perk and I seem to relate to each other's lifestyle . . . girls!

Like all good privates, we arrange to have good times, doing whatever, whenever, wherever, and doing that any which way we can. We are soon to learn that the 511th Parachute Infantry Regiment logo is a wolf behind an eight ball. That there logo seems be just the right fittin' for Perk and I.

Seasick at Sea

Let me tell you sailors this! I am extremely grateful to you for not lettin' me in your navy-and sincerely want to thank you for that! I would have made a poor sailor for Uncle Sam. You can keep your navy! I would rather walk on water! I don't ever want to be out again on one of your big ol' boats in the middle of this ocean- *I am seasick!*

Down below the bunks are stacks of four on top of each other. I am lucky as I am on one of the lowest bunks; I could not have climbed any higher. After four days, I am feeling a little better and it is Thanksgiving Day. The Army always feeds privates good on Thanksgiving Day and Christmas Day.

These people that work on ships, travel back and forth bringing troops to overseas locations sure do enjoy their Thanksgiving dinner. They say they have what they call *sea legs*. That is one thing I never did acquire.

I hope the fish enjoyed my Thanksgiving dinner. It is a daily occurrence for me to feed the fish over the side of the Breckenridge! The only good news on the Breckenridge is when Floyd Perkins tells me that he has overheard them saying,

"We are docking in Honolulu, Hawaii in three hours!"

Paradise here we come- a land of hula girls with lovely hula hands; graceful as a bird in motion, palm trees, sunshine and beaches. Oh, and did I mention the girls? Perk and I are excited as can be. Before, we could only dream about going to Hawaii and now here we are- ready to explore the warm exotic waters- and . . . did I mention the girls?

Paddle like a Dog

It is a warm sunny day as the Breckenridge docks in Honolulu. It will sure be good to get off this boat! Back in California, a navy sailor chief done told me, “Don’t call a ship a boat because a boat is a ship.” *I thought . . . “Figure that one out! If you know what that means.”*

Floyd Perkins, Running Horse, John Russell McFarland, and I catch a bus and go to the world famous *Waikiki Beach. Alohaaa!*

We country southern boys can swim by the time we can walk, but I don’t know nothin’ about tides; tides only happen in that there ocean water. That ocean water comes in and that ocean water goes out. The problem is when that there ocean water goes out, it is sometimes stronger going out, than when that there water is ah comin’ in! *You know what I mean!*

To show the girls at *Waikiki Beach* that I am a good swimmer, I swim way out from the shore. Nobody else swims out as far I do. I don’t think about sharks. The biggest thing we have in Kings Creek is big ol’ catfish. I’m wantin’ the girls to wave at me, but none of them do. I am ah thinkin’ that they just can’t see me. I am gettin’ hungry. I had seen a sign, ‘SPENCE WEAVER’S HOT DOGS’. I want one of them hot dogs and a cold RC Cola. When we get to the beach this morning, I ask for a Moon Pie and an RC Cola, but they don’t have none. *What kind a place is this here Hawaii, no Moon Pie?*

Like I had told them navy people in *Nu Awleans*, I can swim real good. What I was ah talking about is in the creeks and ponds of Missippi’. Now, what I am finding out is this here ocean water is different. You can’t even drink the stuff! I don’t know nothing about tides, and this tide at *Waikiki Beach* is a mighty powerful tide. Here I am, way out in the ocean swimming and waiting for the girls to wave at me.

Every time I take a stroke with my right arm and then take a stroke with my left arm, I am right back to where I took a stroke with my right arm. *“Y’all know what I’m ah talkin’ about!”*

I am not gettin' nowhere and the girls are gettin' smaller! Pretty soon, I am all tuckered out, so as to rest a little, I begin to dog paddle.

As everybody knows, dog paddling is the first thing in the south we learn about swimming. Our older brothers and cousins throw us in the pool *(Yankees say pond)* to learn us how to swim. They would yell,

"Paddle like a dog; paddle like a dog!" The girls on the beach are gettin' smaller and smaller, and they aren't looking at me. I decide maybe I ought to get a little closer to shore so I could wave real friendly like at them. *Have you ever swum against a strong tide? Well, common sense taught me something in that ocean, something that saved my life in later years in Bali, Indonesia.*

If you can't beat 'em, join 'em! And that's what I do with this powerful tide. I stop fighting the tide. I slowly swim towards a curve in the coastline by swimming at an angle, often resting by dog paddling. Reaching the curve in the shore, far from where I started, I am exhausted from fighting the swiftly withdrawing tide. I swim, swim and then dog paddle a while; at last . . . crawling up on the beach, I lie on my stomach and go right to sleep. Later, I wake up sun-burned and hungry. I walk along the beach, hoping to see the girls, but when I get to the place I last saw them-they are long gone!

"In life, it is easy to go along with the tide, which eventually leads to being swept away by the tide. If you want to excel, you must show the strength and desire to fight against the tide, to achieve what you want."
Wayne Cheng

Upon landing in Hawaii, we discover that we don't have much money, as we had spent most of it on the girls in California. *Girls sure like money*!

Going Bananas

Perk and I walk along River Street to the end of Hotel Street where all the bars and the pretty girls are. Savory smells are coming from the local restaurants and are mighty inviting to us. We see a big red sign over a Chinese Restaurant with the name, Won Huang Lo. We stop and put our nose up to the window . . . we see roasted ducks, chickens and pork ribs hanging from hooks; with our eyes widening and our mouths drooling, we gaze upon the wonderful sight of sweet pork dumplings steaming in bamboo baskets. We are so envious- people smacking their lips and eating hot noodles with two little wooden sticks. The food looks so delicious and we are so hungry, but we don't have no money, so we can't go in.

Perk and I, bleary-eyed, heads hanging, sit on a low wall. After the California girls, the pretty girls in Hawaii sure know how to get what little money we have left **. . .** *Alooooha!*

I look over at Perk,

"Perk, I'm so hungry. You got any money left at all?"

"I got a nickel."

"Well, I got a dime."

"Perk, look across the street! Do you see them big ol' green yeller *bananers* hanging at the front of that grocery store? Let's go buy some."

"Ma'am, can we buy some of them big ol' *bananers*, if you please?"

I hand her our fifteen cents. She hands us a bunch of bananas with a look of wonder in her eyes. Some more things in Lee County, Mississippi that we just don't have- and that's green bananas in the stores. Ain't *bananers* **. . .** bananas*?*

These *bananers'* don't taste all that good, but nevertheless we are powerful hungry and we eat 'em all! Soon, I notice that Perk's words are becoming mumbled. I try to say,

"Perk, I know I shouldn't have drunk all those Mai Tais just 'cause that pretty Hawaiian girl said she was in love with me, and then she asks for another drink!"

My mouth is ah tinglin' and puckerin' up. My tongue will not cooperate. I am mumblin' but the words won't come out right. We don't do any talkin' while we are ah walkin' back to that boat. Well, I had never heard of green *cooking* bananas before in my life. But guess what! I have just discovered what they are. I say to myself, *this is my first time eating cooking bananas and it will be the last time I eat cooking bananas!*

"Approach love and cooking with reckless abandon."
Dalai Lama

That night I have a dream . . . I have been invited to the house of Won Huang Lo . . . be there by eight the invitation read . . .

Won Huang Lo
Be There At Eight

The Chopstick

Be there at eight,
The invitation read
The famous house of Won Huang Lo
Is where you will be fed.

Oh! A Chinese dinner
More precious than gold
Is food for the gods-
So I have been told.

I hurry down to China Town
Not wanting to be late
With great anticipation
Of the food I will partake.

It all seems so innocent enough
Exciting to be sure-
Fried rice, Peking duck
And all kinds of other good stuff.

Thoughts of sweet sour pork
And stuffed pig's feet
Make me quicken my pace
As I hurry down the street.

The famous house of Won Huang Lo
Shone brightly in the night
Like a giant pagoda
With flashing neon lights.

The sound of Chinese gongs
And fire crackers splitting the air
Rang through the night
With laughter everywhere.

My host bids me welcome
And I thank him with wonder
Seeing all that food
Trying to conceal my great hunger

The table is large and round.
Everything seems to be there
With the exception of a knife
Nor a fork anywhere.

Much to my surprise
Out of the corner of my eye
Laying innocently by my plate,
Two little sticks I do spy.

Anxiously I glance around
Not believing what I am seeing.
Everyone is holding those little sticks
And with smacking lips, they are eating.

Not to be outdone by anyone-
Oh! It seems easy enough.
I grab hold of those sticks
To get my share of good stuff.

I lift them slowly up
Hoping no one will see
It is then that I spot
That little green pea.

Like flashing crossed sabers
Held high in the air
I make my approach
With a confident flair.

It is the damndest thing
I have ever seen
This little green pea
Is part Mexican jumping bean.

I fare no better
With the Peking duck
And watch all that good food
Being eaten up.

With hungry disappointment
And much despair
My nose perks up
With hot noodles steaming the air.

Hot delicious noodles
Coming through the door
And after all
I have eaten spaghetti before.

Have you ever held
greased lighting on a stick?
Those noodles flew away.
Believe me of what I speak.

I look at the table
With a painful frown,
Like fallen soldiers
My food lay all around.

Again I look around
To see that everyone is through.
Why! I have not even started
Oh! What will I do?

My host said, "How was it?"
And I softly moaned-
Oh! So delicious.
Can I take some home?

Be there by eight
The invitation read.
The house of Won Huang Lo
Is where you will be fed.

I touch my pocket
and smile with glee,
for me and my fork
Is gonna get that pea.

Private Payne- 1946

Privates Are Cunning

What did General Black Jack Pershing say during World War I? *"Army Privates are good soldiers, but very clever and bear considerable watching."*

"There will be no whiskey on this boat!" the ship's Captain had said!

There is one lone Navy S.P. (shore patrol) searching everyone in line as they are going up the gangplank to board the U.S.S. Breckenridge. The S.P. pats each soldier from the calf of the leg to his waist. He does not have time to look up and the line moves on. Three soldiers ahead of me, I see a paratrooper with his treasure, a bottle of Tanduay Rum held high over his head as if weightless.

"Learning is weightless,
a treasure you can always carry easily."
Chinese Proverb

"Next!" says the S.P. . . . and the line moves on.

"A paratrooper knows a good bottle of rum, when an S.P. does not know of a good bottle of rum."
Joshiki

General Black Jack Pershing was right. *Privates are not only clever, but also extremely cunning.* As the soldier walks up the ramp, he conceals his treasure of Tanduay Rum beneath his shirt!

Those of us destined for the 511th Parachute Infantry Regiment of the 11th Airborne Division have our bottles of Tanduay Rum on board; the U.S.S. Breckenridge departs for Yokohama, Japan.

Part II

The Chocolate Bar Days

RIDE THE EAST WIND

Motherly Love

Although the sun is out, it is a very cold December morning as the U.S.S. Breckenridge moves into Tokyo bay, slowly approaching Yokohama Harbor. Our ship pulls into the harbor and docks. Weary soldiers from the long journey across the Pacific, are now descending in a single long line down the ramp of the ship. We climb into the back of the trucks and are taken to transient barracks where we will stay a few days prior to departing for Camp Zama REPO DEPO- Replacement Detachment. My friends do not want to leave the comfort and warmth of the barracks; they also want to stay for chow, but not me! I am ready to see the city and the people of Japan.

As I walk along, I see many damaged buildings. The war left destruction and rubble everywhere. I can see reconstruction-taking place as the people are rebuilding their stores, homes and their lives. Seeing sad determination on the faces of the people as they set about to restore the life that the war has taken from them. I cannot help but feel sorry for them. Their lives are devastated by the ravages of war. They move slowly carrying their belongings in and out of the rubble.

I am surprised to see that Yokohama has some old drab streetcars running with bells clangin'. People are riding these streetcars, coming and going. I, too, hop on a streetcar, not knowing whether I am coming or going and I don't care! I am on for the ride- the thrill of being in Japan. I look around at the Japanese citizens on the streetcar. I am not afraid.

Not once am I ever afraid during my entire occupation years in Japan. With the war over, Japan is the safest place I have ever been in my life. I can walk down the darkest of streets at night without having to look behind me. Don't we wish we could say that about large American cities?

Clickety clack, clang, clang - the old streetcar rumbles along. I hang onto an overhead strap in the crowded streetcar. The cold winter wind blows right through the open windows of the car. The Japanese look straight ahead, almost through me as if I am not there.

Sometimes there is a nervous glance out of the corner of an eye, and I smile, *the war is over . . . I am your friend! It is the winter of 1946/47; it is severely cold . . . one of the coldest winters in Japan's recorded history. There is a severe shortage of food, clothing, housing and medicine. The war has taken its toll. There is much suffering and the hardships for the Japanese people are almost too much to describe.*

Standing next to me in the streetcar, is a young Japanese mother with a little red-faced baby wrapped in a small gray blanket. This little baby is very sick and having a hard time breathing. She tries to comfort the little one, but the baby is crying and gasping for breath. I fear for this little baby's life as it struggles to breathe. The baby's mother with so much love in her heart, puts her mouth over her little baby's nose, sucks out the snot and spits it out the window. She repeatedly opens and clears the air passages so that her little baby might breathe. I am overwhelmed with compassion for the mother and her little baby. I find I have much admiration for the mother whose only thought at this moment is that her baby might live. *Clickety, clack, clickety clack, the old streetcar . . . and life . . . moves on.*

"Where there is love, there is life."
Mahatma Gandhi

Better to Never Have Met You in My Dream

Yokohama is an intriguing and different world. A world I had only seen while watching newsreels at the Strand Theater in Tupelo. I have never been far from my home in Mississippi. I now stand in the street here of Yokohama as an eighteen year old soldier- as I look in awe and wonder.

Homeless people gather in small groups at train stations looking forlorn and destitute. I see makeshift houses built along the riverbanks and shacks arranged under bridges to help block the cold winter weather. Adults and children hug tattered blankets to keep warm. I stop and stare with amazement at the bombed out buildings- many now call home.

The Japanese soldiers are still wearing their war torn uniforms, as this is all they have to keep them warm through the cold winter months. At the entrance of a temple, I see former Japanese soldiers missing arms or legs. Some have bandages- leaving their wounds festering, hoping for donations of food or money.

A few months ago, these Japanese soldiers were our deadly enemies. Now, I see them through different eyes- eyes of compassion. I realize the impact of war on these soldiers and their families and children.

Some soldiers are making toys out of empty American beer cans that they have salvaged from garbage bins outside of the empty beer cans into colorful Kawasaki Zero fighter planes and Mitsubishi heavy bombers. The planes have propellers that turn and wheels that roll. Attached to the front of each toy is a string for pulling. I cannot help but smile when I see these colorful markings on the sides and tails of the planes: **BUDWEISER BEER- Where There's Life, There's Bud**

SCHLITZ BEER- The beer that made Milwaukee famous

As soon as an American soldier throws down his cigarette, young boys scamper to be first to grab what is left of it. There may not be much tobacco left in the smoked cigarette . . . the remaining tobacco is precious. Throughout the day, a young boy accumulates tobacco that he then sells.

He does whatever he can to help feed his family.

Near the entrance to the temple a young Japanese girl steps in front of me and says,

"You come my house. I like you. You come my house.

I like Amelikan' soldier. My mama like Amelikan' soldier; little brother, little sister like Amelikan' soldier. Come, we go PX . . . hungry!"

She looks into my eyes with a pleading smile. As surprised as I am, the soft plea in her voice is hard to resist.

As I notice more about her, charmed by her voice and smiling eyes, I see that she is wearing what I imagine to be a young girl's high school uniform. Her rosy cheeks chilled by the winter air and her beautiful jet-black almond eyes are compelling, erasing any lingering doubts of reason within me. She gently places her hand into mine and says, "Come!"

She leads me to a small Army PX around the corner. Near the entrance of the Post Exchange, she stops and gently takes my hand. She again, looks deep into my eyes with those beautiful black almond eyes and says,

"Little brother, little sister hungry!" *I am overcome by the enemy.*

As we walk hand in hand to the PX around the corner from the temple. I begin to think of her as one of the loveliest young girls I had seen, since the love of my life, Dorothy Ann Brown. In my heart, I am happy to see she does not have . . . yellow skin!

I squeeze her hand gently and turn into the PX as my new friend waits outside the entrance. No doubt, she is crossing her fingers that I will return and return I do, with two large paper sacks of food. Her eyes filled with gratitude of love.

"We cannot all do great things, but we can do small things with great love."
Mother Teresa

She takes one of the bags, places her hand into my free hand and softly says,

"You come my house."

She leads me down the street to a train station. She pulls out two small coins, buys two tickets, we board a train bound for

. . . I do not know where and I do not care. We smile at each other. We are happy as a couple of kids at the fair sharing cotton candy. *What a wonderful day!*

From the inside, looking out the window I see an elderly Japanese conductor in a black uniform standing on the platform. He looks at his watch, looks up to the front of the train at the engineer, waves his hand and times a long blow of his whistle to the exact second for the train departure. With a long low whine, the train pulls out of the station. Soon, we are going fast. I see other trains whizzing by. I am on my first electric train.

"How old are you?"

She turns her head a little to the side. I receive a soft smile.

I point to myself and say,

"Me, eighteen." She turns her head

to the other side and smiles again. I point to myself and count

to eighteen on my fingers. Pointing to her, I make the motion for her to count on her fingers. She smiles and counts on her fingers- sixteen. I say,

"You are sixteen."

She laughs and says,

"Me, sixteen!"

It must have been about a half an hour out into the countryside when the train begins to slow down. We stop at a small station built of wood and covered with a gray slate roof. The roof blends into the grayness of the winter day.

As we leave the train station, my new friend points out into the distance. I see a small house made of wood with a straw-thatched roof. The house sits under a large persimmon tree. High up in the upper branches of the tree I can see a few shriveled persimmons that have not yet surrendered themselves to the cold winter air.

We each carry a sack of food, holding hands as we walk between the frozen rice paddies on to a small path leading to her home. In the warmth of her hand, I feel the pleasure of happiness in her heart.

"To give pleasure to a single heart by a single act is better than a thousand heads bowing in prayer."
Mahatma Gandhi

A gray, weather-beaten wood door slides open. A middle-aged woman bows low from the waist, politely smiling, as she greets me in the Japanese language. A shy little boy and girl peek from behind their mother, happily grinning and grateful to see me. Fortunately, I have brought along some Hershey chocolate bars.

Her little brother and sister run out from behind their mother excitedly looking at the bags of food that we have in our arms.

My new friend lovingly greets her family. I can see that it is true, "Home is where the heart is." It is obvious that her heart is her family. *My heart goes out to them.*

After an attempt at an introduction, with lots of smiles and giggles, my very first Japanese friend points to my boots and motions for me to take them off. *Shoes are not worn in Japanese homes; I will be taking my boots off a lot during the next few years.*

We eat well as the evening begins to settle over the little house. Little brother and sister are all smiles, with chocolate smeared around their mouths. There is food for nights to come. The old wooden house is unheated. It is bitter cold. We all sleep together under a heavy quilt. They call it a "futon". With mother and children asleep . . . or pretending to be, my new friend reaches out with her hands, snuggles close to me and whispers into my ear,

"You like me?"

I have only recently turned eighteen. She is sixteen. With a father lost in the war, this cold winter night at the age of sixteen, she supports her family in the only way she knows how.

Like a lingering dream, I have my precious memories of this time gone by, many nights of reaching out for hands . . . that are not there.

"Better never to have met you in my dream, than to wake and reach out for hands that are not there."

Otomo No Yakamochi

The 11th Airborne Division

If anyone ever wants to know how to build smoke stacks, ask the Japanese. As we travel across the Kanto plain, I see an assortment of tall black smokestacks decorating the horizon, like fingers sticking up into the sky. Our B-29 long-range bombers have leveled the factories to the ground, but the smokestacks remain standing- pointing skyward with defiance.

We arrive at Camp Zama REPO DEPO. All Army troops process in and out of Zama. Camp Zama is the West Point of Japan for Japanese Army officers. *We privates know that our NCOs' (non-commissioned officers) are the backbone of our military. That is why we have soldiers, sailors, marines and . . . officers.*

The military passenger train that goes north out of Tokyo has the name '*Yankee Flyer*'. The train that goes south is *'The Dixie Rebel'*. Whoever named these trains has a lot of common sense- it must have been an *army private!*

I board the *Yankee Flyer* with other paratroopers leaving Camp Zama, heading north for Camp Haugen in Hachinohe, Aomori Prefecture- home of the 511th Parachute Infantry Regiment. One of our Regiments, the 187th P.I.R. and our 11thAirborne Division Headquarters are at Camp Crawford, Sapporo, Hokkaido. Our 188th P.I R. is stationed at Camp Schimmelpfennig, Sendai, Miyagi Prefecture. Our division's 457th Parachute Field Artillery Battalion is at Camp Baker in Yamagata Prefecture.

Our division occupies northern Honshu and Hokkaido. The 11th Airborne Division occupies forty percent of all of Japan and that to me, is the most dangerous part. Stalin knows where we are and he is upset! Stalin wants Hokkaido as part of the occupation, but President Truman states emphatically,

"No way!" Stalin has a massive land army just across the Sea of Japan. He has troops that are still in China and of course Siberia only a few hundred miles away, but he lacks one thing: ships for transportation.

The 1st Cavalry Division is stationed in the Kanto plains- the plum of locations- Tokyo and Yokohama area, where all the big fancy nightclubs with many exotic, beautiful girls all eagerly wanting to entertain the American troops with their charms and cunning tricks of the trade.

After the surrender of the Japanese Imperial Army signed on the USS Missouri, ending WW II, Joseph Stalin was clamoring for his Russian forces to occupy Hokkaido. The 11th Airborne Division is ordered to move north to occupy northern Honshu and Hokkaido. Most railways are knocked out, and transportation is scarce or non-existent; it has been said a number of times that General Joseph Swing, our Division commander and his remaining 10,000 thieves, commandeered every Japanese vehicle that they could get their hands on and went north.

A Japanese conductor blows a long blast on his whistle.. The *Yankee Flyer* grunts a few times, belches clouds of black smoke into the sky-the old steam engine comes to life. This tired train has survived the war; it moves slowly on up the tracks with bells clanging, gaining speed with each stroke of the old pistons. The Japanese engineer often blows the whistle and clangs the bell. The fireman shovels in coal for more steam. The groaning engine begins to bellow.

As we come near a crossing, the engineer is clanging his bell and the old steam engine lets out a long whistle. Someone runs out from a shack alongside the track and lowers a long bamboo pole to stop traffic, so that the train can keep moving.

The *Yankee Flyer* keeps moving on to the northern camps of the 11th Airborne Division. We travel throughout the night, sitting upright with our rifles between our legs. The window curtains are drawn to block vision from the outside.

We arrive at Camp Haugen in Hachinohe around midmorning. Camp Haugen, named after our former 511th Regimental Commander, Colonel Orin D. Haugen, killed in battle in the Philippines. Parts of the camp are still under construction.

Disabled Japanese Zero fighter planes are parked in rows at the end of the runway near the hangers. The engines of the Zeros have been blown, no doubt by the Japanese themselves. Large Japanese coastal guns overlook Hachinohe Bay . . . no longer a menacing threat, but now only a silent reminder of the once mighty Japanese Imperial army.

I am assigned to Easy Company; second platoon-first squad, as first scout. The 511th is no picnic. I have some idea that the Russians are denied any part in the occupation of Japan as it slowly unfolds in a series of well-placed camps and unit deployment facilities across the landscape of the "Rising Sun". *(Many of these same original camps are still in use over 50 years later.)*

The 511th Parachute Infantry Regiment

The Soviets entered the war only eight days prior to the Japanese surrender. Eastern Russia is just across the straits from Japan. The Soviets occupy four small Japanese islands off the northern tip of Hokkaido. These islands can be seen in the distance from northern Hokkaido. The Russians continue to occupy them and refuse to give the islands back to Japanese control; I imagine that Stalin is furious his armies cannot take part in the occupation of Japan. He knows and Truman knows that the Soviets are a large land army.

They do not have enough ships to occupy Hokkaido. *However, one never knows what that mad man Joseph Stalin is going to do next!* Our 11th Airborne Division occupies Northern Honshu and Hokkaido just in case Stalin tries anything funny; of course, our vast naval fleet and army air force keeps him at bay. *I like to think that if it were not for the 11th Airborne Division the Japanese people of Hokkaido would be speaking Russian today.*

We privates have a network that keeps us in the know-how as to what is going on, and this network reaches all the way up into Regimental and Division Headquarters. The 511th is well-trained, as is the rest of our division. We engage in long marches with full field equipment, endless training, night maneuvers, and simulated combat jumps.

When in camp, our day starts with our early morning five-mile run before breakfast. Our 1st Sergeant, slim and wiry sets a fast pace, sounding off at the top of his voice.-he has us singing traditional airborne songs as the earth flies beneath our feet.

Run, run, run . . . As we run, listen to us this day
We are America's Airborne . . . what more can we say?
We are America's paratroopers . . . descending from the sky.
Ours is not to reason why . . . but to do or die.
Airborne! Airborne!

Airborne- all volunteers- are without a doubt, the best-fit troops in the entire military. We are paratroopers, well-fed with only the best chow, especially our desserts. We deserve the best! We go through the chow line with a compartmentalized metal tray; the cooks behind the line spoon meat loaf, mashed potatoes, and canned vegetables onto our trays.

Life could not be better! We also have slices of bread, unlimited refills of iced tea and coffee. We are so fortunate, as often we have powdered milk. For dessert, a slice of sheet cake with icing- this is a special treat! Today the sheet cake may have vanilla icing, tomorrow, strawberry icing, the next day chocolate icing, and then back to vanilla icing. *It sure is nice to have a variety for dessert.*

Thanksgiving and Christmas are special days. We have ham, turkey, stuffing, cranberry sauce, apple pie, pumpkin pie, apples, oranges, some nuts and sometimes ice cream. *What wonderful treats! What a wonderful life!* There is no meat loaf on these holidays. Life could not be better; the ranks of the 511th Parachute Infantry Regiment are in high spirits!

"He, whose army is animated by the same spirit throughout all the ranks, will win!"
Sun Tzu

We might've had roast duck for Christmas, if I was a better shot on this cold winter night, the winter of 1946/1947, *Year of the Dog.*

Song of the Wild Goose

It is not long after arriving at Camp Haugen, on the E Company bulletin board there is a notice for those scheduled for guard duty. Would you believe it! Private Payne is one of them!

"Who me!"

"Welcome to the 511th, Private Payne.

I see that this is your first guard duty with us at Camp Haugen.

From the way you talk, I can guess that you are from the south?"

"That's right Corporal; yes, I am from the south, Lee County Mississippi!" I proudly say.

Hawk nosed, beady eyes, wide mouthed, showing tobacco-stained teeth, the corporal sarcastically says,

"Well, Private Payne I am Corporal Yerrell. I'm from New York and I am . . . your Corporal of the Guard. You will be pleased to know, I have a special guard post picked out especially for you. It is nice and quiet . . . with no one around!"

My first guard duty, especially chosen by Corporal Yerrell, is the gasoline dump on the other side of the airfield. I am driven out to the dump with the Sergeant of the Guard who don't have much to say. Corporal Yerrell is doing the driving. I'm sitting in the back of the jeep with my M1 rifle held upright between my legs. I need my hands to hold on to the jeep as I watch the shadows go by. Corporal Yerrell never misses a bump in the road. *I don't like him, and he knows it.*

As the jeep bounces up and down, he watches me in the rear view mirror with a perpetual Mona Lisa smile on his face. He knows all about this gasoline dump out in the middle of nowhere. He is enjoying this as he sees the anxiety building on my face. I am soon to find out the fuel dump near the ocean- is way past the airstrip. Fifty-five gallon drums full of gas, and *I* am to guard this assortment of containers, row after row stacked high . . . with my life. I am to guard the fuel reserves from thieves, or whoever may want to blow up this dump and maybe even me too! As we go down the dirt road along the beach, I can hear the lapping of waves and I think . . . *what's out there?*

The jeep brakes to a sudden halt that almost knocks me off my seat. Corporal Yerrell points at the large dark foreboding gas dump nearby, smirks and says,

"Here you are, Private Payne; you can get out of the jeep now. Your responsibility is to protect this gas dump. With the war over, there is a great shortage of gasoline for the Japanese. Thieves are operating around American military bases; they will go to any extreme to get this gasoline- so keep your eyes open. Oh' yes- don't forget, Stalin is clamoring for the Russians to occupy Hokkaido, the situation does not look good. One of the first things Russian commandoes will do is

. . . blow up our gasoline dumps. Be on the alert- watch that beach! Now Private Payne- this gas dump is all yours, please enjoy the peaceful quietness of the night!"

With a sarcastic sneer,

"Don't forget your rifle . . . you may need it!"

The old sergeant gives me the password. Corporal Yerrell quickly turns the jeep around. *It is clear that he wants to get the hell away from this gas*oline *dump and maybe me too, as he knows I am mad.* As he spins the jeep around, Yerrell sarcastically yells,

"Nighty-night. Have a nice night, Private Payne!"

I want to *nighty-night* those corporal stripes right down that Yankee's *nighty-night* throat! I thought about blowing out the tires on his jeep with my M1, but that is against military regulations, besides the old sergeant has a southern accent and seems like a nice person.

Here I am all alone in the darkness. They have left me to walk around this large gasoline dump, facing imaginary Russian soldiers, thieves and other ghosts of the night. I watch the taillights of the jeep as it goes winding back down the road. The taillights become a faint glow in the distance and disappear into the darkness of the night. It is pitch black out here. I cannot open my eyes wide enough trying to see beyond the darkness.

This gas dump looks about the size of a football field. I begin my first (and only) walk around it. I do not like this one bit- barrels stacked on top of barrels and lots of shadows. Not knowing what is around the next corner has me jumpy and anxiously looking all around . . . I move about fifty yards away from the dump, out near the dirt road and sit down. I do not want to be easily seen; after all, if something were to happen to me, who is gonna' guard this gasoline dump? Besides being away from the dump, gives me a better vision to guard the entire dump and myself. From this position, I am able see if anyone is coming for me; I have a better chance of any action needed with my M1 rifle.

A large dark cloud overshadows the half-moon. The mournful lapping of the waves coming from the beach don't help none neither. I am all by my lonesome self; it is getting darker and darker, and my eyes are getting bigger and bigger. I look around wildly, as I think to myself, *"What's out there? "I* look around; it's like a nightmare. I nervously keep my finger on the trigger; I must be ready for action!

"Vision without action is a daydream.
Action without vision is a nightmare."
Japanese Proverb

High up in the sky is a flock of geese passing through the clouds. *Honk, honk, honk!* This gets my attention.

I just cannot help myself; they make me do it, ah honking like that. Again, I am a country boy back in Mississippi. I jump up and take action, letting go with three rounds from my M1. The shots are loud and clear in the cold crisp air. Surely, they were heard around the world. I'm gonna' be in big trouble. I am gonna be in the flames of hell and Corporal Yerrell is gonna be fanning the fire. He is also gonna be in heaven knowing that I will be washing pots and pans. I listen for the whine of the jeep.

I grew up with a gun in my hands. In basic training, I fired expert. You can't get any better than that, but I missed with all three rounds; was it the dark clouds that blocked my vision? I can't believe it; those geese just kept right on flying, singing their song. Thinking about those geese flying south for the winter, my mind begins to wonder. A thought comes to my mind . . . *If a goose is a goose and two are geese, then why is a moose a moose and two* **. . .** *are not meese?*

Reality hits me. The Sergeant of the Guard and

Corporal Yerrell are ah gonna' come and get me!

I will be washing pots and pans for the rest of my life. Maybe I can tell them,

"I thought the Russians were attacking!"

I keep waiting for the whine of the jeep. It is late . . . No doubt, Corporal Yerrell is driving the jeep **. . .** in low gear. That Yankee has made sure I do double guard duty.

The jeep never comes until six in the morning. The old sergeant jumps out of the jeep and starts walking towards me. The lights of the jeep are casting his long shadow ahead of him as he approaches. Goose pimples are running up my back. I am trying to act calm.

"Halt! Who goes there?"

"Sergeant of the Guard!"

"Advance to be recognized!"

"What's the password?"

"The ol' red rooster!"

"Step forward to be recognized!"

Corporal Yerrell must be thinking that it is safer in the jeep. He sits there with that smirk on his face. I say to myself, *someday I'm ah gonna' knock that smirk right down his cotton pickin' throat!* My mind goes back to the sergeant in front of me . . . what is he gonna' ask? I think to myself, it may be better if the Russians were to attack, as the situation is gettin' real serious! The old sergeant says,

"How was the night, soldier? All is quiet?"

Hearing these words, I breathe a sigh of relief.

"Yes Sir, all is quiet- mighty quiet, Sergeant.
It was a mighty calm night!"

"Learn to be calm and you will always be happy."
Paramhansa Yogananda

Privates Have Responsibilities

Our captain is announcing in a loud voice, as we listen to him in formation,

"E Company will lead the attack . . . We will keep a good formation. . . We will stay on target with our responsibilities.

We will do our duty as airborne troopers of the 511th!"

He glances over at Perk and me; I wince, saying to myself,

"*Oh, my goodness gracious, not another night on maneuver! Who do they think we are- night owls?*"

It is a cold winter's night. Our breath is curling like smoke in the frosty air. Perk and I maneuver with the rest of E Company, knowing our responsibility is to do our duty and that duty is to scout out and find the enemy. Perkins and I are now lost from the rest of Easy Company. Getting lost is not too difficult for Perk and me. *You know what I mean.*

The 511th Parachute Infantry Regiment is on maneuver. Private Payne as 1st Scout, and Private Perkins as 2nd Scout of the 1st Squad, 2nd Platoon of Easy Company . . . we are now lost from the rest of the regiment. As scouts it is not unusual for Perk and I to get lost in the line of duty.

Instead of going on the attack with the rest of Easy Company, Perk and I maneuver off down a little narrow road seeking the enemy . . . doing our duty.

Looking around to see where we are . . . as if we do not know, off in the distance down in the valley, we see the soft glow of lights. Following a dirt road leads us to the banks of a small river and *a suspicious looking little thatched roof village.*

We can smell that something is cooking down there. Something is going on . . . something we *should* investigate. In the darkness of the night, we hurriedly make our secret approach. The musical sound of the samisen and the sound of girls laughing are incriminating sounds of evidence . . . *that something is going on and we need to get involved. After all, as good scouts we do have our responsibilities!*

"Perk, let's scout out this here village as our part in this here maneuver. After all, we are scouts and scouting is our responsibility. We had better check this village out. They might be ah doing something down there . . . that we should know about."

We hasten our steps. After all, we do not want anyone to get away; the girls need to be interrogated; what if they are wearing *black market silk* panties?"

"You're right, Ray. We best go check this out!"

Perk says, with a squint in his eyes and a cunning smile; by now, Perk is an experienced scout.

Now, we privates know that it is against army regulations to black market PX things such as chocolate bars, cigarettes, or to trade silk panties. We sneak along a stone wall; as good scouts, we silently make our approach. This we must investigate! Something is definitely going on!

"Perk do you hear that music? They are singing! Now they are laughing. What is going on down there? Do you smell . . . sake? Hurry, Perk!"

The tantalizing aroma of hot roasting yakitori chicken fills the night, mixing with the exciting sounds of music and laughter. We throw all caution to the wind. We quicken our pace and hurry down a little dirt lane.

"Look, Perk, there it is . . . Look, look, there's the evidence-that wooden building with rice paper windows. Look hanging by the front door- that's a candle lit red lantern. Do you see it? It is brushed in white, and it says *Yakitori - Hot Sake!" Perk and I are real good at reading Japanese signs that say, "Hot Sake!"*

"That red lantern, is incriminating evidence . . . *something is going on!* As good privates and good scouts, it is our responsibility to investigate the goings on in this sake house!"

Investigate we do and have a great time doing so, after all, on maneuver . . . we privates must keep up our morale.

Mama-san plays the samisen; we all sing Japanese songs, drink lots of hot sake and play games with the girls. We teach the girls the American game of strip poker. Aces are wild! *We interrogate them late into the night!*

The interrogation goes something like, "Do you like your sake hot, or do you like your sake cold? *Remember aces are wild!"*

The next morning the rising sun of Japan is a challenging one. In the middle of the morning, with the brutal red sun glaring down at us, Private Payne and Private Perkins, heads down, feet dragging, come straggling back into camp. As we stand at attention with drooping eyes and slurred voices, we tell our First Sergeant,

"We went scouting in the wrong direction. We got lost and established an outpost in an old abandoned sake house. And First Sergeant, that's where that intoxicating fragrance that you is ah smellin', is ah comin' from!"

I am trying so hard to stand straight at attention, but I wobble a little, look through the squint of my eyes and give a little half- friendly smile.

Our First Sergeant senses that we are not quite telling the truth. He looks at us in disbelief. *Surely, this is one of the best stories, he has ever heard from privates.*

Our First Sergeant gives us that hard look. I can see many endless nights of washing pots and pans in my future. I know that we are in a weak position. I glance at Perk's tired drooping head, and his downcast eyes.

"As circumstances are favorable, one should modify one's plans,"
Sun Tzu

It is then, I bravely say,

"It was a good maneuver, First Sergeant. We accomplished our mission. That outpost was well secured, First Sergeant!

I, Private Payne, as 1st Scout, and Private Perkins as 2nd Scout, did our duty! I am proud to report, Suh,"

As I come to attention and give him a salute, I wobble a little, tilt my head to meet my hand, and then wobble back to attention.

Our First Sergeant's eyes open wide with amazement at what he is hearing. He closes his eyes, opens them again; he looks down, then looks up slowly stirring his coffee. He looks at us, with an amused look on his face, shakes his head from side to side. He looks up at the ceiling, lowers his eyes, waves his hand and says in a soft tone of voice,

"Get out of here!"

I think to myself, *"He is a good First Sergeant; maybe he has been down that road a long time ago, when he himself was a happy private!"*

"Everyone in the world knows that the soft overcomes the hard, and the weak the strong, but no one is able to carry it out in practice."
Lao Tzu

The snow has been falling since nightfall and has not let up. *Now, we don't get much snow in northeast Mississippi. I have never seen skis before in my life!* The next morning our First Sergeant calls for formation out in the company street.

Who in the world would have thought that the army will be sending paratroopers to Hokkaido for ski training?

Ski Training

It is a cold early February morning . . . The Year of the Rat 1948

As we stand at attention, the snowy weather is in tune with what the Captain has to say,

"Now men, we have received orders from headquarters that we are being sent by train to the port of Aomori. From the port of Aomori, we will be going by ferryboat to the port of Hakodate. From Hakodate we will go by truck to a ski training camp in Hokkaido."

The Captain continues,

"Those 9th Corp war planners say, the 11th Airborne Division will learn how to conduct mountainous warfare on skis."

My jaw drops. I whisper to Perk, "*Have they gone mad from the cold or could it be the sake?"*

This is another thing we just don't do in Mississippi. Paratroopers go into battle by jumping out of airplanes and that is what we are paid for. I didn't join the Airborne to slide down a hill on two sticks of wood, and just how am I supposed to get back up on that hill after I slide down?

"Perk, that ski training order must have come from that there headquarters of the 9th Corps. Those people aren't paratroopers. When they were passing out those many medals that those 9th Corps officers wear, you know, like the medal for good conduct **. . .** It's too bad they couldn't qualify for an important one, like a medal for **. . .** *common sense!*"

The Captain hears me whispering to Perk. He stops to look at me,

"Private Payne! You care to share your thoughts about our new orders?" I think long and hard before I speak up,

"No suh, Captain. I recon' not"

The captain turns and continues relaying our new orders in detail. I turn to Perk again and softly continue,

"Perk, do you think we need to worry 'bout avalanches?

What about the girls up in Hokkaido? Are they as pretty as the ones here in Tohoku?

Will there *even be* any girls? It's probably too cold! . . . even for polar bears!"

"Private Payne!" The captain is now ah yelling,

"You have just earned the first place in line to ski down the mountain! We will all see if you like to ski as much as you like to talk!"

"Yes suh! Captain, suh!" *Everybody knows the Russians only enter the war eight days prior to the Japanese surrender. The Russians quickly occupy Manchuria and plunder it. They also occupy the Japanese islands of Etorofu, Kunashiri, Shikotan and the Habomai Islands, just off the tip of Hokkaido. They won't give them back!*

We know that Truman denies the Russians to take part in the occupation of Japan. Stalin is clamoring to occupy Hokkaido. The 11th Airborne Division occupies northern Honshu and Hokkaido. The 11th Airborne Division stands in Stalin's way . . . with the help from a few others, like the U. S. Army Air Force and the U. S. Navy. Thanks to the United States- the Japanese of Hokkaido are not speaking Russian.

Later at night Perk says,

"Ray, does the 9th Corps expect us paratroopers to jump out of airplanes with skis on to defend Hokkaido from Russian ski troops? Can't you just see a sky full of paratroopers with skis on! Why, it will look like a sky full of chopsticks! This skiing paratrooper idea must have been concocted by the Yankees of the 9th Corps or 8th Army officer war planners in some sake house . . . without consulting us privates!"

From the port of Aomori on the northern tip of Honshu for the next four hours, we cross the strait of Tsugaru to Hakodate, Hokkaido. The Tsugaru Strait is a rough body of water. The ferryboat bucks up and down. I don't like water unless it's got ice cubes in it!

I was not born to be a sailor and sure as hell not cut out to be a skier, but at last here we are, ready to defend Hokkaido from the Russians, standing as if in a trance on this snowy mountaintop. Perkins and I look at each other with a look of disbelief that says,

"We just gotta' get out of this some way . . . somehow!"

We stand on top of the mountain and looking down at the valley far below makes it even worse. It is like standing in the open door of a C-47. At jump school, Sergeant Swartz had said, *"Don't look down!"*

Things do get better, in fact much better! It is the 9th Corps "showoff" lieutenant that makes it better and most entertaining! He must have been in on this brilliant planning strategy,

"We are going to go . . . to war on skis!"

I think to myself, "He *is one of those know-it-all types that one only finds in officers. We privates know the kind. That lieutenant stopped being one of us when he went to that there "90 day wonder" officers' school. He is now a newly created officer; you know, like Frankenstein, and he knows it. He is one of those northern Yankee boys, you know the kind-they talk funny English. They don't talk good English like we do down south. Now ain't that the truth!"*

Now, this lieutenant with the look of great importance on his face lets us know right off that he is an expert skier and that we are to do just as he does!

"You can depend on me. You do what I do."

He pushes himself closer to our line of waiting troops. He faces us, and says,

"Now watch this!"

He sticks his poles in the snow, jumps straight up in the air, twists around and takes off straight down that mountainside, like a bat out of hell. I say,

"Hey, Perk, look at him go!"

I have to admit, I am mighty impressed, especially when he hits something hard under the snow. He flies up into the air, goes head over heels, north, east, south and west, becoming a human snowball throwing up sprays of snow as he rolls.

The lieutenant's remarks echo in the frosty air,

"You can depend on me. Do what I do!"

I look at Perkins; shake my head and whispery say,

"Goodness gracious, lordy me! I sho' don't wanna' depend on none of what he did! There's got to be some salvation for us to get out of this!"

"Yeah, I ain't lookin' to be a human snowball."

"Work out your own salvation. Do not depend on others."
Buddha

Everyone assumes a quiet stance, as the Yankee lieutenant slowly recovers, shakes off the snow and hobbles, head down leaving his skis behind. I look down the backside of the slope- I can see there is a way for things to get better for Perk and me. It won't get any better for that show off lieutenant as he is . . . out of action! With everybody standing around bugged-eyed, silently watching all that is a going on, I pull a little on Perk's sleeve; he nods and we slowly back up leaving our skis on the ground. We turn around and melt like spring snow down the backside of the mountain trail towards a little village that we have seen not too far off in the distance. Over the village there are little white clouds floating like signal flags. They seem to be calling to us. *Come on . . . come on!*

I pull my cap down over my ears,

"Come on Perk, they've got to have a sake house down there. Every Jap village in Japan has one!"

Buddha is kind!

Like I have said before, Perk and I have lots of experience in finding sake houses. Sake houses are our specialty . . . not skiing. We soon see a familiar red lantern, beckoning . . . leading us straight to the village sake house.

We slide open the wooden door of the sake house; the Mama-san is happy to see us as she greets us in Japanese and then says in perfect English,

"Howsyomamanem' Y'all got any money?"

I look at Perk out of the corner of my eye and whisper,

"Lordy' me Perk, we ain't the first southerners to come to this hea' sake house."

The girls greet us and sit close . . . the hot sake begins to flow, and the pretty Hokkaido girls take the mountain chill away. Mama-san makes us some fried dumplings that she calls *gyoza.* We like Mama-san's place so much that we decide to spend the night. *After all, it is snowing; it is cold outside; the sake house is warm inside and . . . aces are wild!*

Our First Sergeant, Sergeant Summerfield is out of those hills of West Virginia. I know he too, likes sake. However, I guess he thinks that there's a time and a place for sake. This time he will not cater to another excuse that . . . *we got lost!*

Sometimes sergeants just do not try to understand us privates. I wonder why, as they themselves at one time were privates, not like those officers, many of whom have never experienced the good times of being a happy private.

Of all people, First Sergeant Summerfield should understand us privates. We got lost and it was freezing cold. For good soldiers to stay alert, we had to drink lots of hot sake just to keep warm and . . . to stay alive!

After an evening of washing pots and pans, we are back on the ski slopes again. First Sergeant Summerfield has told our platoon sergeant, Sergeant Crackenbush,

"Keep an eye on Payne and Perkins! They got that look on their faces! It is a cold day and they may disappear to look for something to keep them warm. They sometimes use this as one of their excuses!"

On that cold ski slope, I got the name 'TPP' (Three-Point Payne). "Look at him go! Two feet and one rear end sliding down that mountainside- look at him go!

Three point Payne!"

Ninth Corp war planners soon realize that paratroopers and ski troops are two different animals. Like our daddy had said,

"You can take a fish out of water, but you can't make it fly."

Now, when things get real serious, I mean real bad, I always tell myself that *this too shall pass*, and it did!

I take the long view, turn and leave those skis on the mountain. We go back home to the comforts of Camp Haugen where there are no skis!

"The world will right itself,
take the long view and you are comforted."
Lin Yutang

I nearly froze to death on that mountainside, and I never want to see a pair of skis the rest of my life; however, Perk and I liked that little village. We enjoyed Mama-san's deep-fried dumplings, hot sake and most of all, we sho' did like those pretty girls of Hokkaido!

Thank you, Buddha!

Skiing did not suit me; however, I am in high demand on our long marches through the countryside. When our company commander gets lost and needs directions from some local Japanese, he seems to know who to call. He sends word down the line to fetch Private Payne.

Now, for our officers gettin' lost, it ain't that difficult at all. You see, they and their wives mostly stay in Camp Haugen, whereas some of us privates go outside the camp looking for culture, *always with a deck of cards,* in the surrounding villages. I know the area well and learning Japanese has paid off. I may be only a private, but now I am a private . . . of importance!

Qualities as a Soldier

"Hup, two, three, four!" It is never boring in a line company. Early morning reveille, fall out in the company street, the five mile run, jump today at Misawa, march twenty miles back down a railroad track.

"Hup, two, three, four . . . dig that foxhole!" We come to a halt. The captain sends word down the line,

"Get Private Payne up here." I hot-foot it to the front.

"Private Payne, ask this Jap where Kuraishi is?"

My spoken Japanese is pretty good. I learned Japanese on the streets of Hachinohe and pillow talk at night. It kinda' makes me special for a private and I like that! After all, there is more to life than washing pots and pans! *Privates know what I mean.*

What makes the jumps and long marches a little more comforting is instead of extra socks, first aid kits and all those other essential things that the officers say all good privates should carry, my friends and I cram bottles of R C Cola, cheese and crackers, and Moon Pies into our packs. *Remember what General Black Jack Pershing said about us privates!*

Our officers are well trained; they closely follow Army regulations, *as officers they should.* They never step out of line. They don't have as much fun as us privates, but that's what you get when you are an officer. Officers eat only C-rations. Marching back to camp, we privates also have C-rations plus the goodies in our backpacks.

Most soldiers don't care for C-rations. Having grown up hungry most of my life, I think the qualities of the tightly packed rations are good- a little can of potted meat, some beans, crackers, a small Hershey chocolate candy bar (*that I have an affection for*), powdered coffee and a little pack of four cigarettes. I don't smoke, so I trade my cigarettes to some Yankee tobacco addict for another Hershey bar. With such qualities of luxury, I am a happy soldier!

"One must not judge everyone in this world by his qualities as a soldier; otherwise we should have no civilization."
Field Marshal Erwin Rommel

In spite of all this rigid training, simulated combat jumps and night marches, would you believe this: The 511th Parachute Infantry Regiment has the highest regimental

reenlistment and extension rate, higher than any entire division in the whole United States Army . . .

Inspiration

The Year of the Pig-Autumn, 1947

Our regiment, the 511th Parachute Infantry Regiment, has an enlistment rate higher than any entire division. Stars & Stripes newspaper reporters want to know why, so they make the long train ride from Tokyo to Hachinohe to find out why a remote regimental camp of paratroopers has such a high re-enlistment record.

What they find is an elite well-trained and very proud parachute infantry regiment. The 511th paratroopers maintain a high morale that spreads inspiration throughout the entire. regiment. Could these paratroopers also be getting energy and inspiration by setting a record, no doubt a world record, for eating more chocolate bars than any unit eats in the entire United Stated Army? *Only one private knows the answer to this and he ain't gonna' tell!*

Could it also be the cultural exchange and the friendly inspirations of the beautiful Japanese girls of Tohoku that help generate the reenlistments? The Stars and Stripes reporters interviewed some of the girls. The girls answers were: *"Aces are wild!"*

Japanese girls of the Tohoku region in northern Honshu have healthy soft jet-black hair, no doubt from eating lots of seaweed. They have intriguing, beckoning almond-shaped eyes, lips like Yamagata apple blossoms in the spring, skin as soft and white as milk that gives inspiration to whomever they touch. *I will always remember well the beautiful girls of Tohoku. I will always be proud of the 511th Parachute Infantry Regiment. I proudly wear the pin of the 11th Airborne Division.*

"Inspiration generates inspiration.
It gives of itself to whatever it touches."
Paramhansa Yogananda

We are an unpretentious, confident, parachute infantry regiment. We love who we are and what we do. At times, it can be very challenging; however, our morale, playful spirit, and camaraderie keeps one another going strong; all of that and of course not to forget to mention the pretty girls of Tohoku, are what gives our regiment a higher enlistment rate than any division in the United States Army.

A few months later, heading for a simulated combat jump, flying at about twelve hundred feet, the weather is terribly cold, windy, and it is snowing. Today is the day we jump on Yamoto, and I say to myself,

"I must have been crazy to have volunteered for this hea' Airborne."

The Jump on Yamoto

The year of the Pig . . . January1947

Our C-47 is bouncing around in the air just like Aunt Grace's little red bull, Ferdinand. I am ready to jump at any time, wanting to get the hell out of this airplane! As first scout, I am second in our stick to go out the door. Fully loaded with combat gear, I go out the door into the cold winter wind shouting,

"*One thousand . . . two thousand . . . three thousand*" and then- the jolting shock of my opening chute. *We will earn our jump pay today . . . there will be many casualties.*

We are fully loaded with main chute, reserve chute and full field pack. Not only are we jumping with our own weapon, some of us are carrying the barrel of a .30 caliber machine gun, someone else is carrying belts of ammunition or the base plate of a mortar. We also have a trench knife strapped to the calf of our legs. Although it can be used in close combat, it is mostly used to cut ourselves free of shroud lines should our landing be hung up in trees, or other obstacles.

I am trying to slip wind to control the direction of my fall, but the strong winds are pushing my chute wildly. I must not miss the DZ (drop zone) as this is not a good day to go into freezing water, fully loaded with combat gear. I feel the stinging rush of cold air on my face, I look down noticing snow on the ground and as if this is not enough to worry about, there is a strong ground wind out of the northeast threatening my chute into a bad landing.

My chute is difficult to control because of the strong force of the wind. Looking at other paratroopers descending, I can see helmets and equipment falling from the sky. With the last oscillation, I slam hard onto the Yamoto runway. As I am being dragged by the ground wind, I pull hard on my risers to spill the wind and collapse my chute. My head hits the runway hard, but thanks to my steel helmet, I am only spitting blood from a cut in my mouth. However, there is a throbbing pain in my left hip. Fortunately, I hit the DZ. On this harsh winter day, not all of us hit the DZ. Our sticks are wide and scattered. Some troopers go into the canals, others on rooftops of a nearby village, a few unfortunately are hung up in trees.

Little L-5, single engine airplanes, are busy today at Yamoto, flying paratroopers back and forth to the army hospital in Sendai.

They lay me on a canvas stretcher and load me into one of those little planes. I am flown off to the hospital at Camp Schimmelpfennig. My left hip is pulled a little out of socket. In the hospital, with treatment, it is now mending well. Running Horse has a broken ankle and it is healing. Our captain has a broken back. I am sorry to hear of this. I do not know what happened to him after Yamoto. Our captain had been in the invasion of Luzon, serving under Col. Haugen in the 511th. He is a good captain.

Although that day in Yamoto had been a day of fear, Running Horse and I will not be running away. We will stay11th Airborne!

Down from heaven comes Eleven
And there's hell to pay below
Shout Geronimo!-Geronimo!
Hit the silks . . . check your canopy
And take a look around
The air is full of troopers
Set for battle on the ground
Till we join the stick of angels
Killed on Leyte and Luzon
Shout Geronimo!-Geronimo!
It's a gory road to glory
But we are ready-
Here we go!
Shout Geronimo!-Geronimo!
LTC Byron Paige

"What is needed, rather than running away, controlling, or suppressing or any other resistance, is understanding fear; that means watch it, learn about it, come directly into contact with it. We are to learn about fear, not how to escape from it."
Jiddu Krisnamurti

The 511th Is on Parade
General Douglas MacArthur

At Camp Haugen, it is Saturday morning, and the 511th is on parade with colors flying. The 511th is a grand sight to see. Colonel Cochran on the reviewing stand calls out "Regiment!"... Battalion Commanders call out, "Battalion!"...

Company Commanders call out, "Company!"... The order goes out to march and march we do, as our regimental band strikes up rousing music. Company after company passes with army guidon flags flying high. We are proudly passing in review. The 511th – is on parade! We cover the parade field in perfect formation and pass the review stand with a strong sense of pride in our units. We are paratroopers!

General MacArthur holds an Armed Forces Day Parade in Tokyo each summer. Elements of our 11th Airborne Division always take top honors. In crisp sharp uniforms, highly polished jump boots, never out of step, we march with precision. Pride among the paratroopers in our airborne division comes from a combined effort to be the best. The 511th displays the close comradeship that we have developed through loyalty, pride and friendship, commonly found in elite military units- ours to cherish and remember forever.

Perk and I are in Tokyo for the Armed Forces Day Parade.

"Hey Perk! Let's go salute General MacArthur at his headquarters; it ain't far from here."

Perk grins and says,

"Do you think he will remember us, so as we can make Private First Class?" *It is an honor to salute our Five Star General, General Douglas MacArthur.*

A black Cadillac, chauffeured by an army master sergeant pulls up in front of General MacArthur's headquarters in the Dai-Ichi Building at exactly 6:00 P.M ... McArthur, tall and stately exits the building; Perk and I are among those gathered to pay respects to the great General. We stand tall and as he exits the building; we proudly salute him. He looks at us- stops and returns our salute before entering his car. The master sergeant stands upright as he salutes the general, and then opens the rear door of the Cadillac. General MacArthur and his aide enter the car. The master sergeant closes the rear door of the Cadillac. The elegant black car slowly maneuvers into the traffic without an armed escort, taking him to his home at the American Embassy. *Years later I thought to myself, "You could not do that in Iraq or Afghanistan!"*

Upon arrival of General MacArthur, paratroopers of the 11th Airborne Division escort him to his temporary headquarters in the Dai-ichi Hotel in Yokohama.

To this day, in Tokyo, General MacArthur's office is intact on the sixth floor of the Dai-Ichi, Seimei Life Insurance building in Yuraku-cho Chiyoda-ku.

Again, I will say it right here and now, elements of our 11th Airborne Division combat troops and elements of General MacArthur's headquarters communications' people are the first troops to arrive in Japan, landing by air at Atsugi Air Station **. . . .**documented as true history.

Pretenders are spinning stories, like fairytales, of being the first troops to occupy Japan.

Fairytales

August 1945, American army troops and marines are loaded on ships in Tokyo Bay waiting for the order to go ashore. They are spinning stories like fairytales of being the first American troops to enter Japan, but this is not so.

One group of the many *pretenders* is the 4th Marines. They call themselves the *"Magnificent Bastards"*. Now, you heroic 4th Marines have a lot to be proud of, but you were not the first to arrive in Japan, so just be yourselves."

"The snow goose need not bathe to make its self-white. Neither need you do anything, but be yourself."

Lao-Tzu

No doubt, some clerk in the 4th Marines sitting out in the bay on a ship, writes home, *"Mama, mama, we are the first troops to enter Japan."* Other 4th Marines on the ship pick up on it and write home. "*Mama, mama, we are the first troops to land in Japan! Joe says so!"*

This fairytale goes around the Marines Corps-The 4th Marines write much about their fairytale, and they talk about it endlessly- they are now beginning to believe this trumped-up fairy tale themselves and repeat it to their sons, daughters, grandchildren, relatives and anyone else who will listen.

"The foolish reject what they see, not what they think; the wise reject what they think, not what they see."

Huang Po

But, don't you 4th Marines worry too much about your fairytale; like I say, you are not alone. There are others out there as misguided as you are.

Some Army troops have written the same passable scenario. This is told to their sons and daughters and anyone who will listen. To you *pretenders:* keep your heads up. Like I say, you have a lot to be proud of. Your fairytale makes a good bedtime story . . . just like Hansel and Gretel or Snow White and the Seven Dwarfs! Now, you 4th Marine *Magnificent Bastards* sleep well and just remember this: it is the 11th Airborne Division . . . that paved the way for your safe landing. *"Nighty, Night!"* . . . *Geronimo!*

The Copacabana

The staff calls her Mama Copa. The Americans know her as "The Dragon Lady". She is the Tokyo nightclub Queen! Nightly, she watches over the club, teaching her girls the tricks of the trade to sell more drinks and make money from the eager customers. She is dressed in a long black silk Chinese cheongsam gown, greeting her customers with an enticing seductive smile. Over her right breast embroidered in white is the Imperial Dragon.

As she gracefully walks from table to table, the long slit on the side of her gown exposes her lovely leg from ankle to thigh, like new fallen snow, lending an aura of mystique to her gliding manner. From one table to another, sensually and provocative, she is well sought after by her many admirers . . .

The cathedral inspired dome ceiling portrays a look of sanctity within the Copacabana. Hanging from the center is a large slowly turning ball inlaid with colored glass chips- casting colors of the rainbow sparkling over the dance floor below.. The seventeen-piece orchestra is dressed in formal black tuxedos. A male vocalist softly croons Hoagy Carmichael's "Stardust"

Sometimes I wonder why I spend
The lonely night dreaming of a song
The melody haunts my reverie
And I am once again with you
When our love was new
And each kiss an inspiration
But that was long ago
Now my consolation
Is in the stardust of a song

Mama Copa staffs many beautiful girls who have arrived from all over

Japan to get their share of the G.I. gold mine.

From far away Okinawa in the Ryukyu Islands are some of the most exotic girls: large beautiful eyes, golden sun-tanned skin, often speaking a language among themselves unknown to other Japanese girls.

Night after night, the Copacabana's tables are overflowing with well-heeled customers looking for fun and romance. The Copa's beautiful girls are also looking for fun, romance . . . and money as they smile and teasingly say,

"You buy me drink?"

As Perk and I leave the Sunshine Hotel, I surprise him by saying,

"Hey, Perk, tonight we are gonna party-we are goin' to the world famous Copacabana club!"

A shocked look on his face, wide-eyed Perk blurts out

"Are you crazy? The Copacabana is a high-class nightclub.

Only military officers and rich people like them there government civilians can afford to go to the Copacabana."

"Ah, come on, Perk, we just got paid. We have lots of money. We also got our jump pay. We're kinda' rich right now, Perk, kinda' like them officers and them rich government people. Come on, Perk! Let's grab a taxi and head out for the Copacabana!"

The Copacabana in Akasaka has many beautiful hostesses who make more money in one night than the average Japanese worker makes in one month.

At the Copacabana, we choose two of the prettiest girls to sit with us . . . *or is it, the girls choose us?*

"Hi there, soldiers; we see you are paratroopers. You must have just got paid!"

"That's right beautiful; we got paid all right! We have plenty of money. We also got all of our jump pay, ain't that right Perk?" I say with a millionaire's smile.

"Would you girls like a drink?" *Now this is like asking a bank robber if he would like some money.*

Over the left breast of one of the girls is a tattoo of a cobra, coiled and ready to strike. She orders an expensive house cocktail she calls *"Anticipation."* The girl with dimples and eyes of wonder orders the house specialty called, *"The Gold Mine"*

"Make it a double!" she says.

"Perk, they sure like these special cocktails, but they don't

seem to get drunk. Maybe they will get drunk, after they have some more drinks."

The girls are getting happier and happier every time Perk and I buy another round of drinks! We are so lucky, as they also kindly introduce us to the Copacabana's most expensive house sake called ... *The Kamikaze.* Perk and I toast to each other as to our good fortune. We are two happy privates having a wonderful time, laughing, letting out long whistles, clanging on our sake bottles, keeping time with the drummer, as we sing along with the band. The officers and government civilians looking at us are open-mouthed with big eyes; they have that envious stare ... they must be very envious of us privates... we do know how to have fun.

Perk is real good at jitterbugging. He is a sight to see! Perk is all over the place!

Dance! Dance! Dance!

"You know, Perk, I think these girls are mighty impressed with my romantic slow dancing steps. You remember, Perk, I learned that in Hachinohe, like shifting gears driving a truck?

I bet those boring looking officers in this hea' Copacabana can't do that!" They sure look jealous of our fancy dancing with the girls here tonight.

"We are fools whether we dance or not, so we might as well dance."
Japanese Proverb

"You paratroopers are very handsome and we like you very much."

Snuggling closer, cheek to cheek, with a hint of jasmine that makes Perk and I swoon ... looking into our eyes they say,

"To celebrate our good fortune in meeting you, let's order two more doubles of *Anticipation* and *The Gold Mine,* and of course another bottle of our excellent *Gold Label Kamikaze Sake."* ... *And, the band plays on.*

The girl with the cobra tattoo says,

"You will be amazed as to what we are going to do to you after the club closes at twelve o'clock. Meet us outside, little door- small side street."

Perk and I are having wild imaginations as to what they are going to do to us. We are excitedly smacking our lips with hearts skipping beats as we lean towards them and I whisper close to her ear,

"Darling, I am your one and only, you don't have to worry
... We will be on time!"

"Much of our money is gone, Perk

"I wonder if the girls know that," Perk says, slurring his words.

As we unsteadily head for the door, I burp and say,

"Money does not matter to them because they like us; they said so themselves, every time they ordered another drink!"

Perk and I stagger out the front entrance of the Copacabana, bumping into two army officers waiting at the front door. They are grinning at us with amusing looks on their faces, as if they know something . . . that we privates don't know.

I whisper to Perk, "I wish those officers would stay out of the way. Who in the world could they be ah waiting for? I bet they wish they had . . . what we are gonna' get."

Perk and I hurry to the small side street. We are on time at the side door to the minute . . . twelve midnight. My pulse is racing; with great anticipation, I am wondering if the girl with the cobra tattoo has any more tattoos.

It is freezing cold and beginning to snow; we are jumping up and down, waving our arms, stomping our feet trying to keep warm.

"Perk, its twelve-thirty now. It looks like they are a little late."

"That's ok, we can wait for them. Japanese girls are never on time. They like us ah lot. They love the way we sing and dance, and the way we keep time with the drummer! That's why they let us buy them a lot of drinks."

"You are so right, Perk; we are two lucky privates!"

"Ray, it's after one o'clock now! Do you think, they forgot about us, ah waitn' out here?"

"Pretty Japanese girls and rich army officers are sometimes more cunning than poor army privates!

Joshiki

The very next day Perk is telling me,

"Hey, I know a great little club where all the girls go crazy

over my jitterbug dancing. They all say they have never before experienced anything like my jitterbugging. It is easy for them to see, that I am the best! Nobody in the clubs can jitterbug like I do . . . all the girls say so.

They say it is so thrilling when I twirl them around and throw them over my head. I don't miss too often! Come on, Ray, its early . . . let's go to *the Pearly Gates*"; it's just two blocks off the Ginza."

What a Night
The Pearly Gates are Open

We arrive early. Perk and I are escorted to Perk's favorite table... next to the dance floor. The smarter girls, recognizing that we are paratroopers, come flocking to our table. They have learned that army paratrooper privates make double the money of other army privates. Also the girls know that paratroopers are quick to fall in love and easy to part with their money.

Soon after we arrive, we each have a girl on our laps and one on both sides. The girl on my lap is wearing a red long slit cheongsam gown embroidered with white chrysanthemums. High up on one of her slim legs she reveals a small tattoo of an angel with a golden halo. Each time she crosses her leg, the angel's wings flutter. I cannot take my eyes off her tattoo.

Perk's favorite girl is dressed in a short silk happy coat embroidered with goldfish. A short skirt reveals black fishnet stockings that end above her knees. In her right hand is a black lace fan decorated with pearls. She raises the fan to her face and then slowly lowers the fan, flashing her beautiful dark cat eyes, with a captivating smile.

We order, *recommended by the girls,* the club's special sake, *"Cloud Nine."* It is expensive, but who cares, we're paratroopers and we deserve the best! So the girls say!

It is a romantic evening; the band plays on. A lovely female singer in a low cut white evening gown sweetly croons,

"Pennies from Heaven"
Every time it rains, it rains pennies from heaven
Don'tcha' know each cloud contains
Pennies from heaven?
You'll find your fortune fallin' all over town
Be sure that your umbrella

Is upside down.
Trade them for a package of
Sunshine and flowers
If you want the things you love
You must have showers
So when you hear it thunder
Don't run under a tree
There'll be pennies from heaven
For you and for me
Johnny Burke and Arthur Johnston

In a thundering voice- I yell at a sailor who moves over to our table and begins caressing my girl, looking at her angel tattoo as she crosses her legs.

"Get your cotton pickin' hands off my girl! No one dances with my girl when I'm ah buying the drinks . . . do you hear me?"

I grab the front of his shirt and shove him away. He don't like that. He and his sailor friend grab both my arms. *I am in big trouble . . . this is not my night*!

Perk is jitterbugging up a storm. All eyes are on Perk. He looks over my way and sees two sailors holding my arms. Another sailor is poking me in the chest, yelling at me. Perk comes ah running, knocking over the table, spinning sake bottles around on the floor like scampering mice. The girls are screaming. Perk kicks the biggest sailor between his legs; the sailor lets out a big scream, like a stuck pig, bending over holding his balls . . . that's when Perk gives him a karate chop. At the same time, I stomp on the other sailor's foot. Now, he's ah hollering and hopping around like some kid skipping rope; with my left hand I punch him hard in the stomach and with my right hand I give him a right cross to the head.

All hell breaks loose in the club. Sailors and soldiers rise up out of their seats, joining the fight; some rush from the dance floor, wildly swinging at anything wearing a different uniform . . . a regular free-for all in the *Pearly Gates* is now in full swing. I hastily look around and see Perk swinging into a drunken sailor. I grab his arm on the backswing, yank him around and yell,

"Come on Perk; let's get the hell out of here. We didn't start this fight with those swabbies . . . and we ain't gonna' stick around to see who finishes it, neither. Hurry, Perk, run!" I yell as I run out the front door.

I am now running ah mile a minute, ah headin' for the Ginza subway. Looking back, I see Perk is right behind me.

It is late as Perk and I board the Marunouchi subway heading back to our hotel- Hotel Sunshine. As we enter the car, there is no one seated except for four 1st Cavalry soldiers down at the end of the car. They are as drunk as skunks and giving us mean looks with envy- looking at our jump boots.

The Meanest and the Kindest

As we enter the subway, the big one is pointing a finger at Perk and me, like what are paratroopers from the 11th Airborne Division from northern Japan doing in 1st Cavalry Division territory in Tokyo? Again, the big one points to my boots and says,

"They are mine!"

"Not if I get them first!" says the ugly one with the Jimmy Durante nose.

"Wait a minute, they're my size!" whines the little fat one.

The situation is heating up as the subway spills in and out of tunnels, and the Tokyo night lights go flashing by. Tension is running high-there are four against two. I think the odds are about even, but I can see they have a hard look of determination to take our jump boots. The sound of the wheels of the subway *clickety-clack, clickety-clack* along with the ghostly wail of the engine adds to the eerie feeling that I have. Perk begins to squirm in his seat. To get out of this in one piece with our boots on, we will need a miracle right here and now. *Unexpectedly, out of the darkness of the night, the miracle appears!*

The subway comes to a halt at Toranomon station (Gate of the Tiger). The doors fly open. In the station . . . out of the dark night, *who steps into the car . . . none* other than my Fort Benning Cadre Sergeant, Sergeant Swartz.

He immediately recognizes me. With that swinging gait that I remember so well, he comes over to our end of the car.

"So, we meet again Private Payne."

"Sergeant Swartz, it's you!"

"It's me alright; how you doin'?"

"Not so good, Sergeant Swartz!"

As I motion towards the other end of the car.

"Those 1st Cavalry soldiers want our jump boots!"

The 1st Cavalry Division is always in competition with the 11th Airborne Division as to who was the first to arrive in Japan. The 1st Cavalry was the first to arrive in Manila.

Elements of the 11th Airborne Division were the first American troops to arrive in Japan. When the 1st Cavalry Division unloaded from their troop transport in Yokohama Harbor, the 11th Airborne Division Band was on the dock welcoming them with,

"The Old Gray Mare."
Oh, the old gray mare, she ain't what she used to be,
Ain't what she used to be, ain't what she used to be.
The old gray mare, she ain't what she used to be,
Many long years ago.
Many long years ago, many long years ago.
The old gray mare, she ain't what she used to be,
Many long years ago.

Sergeant Swartz swings around facing the 1st Cavalry soldiers, spreads his legs, places his hands on his hips, shakes his head from side to side and curls his lips. He stands alone, undaunted, unconcerned, as if to renounce the world.

"So, they want your jump boots, do they? Well, let them have mine!"

With that Richard Widmark sneer on his face that I know so well, he swaggers down towards the other end of the car, smirking and calmly says,

"All right, if you want a paratrooper's jump boots then take mine. Come on! Come on, now! Take my boots!

Who's first or would all four of you like to give it a try?"

He curls his lip in a sneer as he issues the challenge.

At this moment, the subway stops at another station; it may not have been those 1st Cavalry soldiers' station; yet, they get off anyway. They exit the subway car . . . hurry through the station and do not look back.

Perk with wide eyes, looks at them as they hurriedly leave the subway. He shakes his head in disbelief. He truly has seen a miracle.

This is the second time that my jump school cadre sergeant has helped me in times of need. Sergeant Swartz is the meanest and the kindest person I have ever met. I am never to see Sergeant Swartz again. Sergeant Swartz, wherever you are, I would like to say:

"To you, I might have been just another paratrooper that you helped in the line of duty, but from me to you, I am ever so grateful to you for being a part of my life . . . I will remember you forever!"

"The superior man, when he stands alone, is unconcerned, and if he has to renounce the world, he is undaunted."
I Ching

For reasons unknown to all but an airborne army private, Perk is not on the train when we go back to Hachinohe. I suspect the reason is Tokyo girls. Our regimental commander notifies our captain that the MPs at the Army Air Force Base in Tachikawa are holding Private First Class Floyd H. Perkins of the 511th Parachute Infantry Regiment for being drunk, breaking up a bar, punching out some Army Air Force soldiers and he is over the hill. He is AWOL (absent without leave).

Private Perkins is AWOL

Of all people in the camp, the Captain selects me, Private Payne, to go to Tachikawa Army Air Force Base near Tokyo to bring the prisoner, Private First Class Perkins back to Camp Haugen. *By sending me, maybe the Captain hopes we will go AWOL together and he will be rid of us both . . . once and for all.*

"Private Payne, bring back the prisoner Private First Class Floyd H. Perkins. Return him to Camp Haugen under armed escort."

"Yes Sir, Captain! I won't let him get away!" *Now this is like sending the fox to bring back the chicken.*

The orderly room cuts a set of orders for me. The supply sergeant issues me a carbine. Soon, I am on the *Yankee Flyer* heading south for Tokyo. Through the towns and villages of the Tohoku region, the *Yankee Flyer* passes waterfalls cascading down from the mountains, valleys of rich rice fields swaying in the sun- large ripe persimmons and radishes hanging under the eaves of thatched-roofed homes of the farmers- the *Yankee Flyer* speeds on through the countryside.

Upon arrival at Tachikawa Army Air Base, I ask the gate guard directions to the Provost Marshall's Headquarters. Entering, I see they have Perkins ready for my custody. Perk is sitting on a stool looking straight ahead, as if he has something else on his mind. *I am soon to find out what that something else is.* With the flip of my hand, I salute the Air Force MP Lieutenant and show him my orders. Raising my head high, I look the lieutenant straight in the eyes.

"I am Private Payne First Scout-First Squad of the 2nd Platoon of Easy Company, 511th Parachute Infantry Regiment, 11th Airborne Division."

I click my heels and say,

"Here are my orders, Sir. My orders are to return the prisoner, Private Perkins, directly to Camp Haugen . . . without delay, Sir!"

The lieutenant snatches the orders out of my hand, lowers his head, takes a long hard look at my orders, and slowly raises his head and snaps,

"He's yours-get him out of here and don't you two come back on this base!"

"Yes sir, Lieutenant, Sir!"

I flip the lieutenant another arrogant salute, do an about face- out of the corner of my eye, I wink at Perkins. For a little show, I wave my carbine from side to side and with an authoritative voice I say,

"OK, Private Perkins- march! And don't you try anything funny!"
Outside the main gate of Tachikawa

"Perk, what in the hell is going on?"

"Man, you gotta' go see them gals at the *Whoopee Club* and stop point'n that gun at me; that thing might go off!

The Whoopee Club is down on the Ginza about four blocks from the Pearly Gates which I ain't about to go near again!

At the Whoopee Club, the girls are so beautiful and friendly.

A few of the prettiest ones do have those beautiful almond-shaped eyes. They say they are from the Ryukyu Islands in southern Japan,

"Come on, let's go, Ray! I'm staying at a little hotel in Roppongi. You got any money?"

"Yea', Perk, I got some. We just got paid." *Perk's eyes light up; just got paid, wow!*

Now, pretty girls are always the number one priority on my list. We privates do have our responsibilities, and some things can wait, when there is something more important . . . like pretty girls.

At Ueno Station in Tokyo, we get off the train from Tachikawa. Perk hires *(with my money)* a couple of rickshaw pullers. Perk is in the lead rickshaw. He yells to the rickshaw puller,

"Giddy-up'!"

Perk is acting just like he is still plowing a mule back home on the farm,

"Giddy-up', Giddy-up'!"

Perk knows just where to go; down a little side street we come to a two-story pine wood building with a gray slate tile roof. Over the front entrance is a wooden sign:

Hotel Kiiroi Sakuranbo

Hotel Yellow Cherry

Near the entrance of the hotel, over a small stream is a wooden water wheel, slowly creaking the years away. Streaks of fading sunlight shine through a small pine tree, casting shadows telling me the lateness of the day. Perk is greeted by the innkeeper. He is so happy to see Perk . . . like a long lost friend. *There is no doubt in my mind that Perk owes the Innkeeper some money.*

With a big smile, the innkeeper proudly displays his two gold teeth. I think to myself, "*Oh my goodness gracious! He carries his wealth in his mouth!*" Perk anxiously speaks up,

"Pay Mister Takamura for three nights' stay six large size bottles of Kamikaze sake, several bowls of fish head noodle soup and then . . . let's get the hell out of here! We've got to get to the *Whoopee Club*. Those pretty gals are ah waitin'!"

"Wait a minute, Perk, what about this loaded carbine?

I can't run around the Ginza with a loaded carbine in my hands."

"Give it to Takamura-san."

"What? Give my rifle to a Jap! Are you sure he knows the war is over?"

"Give it to him, its ok. What do you think he's gonna' do with it, start another war? C'mon, give it to him! Let's go, the girls are waitin'!"

I turn to Takamura-san,

"You take good care of my gun, you hea? Now, don't you go ah shootin' nobody! Let's go Perk- we is ah wasting time!

Whoopee Club, here we come!"

What a great night it was, singing, dancing and romancing. After paying our hotel bill and buying drinks for girls at the *Whoopee Club,* I am broke.

The old smoke belching *Yankee Flyer* takes us back to Camp Haugen, bleary-eyed and hung over. Again, the captain busts Perk back down to a private. He don't do nothin' to me except make me wash pots and pans, as I am a private and there ain't no rank lower than a private!

The First Sergeant says to himself,

"I can't believe it, they are back!"

The captain never questions me as to why we are one day late; he just wants peace of mind.

"When it comes to privates, for peace of mind, it is best to leave some things private."

Joshiki

We are back in camp- our money is all gone- we have no cash to go anywhere till next pay day. Perk and I long to see the girls- especially in those fancy clubs along the Ginza in Tokyo. Perk and I are going crazy waiting for our next pay day. Eternity goes by and then- it's payday, which includes our jump pay. Lo and behold, would anyone believe it . . . our First Sergeant, out of the clear blue sky has done gone and given me and Perk a three-day pass! We will be gone- away from Camp Haugen for a whole three days. We are going back to Tokyo. As we leave our First Sergeant's office he closes his eyes and lets out a long . . . sigh of relief.

Tokyo is an exciting place for us paratroopers from Hachinohe. When in Tokyo, we help the taxi driver. We crank the handle of the air blower. The taxi driver shovels charcoal into the furnace and we get the little steam engine going . . . belching smoke, huffing and puffing, we are off and running! Tokyo sure is a modern place!

Rickshaws

The war is over- in occupied Japan rickshaws continue to be in use. We GIs in northern Japan ride in them often. The rickshaws are our "taxis".

We paratroopers can run for miles and never get tired. Sometimes we put the Japanese rickshaw pullers in the back, and *we* do the pulling, racing each other back to camp. After we arrive at camp, we pay the rickshaw pullers. They find it amusing that we do the pulling and they get a free ride with pay. I can only imagine what they tell their families when they return to their homes . . . "This occupation of Japan by American soldiers is not so bad after all!" *A rickshaw is a cart that can seat one or two people powered by a human runner. The word rickshaw comes from the Japanese word "jinrikisha", which means human powered vehicle. Rickshaws first became popular in Japan during the 1870's. One of the stories about the origin of the rickshaw is that it was invented in Japan by a European missionary to carry around his invalid wife.*

At this time, Perk and I did not know about the history of the rickshaw, but we do know how to enjoy life, whether we are sitting in the rickshaws or pulling them in a race with each other. We privates know how to have fun! While we privates know how to enjoy life, our senior officers live in a whole different world.

On two of the most famous well-known corners in all of Tokyo, Japan sits the prestigious Wako Department Store that has survived the war; across the street is the large Mitsukoshi Department Store in the famous area is known as the Ginza. The exclusive Wako Department Store is now the U. S. Military's high class PX. This is where all the rich officers, government civilians and their sometimes haughty wives shop. Also . . . it is where we privates like to buy pretty pink silk underwear for our Japanese girlfriends, much to the liking of the Japanese girls and much to the dislike of the officers' wives. The wives take their dislikes out on their officer husbands and their husbands don't like this at all. We privates like that! *Y'all know what I mean!*

Perk and I are shopping for two of the girls at the *Copacabana Club*, *as if we had not learned our lesson,* when suddenly we hear a woman's voice over on the next aisle yelling at her husband. We peek around and listen more. She is upset! *This is the conversation Perk and I overheard at the Wako PX*. . .

"Those Privates Should Be Ashamed of Themselves!"

"Horace . . . do you hear what I am saying? Listen to me, Colonel Herpeck; how dare they let those GIs purchase lingerie in our PX! They are buying up our ladies' silk underwear for those Japanese girls faster than the PX manager can replace them! What in the world is that PX manager thinking of? Can't you stop those GIs from buying up our silk underwear? Horace, ask the General to make a regulation!"

"Honey, we can't do that. Those GI's are in the military and that is what the PX is for, unless the GIs are trading that underwear for something. If the girls are trading something for silk panties, then that's black market! I will do some personal investigating . . . to learn what those girls are doing and how they are doing it."

Mrs. Herpeck blinks twice, is open-mouthed, raising her eyebrows listening to what her husband is saying.

"Well, Colonel, I'm glad that somebody will be doing something! Thank goodness, those Japanese girls don't wear extra-large silk panties! If they did . . . there wouldn't be any left! Colonel, write your Congressman; after all, isn't that what Congressmen are for? Those privates should be ashamed of themselves! They should wait until they get back home to the United States where there are nice decent American girls waiting for them!

Japanese girls wearing *our* silk panties . . . what in the world will those GIs be thinking of next?

Colonel Herpeck! What are you thinking about with that smile on your face! What are you dreaming about? C'mon, it's late! I am tired. I've got my *"extra-large"* panties- let's go check out. I want to go home, go to bed and read a good book!"

"Yes, dear, I want to get up early in the morning and get my work done. I am anxious to start my personal investigation early in the evening. It could be a long tiresome night."

Perk and I watch them walk out of the department.

Perk says, “Extra-large? From what I see, I would have guessed the Colonel’s Missus wears the extra, extra-large.

I can tell you for darn sure what that Colonel is dreaming about!”

“Yea’ Perk, we all have the same dreams.”

“The longer the nights last, the more our dreams will be.”
Chinese Proverb

A Hanging Lantern

Gonorrhea is epidemic! In the early days of the occupation, not only is there a shortage of food, clothing and housing, there is also a great shortage of medicine. Penicillin is not readily available for the Japanese. A large number of Japanese girls are infected with gonorrhea. In addition, many GIs are infected throughout our bases where sizeable numbers of our troops are stationed.

According to reports- as many as 25% of the US troops in Japan have gonorrhea. In some military units, it is estimated that the percentage of those infected is higher.

In our 511th P.I.R, I do not think the percentage to be very high. Actually one good shot of penicillin will quickly get rid of gonorrhea, much faster than trying to get rid of a bad cold.

In our latrine, the urinal is a long wooden trough lined with galvanized tin. At one end of the trough is a sign that says *VD Only.* One toilet has a sign over it that also says *VD Only*. In one corner of the mess hall there is a large sign on a table that says *VD Only.* If one wants to pee or use the toilet and cannot hold it any longer, he must use the VD urinal and toilet before everyone's eyes, eat your meal at the VD table or go hungry. He is in plain view to all, that he has or has recently had VD. It is my opinion that the purpose for these VD signs is for humiliation, a form of punishment . . . for visits and fun times in the off-limits bars of Hachinohe.

The officers and NCOs are always preaching to us privates,

"Control yourselves!" . . . Then they go home to their wives.

The military sets up venereal disease prevention tents by night on street corners in the cities. It is good of the American government to think of the GIs, as the GIs are too busy thinking of the girls.

Inside the tent hangs a kerosene lantern. Also inside the tent, are prophylactics kits for GIs to use to protect themselves from gonorrhea.

In Tokyo, the Ginza is a very popular place at night for GIs and Japanese girls to exchange "*culture and friendship.*"

There are many little side streets with quaint little bars and beautiful young Japanese girls . . . wanting silk panties . . . size, small! *When I tell the Japanese today that one of those tents was set up at night right in front of their prestigious Mitsukoshi department store on the Ginza, they are spellbound, as their thoughts run wild with fascination and imagination!*

In spite of all the goings on in Japan, life is going on also in my little home town of Tupelo, Mississippi. The Red Cross notifies my regiment that I am to go home right away on emergency leave. My older brothers and sisters tell the Red Cross that our mother is not expected to live many more days. An important message I received from my regiment that I must come home gets my full attention. I must go to Tupelo as soon as I can.

We Lie to Each Other

The Year of the Rat, Summer 1948

I am on a large four-propeller engine plane. We island hop across the Pacific to Hawaii, on to California, and then to Memphis. I hitchhike on down to Tupelo. I arrive in time to see our mother alive. Her mind is active, her body, weak and tired.

In the lateness of the morning, we look out the hospital window over the sun lit fields towards Kings Creek . . . and we lie to each other.

"Mama, you will be home soon and I'm gonna' go rabbit hunting with my .22. We are gonna' have fried rabbit."

"Baby Ray, I'm going to make you some black-eyed peas, turnip greens, crispy corn bread that you like so much with sweet milk gravy and banana pudding when you bring home those rabbits . . . just like I always did before you went into the Army."

"Yes, mama; I'm gettin' powerful hungry just thinkin' about it. I nodded and smiled as I reached for her hand.

In the darkness of the night, we lost our mother.

Mama and Daddy have left us. It is hard to think they are no longer with us. They did not waste their short precious lives. They took care of their children through difficult years. They were never angry or thought badly of others. They helped others whenever they could.

"Every day, think that as you wake up, today I am fortunate to be alive. I have a precious human life. I am not going to waste it. I am going to use all of my energies to develop myself, to expand my heart out to others, to achieve enlightenment for the benefit of all beings. I am going to have kind thoughts towards others, I am not going to get angry or think badly of others. I am going to benefit others as much as I can."

Dalai Lama

Mama is no longer with us, so my elder brothers and sisters will care for my younger sisters, Bonnie and Geri. Even though I still have more leave time, I want to hurry back to Japan, back to the 511th, back to Hachinohe. So, I say good-by to my little sisters, other family members and relatives. I pack my bags and walk to the bus station feeling sad, yet looking forward to being back in Japan.

The U.S.S. Sadao S. Munemori

From Tupelo, I go to Memphis by Greyhound bus. In Memphis I get a 'hop' on an Army Air Force plane going west. We are heading for Norton Army Air Force Base in San Bernardino, California. This little twin-engine plane carries about eight passengers. Aboard is the pilot, co-pilot, a few officers and myself, Private Payne. It is night and we are high up over Oklahoma. We enter into dark clouds with heavy, pounding rain hitting the glass pane above the cockpit. Loud booming thunder and streaks of lighting are shooting through the sky. Like a yo-yo, we are going up and down . . . and I do not have a parachute.

The pilot changes course out of the storm and we land in Texas. Texas is where I have my first bowl of chili. Not bad stuff; it's got beans in it, but it sure is different from our southern butterbeans. I must have drunk a gallon of ice water.

Someday, I will tell you how to make Mexican Chili.You start with a Popsicle!

I return to Japan on a small Army troop transport ship, the U.S.S. Sadao S. Munemori. Three days out of Oakland, California, we run into a storm. I am bunked down below under the galley. The ship is bucking up and down, worse than that little red bull, Ferdinand. All hell is breaking loose up in that galley. I sure am glad now that I am not in the Navy; 'cause I sho' can't take much of this stuff!

The USS Munemori is the second roughest boat ride I have ever been on in my life. The roughest ride takes place late summer on the yacht, LONG LIFE, sailing into a super typhoon- a yacht misnamed for sure, (Book II: The Wild Wild East)

The U.S.S. Sadao S. Munemori is named after a Nisei (second generation Japanese person) war hero. Sadao Munemori is an American hero who fought in Europe during World War II.. He paid for our country's freedom with his life. This great American, Sadao Munemori was awarded

America's highest award, the Congressional Medal of Honor after he sacrificed his life to save his fellow soldiers at Seravezza, Italy. After finding his squad leader wounded, he made attacks against the Germans through direct fire. When he finally reached the crater occupied by his fellow soldiers, an unexploded grenade hit his helmet and rolled toward the soldiers. He dived for the missile, stifling the blast that took his life.

"A hero is someone who understands the responsibility that comes with his freedom."
Bob Dylan

I am finally again in Japan. I have resolved to leave the pain of losing my mother and leaving family behind. The turbulent trip back was a difficult and long journey, but I am happy to be back in Japan. I am transferred back to Service Company to work in the PX. This is not my first time to be in Service Company . . .

Sergeant Salvatore Sebastianelli

Sendai is the home of our Division's 188th Parachute Infantry Regiment. The 511th sends me to Cooks and Bakers School in Sendai. I tell the service company captain that I had worked at Whit's Café in Tupelo, Mississippi. He is genuinely impressed when I tell him that Whit's Café is the most famous Café in the entire State of Mississippi. It seems that working at the famous Whit's Café will get me just about anywhere . . . *but it didn't last long!*

The Cooks and Bakers School is run by the 9th Corps. One of the 9th Corps instructors is a fat little Italian-one of those sergeants with one of those funny sounding names . . .

Staff Sergeant Salvatore Sebastianelli. *Everybody knows who I mean.*

He says he is from New York City, from some place those Italians call Brooklyn . . . *wherever the hell that is!*

With feet spread wide apart, rocking back and forth with his funny clipped accent he says,

"Today's a-lesson is-a how we a-gonna' make-a good -a banana-a-pudding." I think to myself, "*This hea' Italian sergeant must be crazy! There ain't no Yankee, especially an Italian Yankee, that knows how to make good bananer 'puddin', cause bananer 'puddin' is a southern thing!"*

Sgt. Sebastianelli smirks, raises his hand, points to himself and says,

"Lo son oil piu grande!"

I'm ah guessing as to what he has said, so I decide to attack his *el grande ego*!

I dig in my pocket for some of those little round firecracker balls that explode when you throw them against a hard surface or step on them. With his back to us, as he is pointing to the blackboard, I roll some of these little cracker balls back behind his boots.

This fat Italian sergeant turns around and steps on one, and it explodes-BAM- with a loud noise! Sergeant Salvatore Sebastianelli jumps a foot up in the air and comes down on a bunch more . . . BAM, BAM, BAM. These little cracker balls are exploding all around! Sergeant Sebastianelli is jumping up and down- dancing around like a cat on a hot tin roof- yelling his head off in Italian . . .

"Siamo sotto attacco! Siamo sotto attacco!"

I am jumping up and down, slapping my thighs laughing along with everyone else in the class. Who do you think has the last laugh?

Well, you know who; that 9th Corps Sergeant Salvatore Sebastianelli has the last laugh. Private Payne washes pots and pans for the evening. *Mama Mia! Non si puo avere il miele senza la pecchie.*

I graduate from Cooks and Bakers School. *Would you believe it?* Well, later on the captain over at Service Company said he did not believe it either!

A week after the all-out Italian cherry bomb attack, John Russell and I are on the *Yankee Flyer* heading north for Hachinohe and Camp Haugen.

Matsushima Is a Beautiful Place

The *Yankee Flyer*, to let an express train go by, stops in a little seaside village resort for tourists by the name of Matsushima (Pine Island).

"John Russell, this place sure is mighty pretty. Look, those girls are smiling and waving at us. I wonder what they want. Let's get off and look around a little bit . . . we should find out something we can learn about their *culture."*

"Culture is the widening of the mind and of the spirit."
Jawaharlal Nehru

We don't hear the *Yankee Flyer* train whistle blow; maybe, we don't *want to hear* it blow- the girls are calling to us, inviting us to join them.

"Come, we go sake house! We have party!"

John Russell and I exchange glances . . . no sensible good private can ever turn down such an enticing invitation

Matsushima is a beautiful place. The young girls are very pretty and soooo friendly! So friendly, that John Russell and I stay overnight. We eat fish cooked on a charcoal hibachi. We drink Tom Tom *Shochu* Spirits, and have a great time playing games with the girls.

I teach the girls my favorite card game . . . *strip poker.* They like this new and exciting American card game. *Kimonos have more layers of cloth than an artichoke has petals.* We drink more *Shochu* spirits and *enlighten* our inquisitive minds. We pass the sake bottle . . . our hearts are filled with happiness as the game continues into the night. We have taught them *"aces are wild"* . . . the girls are feeling very excited and so are we . . . playing strip poker . . . exchanging wonderful new cultural ideas-expanding our minds far beyond the mysteries of Kings Creek.

"Culture of the mind must be subservient to the heart."

Mahatma Gandhi

The sun is descending well into the lateness of its day and we too, are late to getting back to camp. After the *Shochu* spirits, getting back late does not go too well for us. Those Indians are beating their tom toms in our heads and we have a train to catch . . .

The Great Train Race

To ride the U.S. military trains, the *Dixie Rebel* that goes south and the *Yankee Flyer* that goes north, one must have military orders showing the date of travel and our date has expired. I know that we are in big trouble with our captain. We had better get back to camp right away . . . I have run out of excuses. All I have left is my common sense as a private.

A Japanese passenger train makes a stop at the Matsushima Station and it is heading north.

"Come on John Russell, let's go! Let's get on this hea' train. It's ah going our way. We gotta' get back to Hachinohe!"

"Ray, you know we can't do that; this is a Jap train!"

"Never mind John Russell, we gotta' go!

Run- grab the handle on the side of the door! Ok now! . . . Swing up on the train!"

Riding a Japanese train is against military regulations . . . so the officers have told us privates. We are soon to find out that there are others that know this as well . . . like the 9th Corps Military Police!

The clanging of the bell rings out, the pounding of pistons begins, and the mighty roar of the engine pushes the train on its way. Much to our happiness, it quickly picks up speed . . . heading north! A conductor comes by checking tickets. He looks at us with surprise in his eyes and keeps on walking. We notice all the passengers on the train are watching something going on outside with intense interest.

"John Russell, what's going on out there?"

John Russell and I poke our heads outside the window. We are just as curious as everyone else is. What is going on? A jeep's red light is flashing. In that MP Jeep are two very unfriendly looking 9th Corp MPs. They are looking and waving at us as if they want something. That MP Jeep, would you believe it, with sirens whining is racing our train to the next station, and we now know what those MPs want . . . *they want us!*

Holding my head high, squinting my eyes, with a big smirk on my face I say, "Hey John Russell, don't you worry none. This train engineer is ah pouring on the coal and we is ah pulling ahead! John Russell, this is our lucky day!"

Again, we stick our heads out the window and with all the confidence in the world, John Russell and I give those MPs the finger. They seem not to like that! With sirens piercing the air, they shake their fists back at us. Now they are blowing their whistles and honking their horn even more so. They look like they might be a little upset!

Our local Japanese train is moving faster than that there jeep. We are pulling ahead! We are gonna' beat that jeep to the next station . . . way ahead of those 9th Corps MPs. Then, we are just gonna' disappear! The more those MPs honk their horn and blow their whistles, the more excited our train engineer gets. We look up front to see our engineer excitingly leaning over the side, waving his hat, yanking on his steam whistle and yelling,

"Sayonara! . . . Good-bye!"

The race is on! The fireman is pouring on the coal! We are laughing so hard at those MPs. We are leaving them far behind as the train picks up speed. We stick our thumbs in our ears, wiggle our fingers, stick out our tongues and again give them the finger. We are two happy paratroopers. Yes . . . siree! You can bet your bottom dollar; we are gonna' win this here race!

The MPs are not only flashing their red light and honking their horn, they keep on ah blowing their whistles, yelling and again shaking their fists in the air. *Why are they so mad?*

John Russell and I are having a great time. We are laughing so hard-jumping up and down, slapping each other on the back with the confidence of sure winners. Again we lean out of the window and give the MPs the finger. Normally, John Russell McFarland is a quiet sort, but now he is gettin' really carried away with us winning this exciting race.

John Russell yells,

"Catch us if you can! You fat-bellied MPs, catch us if you can!" Again, giving the finger, we are waving and yelling,

"Bye, bye, bye, bye!"

Now, I'm thinking John Russell is gettin' a little too carried away. He is acting a little crazy, like one of them second lieutenants when a private impersonates a private first class.

"John Russell, we are gonna' win this race- you can count on that! I brought my lucky rabbit foot!"

"Depend on the rabbit's foot if you like,
but remember, it did not work for the rabbit."
Anon

The Japanese passengers are watching with intense interest what is taking place outside the train. Sneaking a look at the wild antics of John Russell, by now, the Japanese know

what is going on. This race is bringing a lot of excitement into

their lives and I might add it is also bringing a lot of excitement into our lives ... more than we want, when the train ... starts slowing down. *It is the punctuality of Japanese trains to arrive at the station at the precise minute of the scheduled arrival time. This punctuality ingrained in their culture has cost us the race.*

In the excitement of the race, the fireman really poured on the coal and fired up that furnace real good. This put us way ahead of schedule for our arrival at the station. So guess what the engineer did? He stayed with the time schedule and eased back on the throttle ... slowing that train down to a crawl, so that we would arrive at the station at the precise time scheduled!

Those 9th Corps MPs had kept their gas pedal to the floor at full throttle and they are waiting for us at the station with big MP smiles ... and handcuffs.

"John Russell, I do wish we had been a little nicer to those MPs. I hope they are not too mad at us for just havin' a little fun."

The MPs have won the race and they say,

"Well, if it ain't Jessie and Frank James, the great train robbers!"

I greet the MPs with my usual well-practiced great big friendly MP smile. I say,

"Hi, how y'all ah doin' ... good to see y'all!

Howsyomamanem? Sure looks like a nice day, ain't it? It looks like y'all are ah heading towards the direction of Hachinohe. Honestly, we think y'all feel the need for some nice friendly company to ride back with you."

I glance at John Russell out of the corner of my eye and say,

"Ain't that the honest truth, John Russell?" John Russell looks at the sky.

"If you truly want honesty, do not ask questions
that you really do not want to hear the answer to."

Burmese Proverb

The MPs look at each other- give a big smile and at the same time say,

"Jessie and Frank James . . . you are under arrest!"

The ride to Hachinohe is not as pleasant as we would have liked, handcuffed in the back seat of the 9th Corps MP jeep.

Along the road, someone may find my lucky rabbit foot that I tossed out, because I don't want it no more.

Back at Service Company,

"I'm busting you back down to private," says the captain.

He says that as if it was something new. I had just made Private First Class. *Some officers had said that me, Private Payne, making Private First Class was . . . truly amazing!*

I had not even had time to sew on the stripes. Again, I am going to be Private Payne and put on KP, washing pots and pans. I am getting real good, like say- expert level, at washing pots and pans. I cannot say that I have set a record, but PRIVATE PAYNE, Regular Army 14236468, must have washed more pots and pans than any private in the entire United States Army!

Not to mention my share of peeling potatoes that I should have gotten a medal for or at least . . . a certificate of appreciation- and not to forget the many hours I spent wounded- crying while peeling onions. I know I should have gotten' the Purple Heart, but the mess sergeant said,

"No, Private Payne, you do not qualify! Quit your bellyaching; get back to peeling your onions. Chow is at five! *Life ain't fair to us privates.*

I *had* worn a PFC stripe on my overcoat once before in company formation. That was back when I was in Easy Company . . . my troubles are not over as I about to meet

2nd Lt. Massimiliano Quattrochi, and if that is not enough, I am being charged with the disappearance of Al's Hammer!

The Impersonator and Mussolini
And Al's Hammer

It is *The Year of the Rabbit-* a crisp chilly Saturday morning, cold enough to freeze the balls off an Eskimo. Easy Company First Sergeant Summerfield walks through the barracks yelling,

"Fall out! . . . Fall out! . . . Everybody out on the company street! Class "A" inspection with overcoats!"

Platoon Sergeant Crackenbush yells,

"You heard the first sergeant! Get the lead out of your butts! Everybody out!"

I yell,

"Perk, loan me your overcoat- hurry! I left mine downtown last night in that sake bar. I don't have no overcoat!"

Perk says with a hint of envy,

"What do you mean you don't have no overcoat? What sake bar are you talking about?"

"Perk! You know the one, the one where that MP Jardine's girlfriend works, *The Pink Butterfly!* Don't you remember?

You were with me and I ran out the back door. Quick Perk, gimme' your overcoat!"

Perk is confined to the barracks with the flu.

Perk's overcoat sleeves are so short they end half way down from my elbows. I head for the company street, line up ready for inspection. I am properly dressed **. . .** *so I think.*

Our platoon's new lieutenant is a short bowlegged little 2nd lieutenant wearing size twelve elevated boots. I don't know how he got in the paratroopers, as the airborne normally don't take midgets.

As we stand at parade rest, he yells with an exaggerated shrill voice,

"I am Second Lieutenant Massimiliano Quattrochi. I am your new platoon Lieutenant."

He pulls himself up to his full puffed-up height and yells his orders,

"Sergeant Crackenbush, call the men to attention for my inspection!"

I am staring straight-ahead thinking, *Uh-oh!* We got another one of those Eye-talians, with one of those crazy names that is hard to pronounce. We all know Mussolini, *so I simply name him Mussolini, but he don't know that!*

Out of the corner of my eye, I can see him ah coming . . . struttin' down the line, with the cockiness of a little banty rooster, his size twelve boots leading the way.

Mussolini is one of those little rich kids that didn't have to pick cotton. He got his money from his folks to go to school and to buy RC Colas and Moon Pies. What he received is that weekly money handout from his folks that them there rich kids call an allowance. That's sumpin' us privates didn't get! We had to work for our Moon Pies!

You know the kind of officer I'm talking about? They go to that there Officer's Candidate School for 90 days and then they come out of that school like a God . . . a second lieutenant!

Mussolini is now an officer! He is now *God*! We privates know that officers get double the jump pay that us privates get. *Is it because their head is twice as big?* Coming from Officer's Candidate School "OCS", he is now what us privates call a, "ninety-day wonder!" *and he knows it all . . . so he thinks!*

Mussolini troops the line and he gets to me. Mussolini does a well-rehearsed right smart about left face. *He has learned to do that in that there officer's school.* He smiles, then with a frown he slowly looks me up and down, then looks from side to side to make sure he is getting his respectful recognition from the entire platoon.

Now, that he knows that he has everyone's attention, he looks me over again nodding his head up and down. He acts as if he has just discovered the eighth wonder of the world and I can see that there eighth wonder of the world . . . is me!

Uh-oh! I'm ah thinkin', *there is gonna' be trouble and that trouble is gonna' be me.*

Little Mussolini steps four paces back, throws back his little shoulders, stretches himself a little taller in his spit-shined elevated boots, and screams at the top of his little shrill voice,

"Private Payne- front and center!"

Mussolini rises a little higher on his toes and yells,

"Look, every one of you; look at the imposter! Look at the impersonator!

Private Payne is impersonating a private first class! Look at him closely if you will," he crows.

With one eye closed, I slowly look down at one of those sleeves of Perkin's overcoat, hoping I won't see any PFC stripes. I had forgotten that Private Perkins had made private first class. I don't know how he made it, because if I get in trouble, Perk is in trouble.

Lieutenant Mussolini won't stop yelling. He is swinging from one foot to the other, yelping like a little puppy dog, yelling and ah carrying on about those PFC stripes.

"Private Payne, report to the mess hall at 1700! You will be washing pots and pans!"

"Yes Sir! Lieutenant Mussolini! Oh! Oh! I mean . . . ah yes Sir, Lieutenant, Sir!"

Mussolini is staring at me in complete disbelief. As if he is seeing something unique, a private impersonating with distinction ... a five star general. Mussolini orders Sergeant Crackenbush to dismiss the platoon and as Mussolini walks away, he throws his hands up and mumbles,

"Dopotutto, domani e un'altro giorno!"

"Privates are unique unto themselves with the distinction of holding the only rank that cannot be lowered to a lower rank."

Joshiki

Lieutenant Massimiliano Quattrochi will not be the only one throwing his hands up at me that day. For some odd reason my First Sergeant feels the need to interrogate me on my whereabouts the night before ...

I had lost my overcoat downtown the night before, running out of an off-limits sake house. I had heard the old weapons carrier that our regimental MPs use come to a screeching halt out front of the sake house. No time for coat- priorities first; I grabbed a bottle of sake and ran out the back door!

The next day, red-eyed, head hung low, I find myself standing before my First Sergeant.

"Private Payne, where were you last night? Private Perkins got caught in an off-limits sake house. The MPs said there were two, and one escaped out the back door. Where were you last night?"

"Where I was last night, First Sergeant? I don't remember, First Sergeant."

"What do you mean, you don't remember, Private Payne? Do you have Alzheimer?"

"No sir! First Sergeant, I don't have Al's hammer. I don't have no nails, neither! Besides, I don't even know this guy Al!"

"Do not be afraid of going slowly, be afraid of standing still."
Chinese Proverb

I Am So Proud The General Would Ask Me That!

Anytime I tell an officer that I've worked at Whit's Café in Tupelo, Mississippi, they seem impressed as to how proud I am of this. After all, everybody knows how famous Whit's Café is; well, at least they do around Lee County, Mississippi.

When I tell the captain of Service Company that I had worked at Whit's Café, he seems greatly impressed. So impressed, that he makes me a baker in Service Company. Going to Cooks and Bakers School at Camp Schimmelpfeaning might have helped a little, but *some things are just not meant to be.*

Being a baker in Service Company didn't last all that long. General Miley, our new Commanding General of our 11th Airborne Division is paying our Service Company a visit. Our captain is gettin' real nervous, like an ol' tomcat gets nervous when an ol' coon dog comes around. Captains get nervous when a general comes around; just like us privates get fired-up nervous when a 2nd Lieutenant comes around.

I am standing in front of my oven when the general says,

"What are you baking, son?" *I am so proud the general would ask me that!* The captain is getting nervous. I can hear him shuffling his boots from one foot to the other. He is holding his breath as he shifts his eyes from the general, to the oven, to me.

"Pound cakes, Sir!" I reply with great enthusiasm. I proudly open the oven door, to let the general see my nice pound cakes. You can hear the captain gasp as that cold winter air rushes in and flattens my pound cakes . . . as flat as the captain's feet. The general retreats out through the mess hall door. The captain transfers me back to a line company.

Hup, two, three, four! . . . *Hup, two, three, four!*

Service Company has lost a good baker and this problem does not bother me at all. On the lookout for a better job, I spot an opportunity for success posted on the PX bulletin board. I will soon land the *peanuttest* job that a private could ever dream of.

"Always be on the lookout for ways to turn a problem into an opportunity for success. Always be on the lookout for ways to nurture your dream."

Lao-Tzu

Parting Ways

"Hey Perk, over at the PX, I saw a notice on the bulletin board that that there PX Lieutenant is looking for a snack bar manager."

Perk looks at me quizzically with his eyes wide as if to say, *what are you up to now?* I kinda' straighten my back with the look of importance.

"Perk, I worked at Whit's Café in Tupelo, Mississippi'.

I wasn't exactly a manager, but I could carhop. Sometimes, they would let me work inside to make sandwiches if Earl Moody didn't show up for work- Earl sure did like cat-fishing! I have always wanted to be a business man. I'm gonna' apply for that job. After all, I am well qualified. That PX Lieutenant would be lucky to hire me!"

Perk kinda' hangs his head to one side, looks at me, squints out of one eye, not answering, hangs his head not believing what he was hearing. I can tell he doesn't know what to say. *Echoing down the mountainside, breaking the silence ... is the long eerie wail of a fox.*

The sun is settling down over the hills as Perk shuffles off down the company street, head down, slowly dragging his feet along. *I feel a sense of sadness come over me.* Perk and I have been through a lot together; we are line soldiers. We are paratroopers, but the strong desire to become a manager, a business man overcomes the sadness of parting ways with my best buddy. Perk and I are a legend in the making in our line company-trouble seems to find us or follow us all over northern Japan.

However, I'm not going to be in the line company anymore . . . I'm going to be a snack bar manager!

Until this day, I will always remember Private Floyd H. Perkins as being the best friend I ever had in the 511th Parachute Infantry Regiment. Over all these many years, I have never given up hope nor discontinued my search for Perk. Perk went on to be a war hero in that there Korean War. I lost track of Perk and his whereabouts.

Where are you, Perk? Maybe someday Perk and I will meet again in heaven! Better yet, Perk, how about a 24-hour sake house by the name of, Mama-san's Eternity Sake House, where the sake is free, the girls are beautiful and aces are wild!

Knowing I will always remember the good times with my best friend, I continue on with enthusiasm to be the entrepreneur that I have always been from the day I was born!

First Lieutenant Winfred Montan McWherter
And Mama's Secret Peanut Butter Banana Sandwich

First Lieutenant Winfred Montan McWherter is the 511th Parachute Infantry Regiment's, Camp Haugen Post Exchange Commander. He looks as if he should have been in the cavalry. He carries himself tall and lanky, with sandy wispy hair and a handlebar mustache. He has the air of a debonair southerner. He speaks with a true southern gentleman's accent that distinguishes him from the Yankees. Lieutenant McWherter is from a well-to-do South Carolina plantation family. He is right out of *Gone with the Wind.* As a southerner myself, I feel comfortable with him as I look him in the eye and say,

"I am here to be your snack bar manager. I have worked at Whit's Café!" Now, I say this as if I graduated right out of the Paris Culinary Arts School.

"Sergeant McWherter, as you can see, I do have excellent qualifications. I was on the staff at Tupelo, Mississippi's, famous Whit's Cafe. I was a sandwich maker and carhop, tutored by the Executive Chef, Mister James Ballard. Those big old cars with running boards would pull up and the customer would say,

'Boy, what kind of sandwiches y'all got?'

Without missing a beat, I would speedily say,

'Mister, we got bacon tomater', bacon egg, barbeque', toasted cheese, cheeseburger, hamburger, fried ham, baked ham and chicken salad.' I could rattle off those sandwiches like the rapid fire of a machine gun. Now, sometimes they would say,

'Would you say that again?' They just wanted to hear how good I could say it!"

The Lieutenant slightly cocks his head, pauses for a second to reflect on what I had just told him about my culinary experiences and mumbles under his breath something like, *"Maybe he could at the least ... entertain the customers!"*

Now that I have Lieutenant McWherter's attention, I straighten up more and with much enthusiasm say,

"Yes sir, Lieutenant Sir! I can manage your snack bars.

I made good sandwiches at Whit's Café."

Knowing that he is a southerner, I continue on,

"And my mama taught me how to make the best peanut butter banana sandwich that you have ever eaten in your whole life, and I have mama's secret recipe."

The Lieutenant's eyes widen. *Forget all that fancy food: orange duckling, goose liver pate and caviar! If you want to give a southerner good gourmet food, give him a peanut butter banana sandwich.*

I am happy. I had really gotten' Lieutenant McWherter's attention. It is almost ten o'clock!

"Knowing of the needs of others at the appropriate time
will bring forth results at the appropriate time."
Joshiki

There is something about being a private; there is always a little devilishness in us. We privates seem to have a unique instinct on how to make things happen at the right time and at the right place, all to the puzzlement of officers. Lieutenant McWherter stands up and says with excitement in his voice,

"Private Payne, I will put in a priority request with headquarters today for your transfer to the PX! You are now the PX snack bar manager. On second thought, because of your excellent qualifications *for making sandwiches,*

you will be the manager of both Camp Haugen snack bars, the one in the PX and also the one in the dance hall down town!

The only requirement for the job is that you give me your mother's recipe for her peanut butter banana sandwiches."

The Lieutenant continues on,

"In the mornings, I like my peanut butter banana sandwich precisely at ten and again in the afternoon precisely at three."

"Yes sir, Lieutenant McWherter! Yes sir!"

"Private Payne, you meet my requirements for a great snack bar manager. You have the enthusiasm for management.

Tomorrow morning, you can start work at the Camp Haugen snack bar!" I snap to attention and offer my best salute! I am on my way!

"He who possesses the source of enthusiasm will achieve great things."
I Ching

When Lieutenant McWherter had said, "The dance hall down town", that really got my attention- the dance hall with all beautiful girls . . . *and that is where Perk is gonna to teach me how to dance.*

After Lieutenant McWherter gives me the job of snack bar manager, I move out of the barracks and into a small room in the PX. Dreams do come true and I am about to achieve great things in life.

Job Protection

I am now living in *high cotton. For you Yankees that don't know high cotton. I am living upscale. No more "hup, two, three, four!" and "Dig that fox hole!" I am now . . . living high on the hog!*

Living a life of opulence changes my whole world. *I had to get out a dictionary to learn to spell that there highfalutin' word-opulence.* Sometimes, it is smart for a private to act dumb, especially in front of officers; this makes the officers think that they are smart, not dumb. *Privates know what I mean?*

Lieutenant McWherter sure likes mama's peanut butter banana sandwiches. I am careful to keep mama's famous peanut butter banana sandwich recipe a secret. I call *mama's secret recipe* **. . .** *job protection!*

When I'm not in the snack bar or in the main part of the PX, my friends and I are out riding horses in the afternoons. At night, we are in the bars and dance halls of downtown Hachinohe. Things could not have been any better for a private. I have learned how to live as an army private, scads of useless time with no cares and no worries. We Privates help each other. Worrying is for sergeants and them officers. They spend a lot of useless time worrying about us privates!

"If you can spend a perfectly useless afternoon, in a perfectly useless manner, you have learned how to live."
Lin Yutang

Living the opulent life as a snack bar manager gives me a lot of free time. My friends and I ride horses in the afternoon and see our girlfriends at night. Best of all, I am now in love. Her name is . . . *Aiko Koiwa.*

Cherokee

We country boys, back in Lee County, Mississippi, ride horses. *We are only about ten years old or so, and we have only a bridle. Sitting high forward on the horse, we wrap our legs around the neck of the horse and hold on to the mane.*

With a brisk wind blowing in our faces, it is exciting to ride the trails. We have our favorite places to go; we name the hideouts ourselves, and they are our secret places: Sleepy Hollow, Possum Creek, and the Trail of the Lonesome Pine.

We are young, full of energy and imagination back in Kings Creek days of Lee County, Mississippi!

At Camp Haugen stables, riding horses with a saddle is new to me. Perkins, Running Horse, John Russell and I are close friends in the 511th. We ride almost every day. Just because I have moved into high cotton by becoming the PX snack bar manager, nothing has actually changed. I work a little in the morning, sit around, shuffle papers and drink a lot of coffee. *You know, like those government people do when they are not on vacation.*

We go to the stables and ride our horses exploring the great frontier. Often we ride in the afternoon, drink sake and dance with the pretty Japanese girls at night.

We each have our favorite horse to ride. My horse is a big bay stallion by the name of Cherokee. He is a handsome bay, with eyes set far apart, broad chested and high-spirited. When I saddle Cherokee, he snorts and prances around a little to show that he is ready to go. Out of the gallop and into a full run, Cherokee runs as if he is in the Kentucky Derby. As we race down the road, my big bay is usually out front.

"Go, Cherokee go! Fly with the wind! Go, Cherokee! Ride the East Wind!"

A moving train is a big challenge to Cherokee. In the afternoons, a train runs parallel to one of the dirt roads where we race up and down. I love the excitement of racing the train and so does Cherokee! The fireman keeps pouring on the coal for more power. The train is puffing bellows of smoke. The engineer keeps blowing the whistle. To race next to the train is a great challenge for Cherokee. The Japanese passengers hang their heads out the windows cheering us on. We race down the road yelling, as if we are a bunch of Comanche Indians on the warpath, not knowing that what is waiting for us further down the road . . . is . . . *the fragrance of spring!*

The Fragrance of Spring

You should be able to smell the honey bucket wagon about a quarter of a mile away. As you get nearer, never race past a honey bucket wagon. Reign in your horses, and bring them to a full stop. Quickly turn your horses around, gallop off in the direction from whence you came!

Go back, go back! If you do not go back, you will learn the hard way about the honey bucket fragrance of spring. Have you ever been in contact with the contents of a honey bucket?

For centuries, the Japanese have used human waste as fertilizer. As our horses race down a country road, we are quick to find out Japanese are still collecting human waste. Human waste for the Japanese is not a waste. It is called" night soil." Night soil is collected in wooden buckets, from the village homes. These buckets we call "honey buckets!" This is nutritious fertilizer for the farmers" fields. From the fields, to the homes, the fertilizer is again recycled to the honey buckets.

"The fragrance always remains on the hand that gives the rose."
Mahatma Gandhi

It is a beautiful spring afternoon. Cherokee is in high spirits. The dogwood trees are in full bloom- the fragrance of honeysuckle rose lingers in the air. The sweet smell of the dogwood flowers disguises the fragrance of the honey bucket wagon.

As we gallop around a curve, there is a farmer and his honey bucket wagon. The farmer's horse becomes skittish with four galloping horses rapidly approaching. The farmer's little sorrel mare wants to get into the race. She takes off running. Our horses are now alongside of the honey bucket wagon. The wagon is hitting bumps in the road. The farmer is hanging on for dear life! Honey buckets are splashing everywhere. Off in the distance, we hear the yelp of a fox as we race by the honey bucket wagon, we too become a part of the honey bucket's . . . *fragrance of spring.*

The next morning the sun is slowly rising over Hachinohe Bay. I am up early and ready to go riding again. Cherokee and I leave the stables-bringing to our lives the excitement of another day.

The Sacred Shrine of the Fox

Greeting the morning sun, we find ourselves patterned on a small path as we ride up the mountainside winding higher and higher into the silence of the mountains. Far off in the distance is the cooing of a mountain dove, silenced by the yelping of a fox, as if to announce the coming of strangers.

High up on the mountainside comes the spine chilling call of the fox to announce a human has entered into the sacred mysterious spirit world of the fox.

"But I will lead you through the portals of eternity,
to wander in the great wills of infinity."
Chuang Tzu

Two large stone foxes on either side of the short stone walkway guard the entrance to the shrine. The pine boards are old and withered. The slanting roof shingled with gray slate, lends itself to the reverence and serene tranquility of the moment . . . It looks as if it has been there since ancient times. *Could this be The Sacred Shrine of the Fox?*

I slowly dismount. Cherokee stands solemnly, hooves planted wide and solid, eyes fixed on the shrine. Cherokee is not his usual skittish self. Can Cherokee also feel the mysterious enchantment of this sacred shrine? I rub Cherokee's neck. As if being summoned by the spirits of the Inari, Cherokee gently nudges me towards the shrine's entrance. Fronted by two lines of smaller stone foxes, the entrance of the shrine beckons to me; I pass between them and slowly walk up to the door and go no further.

In a trance, I stand bewitched by the immortality of the godly stone foxes before me. *Can it be possible, the spirit of the fox now possesses me to leave the nature of this human world of man, to run wild in the supernatural world of the fox?*

*"Do not develop the nature which is of man,
but develop the nature which is of God."*
Chuang Tzu

A slight breeze whispers around the eternal foxes of the shrine setting off the tinkling of a small bronze bell, returning me to the human world. *The bell has the mystic casting of foxes upon it.*

I gently ring the bell of the fox to summon the gods, although they already know of my presence. I thank them for letting me enter into their spirit world. Thanking them for my happiness and for the happiness of Aiko, our life together, our future together- I pray to the seven gods of life. *My mind takes me back to our little white planked church in Palmetto Lee County, where as a boy, I had spent many a Sunday with family, cousins and friends. Our little country church in Mississippi, with all-day singing and dinner on the ground, will always be a part of my heart.*

As I ride Cherokee back down the path of enlightenment into the shadows of the mountain **. . .** high up on the mountainside comes the mournful, elusive and mystifying heartfelt cry of the fox.

*"There are many paths to enlightenment.
Be sure to take one with a heart."*
Lao Tzu

Teppanyaki Steak Kobe Beef

After the war, it is comical to see Japanese trying to eat with a knife and fork as most had only eaten with chopsticks. My employees try to eat a whole fried egg by placing it on the back of the fork, trying to slide the whole egg into their mouths. At the Camp Haugen PX snack bar, my Japanese employees eat well. Whatever I eat, they can also eat. They like steak and they like me. I have become the typical government employee, '*who cares? It's not my money!*'

The Japanese people have not eaten much beef for centuries. Steak is now their favorite item on the menu. At Camp Haugen, as in America, there are no fancy char-broilers; most things are cooked on a grill: steak, bacon, sausages, eggs, hamburgers, toasted cheese sandwiches, pancakes, and so forth- all on the grill. The Japanese call the grill a Teppan.

The Japanese prior to WWII rarely ate beef. They mostly ate fish and some fowl. During the military occupation following the war's end, my firm opinion is that with the many American GI snack bars from Hokkaido down to the southern Ryukyu Islands, the Americans cooking on flat grills, introduced teppanyaki steak to the Japanese. Much is written about teppanyaki steak, the Americans call it "Kobe beef".

When the Japanese began to import limited amounts of good tender beef from America, the beef was brought in through the port of Kobe- thus, beef from Kobe became known to the Japanese as good "Kobe beefsteak". To the best of my knowledge, the city of Kobe had never raised beef.

In my opinion, this is not true that teppanyaki Kobe steak is a centuries old Japanese tradition. One well-known Japanese owned teppanyaki steak chain in America advertises and promotes the myth of Kobe beef. There are others responsible for perpetuating this belief. The Americans want to believe the myth of Kobe steak.

In many gourmet restaurants in America the menu proudly proclaims tender, mouth-watering Kobe beef.

So let us get the history of the famous beef straight. It was the American soldier during the occupation of Japan that introduced to Japan the art of teppanyaki steak on a grill.

In Japanese, 'yaki' means to cook, grill, roast and so forth. I am one of those American soldiers that introduced teppanyaki steak to Japan, which is wildly popular throughout the country.

The Japanese now cook steak on these grills, a throwback to the days of the occupation. As I have said, before the war the Japanese rarely ate steak, if ever. After the war, what little Japanese beef that was available was on the tough side. American beef was imported through the port of Kobe, Japan

and cooked to perfection on flat grill surfaces.

With a clear matter of conscience, I have made a lot of money selling to the majority of Americans what they want to hear about . . . and see on the menu . . . Teppanyaki Kobe Beef Steak

Today in our chain of eleven restaurants, we have five teppanyaki Kobe beefsteak restaurants. The majority of our customers are Japanese, as they now have the money for good quality American beef.

"In matters of conscience, the law of majority has no place."
Mohandas Karamchand Gandhi

You can find me at the Camp Haugen snack bar warming up the grill to get ready for our 11:00 o'clock opening. People are already waiting behind the chain to place their orders. On one particular morning, unbeknownst to a certain sneaky buck sergeant, he is in for the shock of his life . . .

The Electrocution

Through the main entrance to the PX, the exchange retail store is off to the right; the snack bar is to the left. The only thing separating the exchange from the snack bar is a waist high chain hooked between the two walls. Each day, when we are ready to open, one of our employees drops the chain and removes it. This lets the crowd waiting behind the chain to enter. Some of the customers that my snack bar feeds and amuses are officers' wives. Shockingly enough, they are the high society of Camp Haugen.

"To get into the best society nowadays, one either has to feed the people, amuse the people, or shock the people."
Oscar Wilde

Some days my buck sergeant is anxious to get his food and drops the chain early and we are not ready.

"Hey, y'all, we're not open yet!" Please stand behind the chain."

Oh, no that buck sergeant has done it again! He drops the chain and every one rushes in. We are not ready to open, but with the chain down, we are open, ready or not. Here they come . . .

"I want a cheeseburger with a Coca-Cola."

"Gimme' a ham and cheese with a chocolate shake!"

The orders are coming across the counter. We are not ready for my Camp Haugen PX Snack Bar to open . . .

It is not opening time! I could kill that Yankee soldier and I almost do!

Red hair . . . hawk nose, beady blue eyes, big ears shaped like the wings of a gooney bird, and he thinks that he is someone of importance. *You know the kind I'm ah talking about*. He is a Yankee who just made buck sergeant. Now, he is of rank. *He is no longer one of us privates.*

As he often does, sometimes two or three times a week, he snuggles up close to the chain. When he thinks no one is looking, he slyly places his hand over the hook and drops the chain. All those people waiting to come in- rush in. Suzuki always has a twinkle in his eye and a mischievous smile. *He is like one of those privates General Pershing was talking about- cunning and needs considerable watching.*

As *electrifying* as this may seem, this is the day Suzuki and I shock the hell out of that Yankee! Suzuki and I devise a plan- come to think of it, General Pershing would have been exceedingly proud of us . . .Suzuki would make a very good private. He salutes every officer that comes to the snack bar counter, plus he washes pots and pans regularly.

I touch the chain we have "fixed" and jump back.

"You know, Suzuki, I don't think there's enough juice in it for a good jolt!" Suzuki touches the chain and jumps back,

"You right, boss! We need more *shocku'!* I can fix'em good!"

Earlier this morning, we wired the chain to a 120 volt outlet, with an on and off switch. So, what can Suzuki do "to fix'em more good?" *I am soon to find out!* Suzuki sets down a water bucket, looks at me . . . sends me a wink and with a big happy smile- begins to mop the floor.

"Suzuki, it doesn't look wet enough."

Suzuki slops more water on! We are getting a big charge out of this. Suzuki and I are accelerated; our current electrical plan is getting us all wired up! The excitement is most contagious!

"Even a hare will bite when it is cornered."
Chinese Proverb

It is nearing eleven o'clock. The smart-ass buck sergeant snuggles up to the chain, puts his hand on the hook and that is . . . when I throw on the switch. Sparks fly! Smart-ass screams, jumping up and down. His bright red hair stands on end. Suzuki's hair stands on end . . . my hair stands on end!

Suzuki screams, "*Jizusu Cristo!*"

I yell, "Oh, my goodness gracious!"

I quickly throw off the switch. The Yankee is jumping up and down, screaming like a stuck pig. Suzuki runs for the safety of the kitchen door. I take off running for the open back door.

"A sly rabbit will have three openings to its den."

Chinese Proverb

The next morning, Lieutenant McWherter receives a call from the regimental commander and as instructed, I receive a stern lecture. With a slight smile on his face, he picks up his coffee cup and dismisses me with a wave of his hand.

Lieutenant McWherter always knows when I'm up to something. Every time I am up to something, he cocks his head to one side, looks at me out of the corner of his eye and wiggles his mustache. He knows when he is about to be *involved*. . .

The Lieutenant's Convertible

I have carefully chosen my well-planned time of approach to Lieutenant McWherter to coincide with the arrival of his ten o'clock mid-morning peanut butter banana sandwich. *This always puts him in a good frame of mind.*

"Lieutenant McWherter Sir, when I arrived in Japan I went to a PX snack bar in Yokohama. They have pretty snack bar girls working in their snack bars down there and I think we should have some, too. All we got working in our snack bar are these here farmers. I know a private over in personnel. He can arrange to find our farmers new jobs, one way or the other." *With an amazed look, he stares straight into my face. The Lieutenant asks no questions. He thinks it is best to let sleeping dogs lie.*

I continue on,

"In Yokohama, there is an 8th Army employment center where we can get some pretty girls for our snack bar. This will be great for the troops' morale." I thought to myself,

"Especially, my morale."

"Sir, how is mama's peanut butter banana sandwich this morning?"

"Fine, except it was five minutes late. I am expecting it to be right on time-ten A.M. on the dot."

"Oh, yes sir," I say. "It won't happen again!"

Lieutenant McWherter is married- he and his wife reside in base housing at Camp Haugen. She is a pert attractive blond, blue-eyed southern girl. I have seen her in the ladies' section of our PX, where Lieutenant McWherter bought her one of those yellow and red polka-dotted dresses for her birthday at the newly inflated price of $4.99.

Before leaving the states for Japan, Lieutenant McWherter bought a brand new 1947 yellow Buick convertible for their wedding anniversary.

When I say 'Yokohama', the first thing that comes to Lieutenant's McWherter's mind is his new 1947 yellow Buick convertible sitting on a railway car at the station in Yokohama. He is notified of the car's arrival, and there it sits waiting to be transported on a flat car up to Hachinohe. It is going to be a long ride in the darkness of the night for the lieutenant's beautiful convertible ... all by itself. I can sense the lieutenant is thinking, *What if it were to get scratched? Worse yet, somebody might borrow the radio for their jeep.*

Lieutenant McWherter is in ecstasy eating Mama's ten o'clock secret recipe peanut butter banana sandwich. My timing is well planned.

"You know, Private Payne this is not a bad idea after all.

How many girls do you think we need?"

"We need about sixteen, sir- for two shifts."

I think to myself, *"This is about four more than I actually need. I figure a few extra is good for my morale. After all, I will give them some on-the-job training and plenty of time off so I can take them out for a little sightseeing around the sake houses in Hachinohe. On their leisure time, I will teach them my favorite card game!* Lieutenant McWherter leans back in his chair, pleased with contentment as he eats the last bite of mama's peanut butter sandwich.

"Private Payne, our customers deserve a first class snack bar. He tips forward, looks right at me and says,

"I'll have orders cut for you right away to go down to Yokohama on the *Yankee Flyer* to get some snack bar girls for Camp Haugen."

"Yes sir, Lieutenant McWherter, sir! Yes, sir!"

I know what the Lieutenant has on his mind, what he's ah thinkin'. *"He is ah thinkin' about his new 1947 yellow Buick convertible sitting all alone on a flat car at the Yokohama Station, and he knows ... what I'm ah thinkin' ... good things- like pretty snack bar girls.*

Sometimes lieutenants and privates do think alike when it comes to the good things in life.

"But, where will we quarter them?" asks the lieutenant.

"We have an empty PX warehouse down by the horse stables that is not being used. We can get some bunks and bedding out of the regimental supply warehouse. Don't worry, lieutenant, as I have the time and patience to take care of the girls. I know some privates that work in supply who can handle the paper work. *"Lieutenants just don't know about the timely wonders of privates!"*

"With time and patience, the mulberry leaf becomes a silk gown."
Chinese Proverb

Lieutenant McWherter sits in his chair, rocking back and forth, slowly swaying his head from side to side. He does not want to know any more about my supply channel, paper work or whatever I might have up my sleeve.

"Don't you worry none, sir! I will help you, sir!"

I practically skip out of his office, but he catches me before

I round the corner.

"Wait, Private Payne! I will have orders cut for you to go down to Yokohama and get sixteen snack bar girls from the 8th Army employment agency in Yokohama. Your return is precisely scheduled to be on the same train as my new 1947 yellow Buick convertible. Private Payne will you be so kind as to sit in my convertible and make sure that no one touches it?"

"Yes sir, Lieutenant, yes sir!"

I say while trying to control my thoughts of that long cozy romantic train ride from Yokohama back to Hachinohe with sixteen beautiful girls.

"Yes sir, Lieutenant! Yes Sir! Don't you worry none about your nice new Buick convertible; it is going to be in real good hands."

The Lieutenant does not know it, but I too, have plans for his brand new convertible. I think the lieutenant can tell that I am getting pretty excited about all this, as I want to see all those pretty girls and choose the prettiest ones to bring back with me for our snack bar. I can tell that the lieutenant is relieved to have his car in such good hands as mine- Private Payne, who is another southerner, from the State of Mississippi.

In his South Carolina accent, he says to me,

"Your travel orders will be ready tomorrow mornin' for the *Yankee flyer*. Someday, you must teach me your mother's secret recipe."

I come to attention; smartly click my heels and salute. As I turn to depart, I reply,

"Yes sir, lieutenant, sir!" *"He ain't gonna' get that recipe!"* I mutter to myself.

The war is over, times are hard and there are many people looking for work. I feel so lucky, as I am soon to choose sixteen pretty girls. I can be very picky as to whom I choose for my snack bars . . . and picky I am.

However, unbeknownst to me, I will soon meet the notorious 8th Army MP rat!

The Great Movie Star Director

1948 The Year of the Rat

The sun is peeking over the distant Mountain of the Fox, full of excitement, and with great anticipation, I am at the station early. I hear the familiar long blast of the whistle, the clanging of the bell, pistons pounding as the old *Yankee Flyer* that had survived the war, rounds the bend, creaking to a halt. I quickly board and it takes off for Tokyo. Passing through the little seaside town of Matsushima, I smile as a fondly recall the girls of Matsushima, and .... *Aces are wild*!

The minutes are as long as hours as the *Yankee Flyer* races on down the tracks bound for Tokyo. In Tokyo, at Ueno Station, I catch another train, *not quick enough,* that takes me on to Yokohama. *I do not waste any time*; after all, I am on a very important, high priority mission. *At least I think so!*

In Yokohama, I sleep in a small Japanese Inn by the name of *Ume no Hana* "Plum Blossom". After a delicious breakfast of fish head soup, fish eyeballs in sea-urchin sauce, broiled eel with fermented bean curd, served with green tea; I have the Plum Blossom Inn summon a rickshaw.

The steady gait of the rickshaw runner *is not fast enough for me as it* speeds me on my way to the 8th Army Depot. Without wasting any time, I go directly to the employment office as directed by the gate guards. I show my orders to an Army corporal at the front counter and say,

"These are my orders. Where are the girls?"

The corporal scans me up and down with disbelief, shakes his head and mumbles, *"Another one."* He points out the window and directs me to a large warehouse down the street where he says hundreds of people are looking for work. I thank him and hurry down the street. Inside the building, I inquire of another corporal as to whom I should talk to about hiring girls for our Camp Haugen snack bar. The corporal points to a staff sergeant and says, "He . . . is the one."

The staff sergeant portrays the look of importance. At least *he* thinks so! You know the kind; they glide around like a ballerina with head high up in the air. *Look at me!* He shows a tight smile and softly tiptoes around with a clipboard in one hand, waving a pencil around in the other. As I look, I stop, tilt my head and think; he *sure would make a good officer!*

As he approaches my direction, I step in front of him- with the voice of authority and say to him,

"I am Private Payne, general manager of all Camp Haugen PX snack bars. With a voice of authority, I say to him,

"Sergeant, these are my orders! I am Private Payne, general manager of all Camp Haugen PX snack bars, near Hachinohe, home of the 511th Parachute Infantry Regiment.

I look him straight in the eye and ask,

"Where are the girls?"

He looks down his nose at me, shifts his glasses, looks *me* straight in the eyes and says,

"I'm busy!"

"But Sergeant, these are my orders. I am here to get sixteen beautiful . . . oh, I mean sixteen girls for our snack bar at Camp Haugen in Hachinohe. I am only following my orders! I need to know where the girls are."

He pushes his glasses further up on his nose, looks at the orders, waves his hand and says,

"Take your pick."

I can feel the excitement! As he walks away, he hands me a piece of paper and a pencil. Over his shoulder he says,

"Write their names and bring me the paper, Private Payne!"

"Yes sir, sergeant! Yeees' sir!"

Now, I am like Cecil B. DeMille, the great movie star talent director choosing a cast for my production on stage at the Camp Haugen snack bar. After all, I also I have some talent. I had been in a school play once when I was in the fifth grade directed by the great, Miss McKinley.

Looking slowly around the room, I do see many very pretty girls with beautiful snow-white skin, black hair, and almond- shaped eyes to choose from, and choose I do. I walk among them confidently, looking them over, and I choose sixteen beautiful girls out of hundreds of girls in the room. Each one of them could have been a star on a movie stage! I say to myself,

"They don't know nothin 'about snack bar work and I don't care. Camp Haugen will be their stage of life as they learn their lines, *"Would you like*

French fries with your cheeseburger?" What is important to me is my part . . . I will be their on-stage director!"

"On the stage of life, your part is just as important as anyone else's is."
Paramhansa Yogananda

The Long Cold Night

At the Yokohama train station, I put fourteen of the girls in a passenger car and take two of the prettiest ones with me. This is not an easy choice as they are all pretty and give me beautiful smiles . . . I cradle an arm around each girl as we walk along the railway track. We are giddy as we seek the comfort of the Lieutenant's convertible. The full moon is bright, truly a beautiful sight . . . a night for romance.

Under the full glow of the moon, we find the car; it is gleaming yellow and bright as can be. *How can anyone miss seeing it?* Nearby, there is a snack bar; I load up with cheese, crackers, RC Colas and Moon Pies- all high-energy food. After all, it is going to be a long, cold night. I do not worry much about the cold, as I know the girls are gonna' heat up the night! We settle into the back of the car for a long . . . *lovely warm night,* I think to myself as I rub my new . . . lucky rabbit's foot, "*Why is Private Payne so lucky in life?"*

The engineer of the *Yankee Flyer* pulls the chain, lets off steam and blows the whistle, letting us know that we are about to pull out heading to the north country and on to Camp Haugen. My beautiful girls and I snuggle close in the warmth of the back seat of the convertible. I too, am like the engineer; I am also ready to let off steam . . . for a beautiful romantic evening on the road to Hachinohe! *Oh! Happy nights are here again. I hope this night will never end!*

I will never forget the screeching of the brakes on the 8th Army MP jeep, as it comes to an abrupt halt right alongside of Lieutenant McWherter's bright new yellow Buick convertible. I peek out the window, and what do I see? . . . I see two fat 8th Army MPs. The MP Sergeant says,

"Soldier, this is a nice yellow Buick convertible". Seeing the MPs, the girls snuggle down closer.

The Corporal says,

"Yea', how could anyone help but notice this shiny yellow Buick convertible? Where are you going?"

"Hachinohe, Corporal! Camp Haugen, 511th Parachute Infantry Regiment."

"So, you are a paratrooper? Well, let me see your orders!" grunts the sergeant with authority.

"Yes sir, sergeant, and here they are. How are you this evening, sergeant? I am Private Payne; it is so nice to meet you, sergeant! Isn't it a beautiful evening?" I say with my most friendly smile.

"Private Payne, these orders are for you and sixteen Japanese girls . . . Where are the other fourteen?"

"They're up yonder in that passenger car, Sergeant Sir."

Again, I give him my best big friendly smile *reserved for MPs*. I'm ah thinkin' "I sure am glad I brought my lucky rabbit foot."

With that all too familiar fake MP smile, the Rat says.

"Well, guess what soldier? These two Jap gals are also gonna' be up yonder in that passenger car with the other fourteen girls!"

Here I sit, heartbroken- me the great movie star director all alone in the back seat of Lieutenant McWherter's 1947 yellow Buick convertible. I sadly gaze out the window at the brightness of what was to be a romantic full moon.

It is indeed a fact whether I like it or not, it will be a cold lonely trip, as the train bound for Hachinohe disappears into the night. I roll down the car window; my lucky rabbit foot **. . .** also disappears- out of the window into the cold winter night.

"Facts are facts and will not disappear on account of your likes."
Jawaharlal Nehru

Dance. . . . Dance . . . Dance

The Hachinohe Snack Bar in down town Hachinohe is Private Payne's branch snack bar on the ground floor of our approved dance hall. The dance hall on the second floor is the only dance hall in Hachinohe approved for us GI's.

Our dance hall has an orchestra with a good-looking female vocalist. The girls sit at one end of the dance floor and the soldiers sit at the other end. Only when the band strikes up, can we meet to dance by walking towards each other. Sometimes, this leads to mad rushes. When the music stops, we go back to our side of the room and the girls wander back to their side. The last dance the band plays and the singer sings:

"Goodnight sweetheart, all my prayers are for you
Goodnight sweetheart, I'll be watching o'er you
Tears and parting may make us forlorn
But with the dawn a new day is born
So I'll say goodnight sweetheart, sleep will banish sorrow
Goodnight sweetheart, when we meet tomorrow
Dreams enfold you, in them, dear, I'll hold you
Goodnight sweetheart goodnight."
Ray Noble, Jimmy Campbell, Reg Connelly

As this is the last dance of the evening, there is a lot of kissing and ah hugging going on! And plans being made for a nightcap and a little romance with our special ladies.

"See you tomorrow, sweetheart! We all have girlfriends that we see on most weekends and holidays. We also have a secret . . . a secret hole in the fence that allows us to sneak in and out late for a sweet nightcap with our special ladies . . .

"*It is at this very dance hall, that Perk has taught me how to dance.*

"Perk, I don't know how to dance! I never danced in my life, and I ain't gonna' do so now!

Perk replies,

"Come on, I'll show you how. Don't you like these pretty girls?" *I say to myself, "Is he crazy, this is like asking a kid in a candy store . . . if he likes candy!"*

Perk says,

"It's just like driving a truck! Now watch me and do as I do!"

Perk explains as he demonstrates,

"You put the left leg in low gear. You shove the left leg forward into second gear. Then you throw the right leg into third gear. Next, you shove the left leg into fourth gear. Then you put the right leg forward into fifth gear. You pull the left leg back into reverse . . . that is to back up, and then you start all over again!

Now, you see it is just like driving a truck. See how simple it is; it is not complicated at all."

And this . . . is how Private Payne learned to dance!

"Life is really simple, but we insist on making it complicated."
Confucius

The Samurai

Perk's girl is from Sapporo, Hokkaido; she's tall, about a foot taller than Perk, and she doesn't speak any English. Perk simply calls her Sapporo.

"Perk, why don't you teach that girl of yours some English?"

"I did."

"What is it you taught her?"

"Let's go to bed!"

On this Saturday afternoon, I cannot go into town until evening; I let Perk have my key so he can meet his girl in my snack bar that does not open until the evening. It is summer time and I have a ton of watermelons in the snack bar, and my snack bar is well-stocked with large bottles of ice-cold Sapporo beer.

By the time I get there, Perk and Miss Sapporo are already drunk. She is wearing a light summer *yukata* embroidered with the mon (crest) of the *Matsumae Warrior Clan* of Hokkaido.

Wild-eyed, she is wielding a big kitchen knife in her hands and using my watermelons to demonstrate to Perk how the Samurai use their swords. She is dashing around, yelling, "Banzai!" slashing watermelons all over the place.

"Samurai do like this! Banzai!" she yells. Bringing both hands high over her head, swirling around, she slashes the air with a downward swift cross cut **. . .** Swish!

Another watermelon splits the air!

Perk is sitting high up on the side of the table, bug-eyed, wishing he had taught his girl more English . . . like, STOP!

"The way of the Samurai is one of immediacy, and it is best to dash in headlong."

Samurai Proverb

Tom Tom

There is plenty of sake, beer, romance and Tom Tom in those wonderful off-limit bars in downtown Hachinohe. These bars are off-limits to us privates. Many pretty girls are serving Tom Toms in these off-limit bars. I learn the hard way real early in my long career as a private that the white innocent looking drink that the Japanese call shochu and we call Tom Tom is mighty powerful stuff, and it will knock your head off. It is guaranteed to sneak up on you and get you into trouble! Many a bar fight over a girl has started with Tom Tom. The reason we gave it the name of Tom Tom, is because the next morning our heads pound like an Indian beating his drum-

Tom Tom, Tom Tom, Tom Tom!

In the Army, not only do they tell us privates where to go, they also tell us privates where *not* to go, and these not to go places are the fun places. Every night the MPs go out looking for us privates in off-limit places. These bars are strictly off-limits! These off-limit places sure do make it hard for a private to make Private First Class.

I have a sweet plan for this coming Saturday night. With their ol' weapons' carrier out of action and no transportation the MPs won't be able to go out looking for us privates. My friends don't know about my plan- *just wait till I tell em'!*

"Privates help privates . . .
After all, it is our own little private society."
Private Payne

How Sweet It Is

Perk speaks up,

"It is Saturday night and we have all got paid- Hachinohe here we come!"

John Russell says,

"Let's go to the *Pink Butterfly* and on to *Yokohama Mama's!"*

I notice Running Horse has that warpath look on his face.

"What's up, Horse? You look like you want to go on a scalping party. What are you thinking?"

Running Horse puts his left hand on his scalp-lock haircut, squints his eyes, frowns and says,

"Y'all pale-faces know, the *Pink Butterfly* and *Yokohama Mama's* is off limits and that's the first place those MPs are gonna' be looking for us. That ol' weapons' carrier is gonna' be all over town looking for us privates and sure enough, they will come to *Yokohama Mama's!* We can't do nothing about that!"

"Yes we can, Horse! That ol' weapons' carrier just won't run on sugar!" I announce proudly. *For those that do not know what a weapons carrier is, it is larger than a jeep but smaller than a six-by truck. A weapons carrier is for carrying heavy weapons such as .50 caliber machine guns, mortars and ammunition. It is like the difference between a mule and a donkey. Southern country boys know what I am ah talking about! In our regiment that ol' weapons carrier is also used by the MPs to look for us privates in off-limits places where privates ain't supposed to go . . . but we do go!*

John Russell speaks up,

"What do you mean that ol' weapons carrier won't run on sugar?"

"Well, you know the MPs on a Saturday night park their ol' weapons carrier on a side street near their favorite downtown restaurant *The Rose Garden* until they are ready to start checking the off-limits places. We are gonna' teach them MPs a lesson! I got packs of sugar in my snack barlet's pour five pounds of sugar into that ol' weapons carrier's gas tank.

It's a sure thing that weapons carrier won't run on sugar!"

Just like I said it will be, I am now telling everybody what to do.

"Horse, you're the scout; stand watch near the front of the *Rose Garden* and if they start coming out, you give out your Indian hoot owl signal. John Russell, you keep an eye on Horse, we don't want no war party! Perk, come with me.

Now, Perk, make a funnel out of this paper sack.

That's it-hold the funnel while I pour the sugar!

There she goes . . . five pounds of sugar right down the tank.

This ol' weapons carrier won't be up to speed!"

"There is more to life than increasing its speed."
Mahatma Gandhi

It is a wonderful night for us privates- this night on the town! We are having a great time, singing and dancing and romancing the pretty Japanese girls. . . from bar to bar all over Hachinohe City. Horse is happily dancing in his best "pow-wow" style, and a whoopin' it up on firewater while drumming away on the table top . . . John Russell is as happy as a pig wallowing in a mud puddle as he raises his Sapporo beer bottle and yells,

"Hey, Horse, everybody . . . we did it, we did it! We are heroes! We escaped the ol' weapon's carrier!

"Heroes are made, not born!"
Private Payne

The Pink Butterfly, Do Drop Inn, Night Train, The Thirsty Pelican, and Yokohama Mama's.

What a night!

What a life . . . how sweet it is . . . for us privates!

Our officers should tell those MPs that officers and privates are different. We privates just wanna' have fun. In the Army, there is discrimination between officers and us privates.

There Is A Difference!

We privates always have to salute first. Why don't we take turnabout and officers salute first? After all, fair is fair. There is also discrimination as well in regards to money. Maybe it is because the officers have rich mamas and daddies. They had food on their table every day and they could afford to go to school. When they graduate from college, they get a piece of paper . . . they call it a degree. That degree says they are now a bachelor. Now, I can never figure out why they are a bachelor as it says on that there degree, as most of the officers at Camp Haugen are married! *Would you believe it!*

Anyway, after they become a bachelor, I guess they leave their wives at home; they go on to that there Officers' Candidate School where they teach them to stand around with their hands on their hips and watch us privates do all the work. This is the difference between an officer and a private.

We privates that grew up during the Great Depression, *we didn't know it was the Great Depression*, thought this is the way life is supposed to be, always hungry. We didn't have no shoes. I work in the cotton fields and later on in town, wherever I can, doing anything I can to make a nickel. Those *rich kid* officers got what they call scholarships and they had shoes. This is why officers get special privileges.

We privates don't get no scholarships. We just have to get along with what we have ... our common sense.

"Common sense is not so uncommon, for a private."
Joshiki

No doubt, common sense is something they don't teach in that there officer's school. An officer will never understand the principles of good marketing as a private does working in the Camp Haugen PX! We privates must be fair to the officers though and try to show them kindness and consideration. We got to show them that we understand why they are officers- that they need to be around just in case the sergeants ever need them!

You know . . . the Army is just like a beehive. There are drones, like officers, to make honey for the queen bee. The queen is like the government. She needs honey, like the government needs money, and us privates are like the worker bees. We do all the work to support the officers that hang around like drones.

We privates must understand this . . . *not everyone can be a private!* Drones live all their lives receiving benefits from the hard-working honeybees. It is like a government person receiving benefits all of his or her life from the hard-working, non-government people. Government people get to retire early in life and keep receiving benefits from the hard-working, non-government people. The non-government people have supported them government people all of their lives, and they will continue to support them government people so the government people can enjoy their wonderful early retirement life style . . . forever and ever!

"Don't go around saying the world owes you a living.
The world owes you nothing, it was here first."
Mark Twain

It is just like those worker bees, all of their lives, supporting those drones! Drones live comfortably all of their lives, living off the honey of the hard-working honeybees. The drones try to get more honey out of the worker bees. Just like officers try to get more work out of us privates, and it seems that us privates are saluting all day long! I must say though that I am proud to say I do get a lot of individual attention as the lieutenants are looking at me all day long.

To get along in this army, it is important to know the proper way of saluting. The main concern of the officers, besides having the sergeants march us up and down, is the salute. One salute they don't like is a private to slowly bring his right arm up and tilt his head to the right to meet the palm of his hand. They think this salute is a lazy private. You don't want them to think of you like that.

Another way of saluting that they don't like is the flip. The flip is when you swing your right hand far out with a wide left return, coming back to briefly touch your head and then flip your hand up into the air. The officers think this is arrogance. If you don't want to call attention to yourself . . . you had better not do that!

The proper way to salute is slowly bring your right arm up- placing the side of your hand over your right eye and pause . . . before bringing your arm down. This makes the officer feel that he is recognized. Don't go spreading your legs far apart- putting your hands on your hips, swinging your head from side to side, looking all around as to do this will land you in the guard house. These positions are for officers only. As I say- if a private wants to get along in this army, he must learn these things. One can figure this out if one thinks about it. No wonder we privates are saluting all day and have to work so hard!

We know that us enlisted have only seven enlisted ranks; whereas, the officers have fifteen officer ranks. We have learned the officers have got us enlisted ranks controlled and outnumbered more than two to one! We privates know we must understand ourselves; to get along in this army, we learn to master ourselves.

"One who knows much about others may be learned, but one who understands himself is more intelligent. One who controls others may be powerful, but one who has mastered himself is mightier still."

Lao-Tzu

The officers could learn something about reverse economics in marketing when it comes to shopping for their wives in our PX.

Beauty Is In the Eye of the Beholder

"Beauty is in the eyes of the beholder", so they say! I reckon they are talking about dresses and the principles of good marketing as seen through the eyes of a private working in the Camp Haugen PX. When shopping for our special ladies there is a difference between officers and us privates especially. The officers buy their wives dresses for a special occasion like a birthday or anniversary and ... they had better not forget!

We privates buy dresses for our girlfriends ... because we are in love!

Now y'all outta' know, that there is a big difference in who can afford, or not afford those $4.95 dresses. Officers make a lot more money than us privates do. I can never figure out why, as it is us privates that do all the work. Officers get one hundred dollars a month for jump pay. We privates only get fifty dollars a month... And, this ain't fair!

Our Camp Haugen PX sells expensive dresses for the ladies for $4.95. Prices for the pretty dresses are printed on small tags that hang from the sleeves on little strings. In our PX, we also sell pretty dresses for a lower price of $2.95 and these $2.95 dresses are benefits on a string for us hard-working, low-paid privates when placed on a $4.95 dress. The privates that work in the PX do have *some* benefits. We quickly learn good business and marketing practices-something they don't teach in that there officer's school. Let me say right now, us privates working in the PX do not steal; we just manipulate the price market.

A $7.25 Bulova watch to some people looks just as good as a $13.95 Benrus watch, and to us privates that $13.95 Benrus watch looks as good as a $7.25 Bulova watch. Some of those $2.95 dresses look just as pretty as the $4.95 dresses and those $2.95 price tags look just fine on those $4.95 dresses. In turn, the $4.95 looks right on the $2.95 dresses. Are you still with me? *Do you know what I mean? Privates know it well!*

An officer says, "Hey, Bobbie Jean, look at that $4.95 price tag on this pretty yellow and red polka-dotted dress. Do you like this one? She smiles at him, and the officer buys Bobbie Jean the increased value dress; while us privates happily buy the $2.95 discounted good looking dresses for our girlfriends.

I don't think officers will ever understand anything about our low-key marketing plans, the way us privates do. No doubt, in that there officers' candidate school, they only teach the sergeants how to march us privates around, up and down.

Hup, two, three, four! Hup, two, three, four

And, for those PX dresses . . . *Beauty is in the eyes of the beholder!*

"Everything has its beauty but not everyone sees it."
Confucius

Life at Camp Haugen is ever rewarding despite the differences in officers and privates. Life could not be better for Lieutenant Winfred Montan McWherter and his beautiful wife, looking ever so lovely in her new yellow and red polka dotted dress as she drives around Camp Haugen in her brand new 1947 yellow Buick convertible. I am beginning to develop in my mind a good marketing strategy for a wholesale business.

The Chocolate Bar Days

"If you must play the game, decide on three things at the start, the rules of the game, the stakes and the quitting time."
Chinese Proverb

The road to riches is right down the road in Hachinohe. Paratroopers have to make their required jumps. Other than that, I am living the good life working in the PX. Using my God-given common sense, I create a strategy for wholesale distribution. I am making big money! Life could not be better for me, Private Payne. I am so in love with a beautiful Japanese girl and the two of us have a successful wholesale business.

Life could not be better for Lieutenant McWherter with his daily delight . . . Mama's peanut butter banana sandwiches. PX sales are increasing by leaps and bounds.

Cigarettes are fifty cents a carton, twenty cartons to a case. Now, I have never smoked a cigarette in my life, but it don't mean that I don't like cigarettes, because cigarettes make Aiko and me a lot of money.

A big ol' large five-cent Hershey chocolate bar makes me a lot of money. I sell them wholesale by the case in down town Hachinohe. It is said that the 511th has the highest chocolate bar consumption of any regiment in the entire United States Army! *I know why, but I ain't gonna' tell.*

"To succeed in life you need two things:
Ignorance and confidence."
Mark Twain

Aiko Koiwa

Young, radiantly beautiful, skin like the purity of new fallen snow, pulsed inquisitive lips, dark almond- shaped eyes, magnetic to all . . . this is Aiko and w*e are in love.* She is eighteen and I have recently turned nineteen.

I buy the most beautiful of dresses for Aiko, *always at the special discounted price of $2.95.* Aiko and I met in our Camp Haugen PX, where we both work. Together, we are learning a lot about business. Although the PX is in the retail business, Aiko and I are fast learning the wholesale business. We sell wholesale to a china store in Hachinohe for three times what we pay the PX. We provide cases of cigarettes, soap, Hershey chocolate bars and other goods that are sought after by the more well to do Japanese. The PX is making money and PX sales are going up. The wholesale business is a volume business by the case, most profitable . . . and exciting! Cases of Ivory soap and cases of Hershey chocolate bars are selling very well. Our wholesale business is increasing. We are stuffing our profits into banks in Hachinohe and Morioka City where Aiko's sister lives- we only accept Japanese yen.

I am an honest private!

The PX always gets paid full retail price on my retail purchases for my wholesale sales. In my distribution channel, it is wholesale to retail, retail to wholesale, wholesale to retail. The success of my wholesale business goes right over the heads of officers. *I call it reverse economics.*

Aiko and I are happy each day and are unafraid of the consequences; my motto is, "Always sell for whatever the market will bear!"

"Success often comes to those who dare to act.
Seldom does it go to the timid that are ever afraid of the consequences."
Jawaharlal Nehru

MPC

"A good manager has a vision and sees clearly what's happening and what should be done to adapt quickly to changes and developments. He can grasp the trends that will evolve, and the market place that will emerge."
Rafidah Aziz

Uncle Sam does not pay in U.S. dollars; we are paid with Military Payment Certificates (MPC). We use MPCs as legal currency on military bases. Sometimes the MPCs change overnight to a new script design. This is to prevent the currency from being of value on the black market. Japanese do not want to be holding MPCs when the script changes. With the help of a private with vision in headquarters, I know when to grasp and adapt quickly the overnight change to a new script, prior to it happening in the market place.

With the foresight of change, but I must act with speed! I tell my Japanese broker that I will buy the old MPC with the new MPC at seventy-five cents on the dollar. With my private connections in finance at regimental headquarters, without difficulty I am able to turn in the old MPCs at full dollar value for the new MPCs.

"The manager with a vision sees opportunities, while the one with blinkers only bemoans the difficulties. The mark of a good manager is the speed at which he acts on opportunities. The better manager actively shapes the vision and does what needs to be done to realize it."
Rafidah Aziz

The U.S. Government does not lose a penny on me. My vision is clear and serves me well. I see the opportunity to realize a twenty-five percent return on my investment in the Japanese market. I only accept the highest denominations; I will not accept 5, 10, 25 and 50 cent MPCs; I accept only $1.00, $5.00 and $10.00 MPC certificates!

I have pre-arranged with the *Hachinohe Fine China Store*

to receive- soon to be out dated MPCs held by some citizens of Hachinohe that are desperate to unload them in exchange

for the new scrip design.

I have a good relationship with the *Hachinohe Fine China Store*; as the owner is my retail distributor for my wholesale products.

Distribution and Compassion

There are no questions asked as I go out the gate in the PX's six-by truck when I furnish my snack bar in downtown Hachinohe with supplies. It is obvious that Aiko is better with numbers than I am. She is in charge of the finances, ensuring the PX gets every penny of the retail sales. She is good at this. PX sales keep going up, and so do Aiko's and my wholesale profits! *We keep stuffing money in the banks.*

Our wholesale distribution system is my job. I drive our PX snack bar truck to downtown Hachinohe to re-stock my snack bar twice a week. I give our Japanese truck driver the day off on these days. In doing so, it is always good to have compassion in one's heart for other people- always thinking of their welfare. *After all, money is not everything!*

Thanks to my loyal employee, Moriyama-san, my personal hands-on operation keeps my distribution system working well, right to the back door of my downtown Hachinohe snack bar.

Moriyama and Horse

The wheels squeak and wobble as the old wagon slowly maneuvers its way down a narrow cobblestone side street in the darkness of the night, pulled by an old gray horse that seems to be as ancient as the old wagon.

Moriyama and the old horse, now both in the twilight of their years, have seen many a spring day supplying honey bucket fertilizer to the farmers for their rice fields. The old horse does not have a name. With deep affection for his friend, Moriyama simply calls him 'Horse'. The old man, the horse and the ancient wagon seem to be as one.

In the cold lightly falling snow, Moriyama pulls his well-worn straw cape closer around his neck to shut out the winter chill. He sits on the tongue of the old wagon not looking up. 'Horse' slowly plods along aware of where he is going, his biweekly stop at the back door of my Hachinohe snack bar. Good jobs are scarce in the winter of 1948, Moriyama now has a job as my garbage collector; also, he is my transporter for my wholesale black market goods. *Moriyama's biggest concern in life is for his old horse . . . so his wife says!*

Moriyama has spent most of his life collecting human waste from the homes around Hachinohe as fertilizer for the farmers. The so-called honey buckets of human waste are not a waste. The waste becomes fertilizer growing crops for the hungry people, and then from the homes back again to the honey buckets . . . *and that is not a waste as this fertilizer grows good nutritious crops!*

Twice a week, my faithful old garbage collector with his one-horse honey bucket wagon collects my garbage to be disposed. He also collects my wholesale goods and delivers them down a small street to the back door of the *Hachinohe Fine China Wholesale and Retail Store,* where my goods go from there, I do not know. After all, I am in the wholesale business, not retail.

The old man, Moriyama, takes great risk and responsibility for my downtown transportation. He handles it well. He is my employee, like a family member in my wholesale business. I compensate him well with the same feelings of responsibility that he has for the old horse.

"We treat employees as members of the family. If management takes the risk of hiring them, we have to take the responsibility for them."
Aiko Morita

Red Crested White Cranes Among Lotus Blossoms

"Welcome to the *Hachinohe Fine China Store*,"

Fujiwara greets his customers with a slight bow.

"May I show you some of my fine china? Our china is of the finest quality and it is properly marked under each piece, MADE IN OCCUPIED JAPAN, as required by General MacArthur's Headquarters. The china is also ready for shipping. Here is a beautiful tea set for six and the price is right. Look what a beautiful design: Red Crested White Cranes among Lotus Blossoms."

The mystique of Fujiwara's crisp English accent I can never figure out. Slim, with a pencil thin gray mustache that matches his salt and pepper hair, neatly dressed in a gray pin-striped suit-he wears a black bow tie. Fujiwara carries himself with the air of luster and mystery.

One evening, in the soft breeze of a clear night sky, as I
greet Fujiwara . . . I say to him,

"Fujiwara-san, were you in the Japanese military?"

"No, I served in His Imperial Majesty's Service. Please come in and we shall settle for your last night's shipment."

With a respectful smile, and slight nod of my head, I inquire no further. I observe the risk that he is taking in distributing my wholesale products; I am assuming that Fujiwara has been involved in mystery and intrigue and has taken suspenseful risks for His Imperial Majesty. *In Japan, for centuries the mysterious, shadowy elite Fujiwara clan has an ancient history of intrigue.*

On my drive back to camp, my mind creates a scene: *Why is he in this small seaport city of Hachinohe, so remote in northern Honshu? Why is he listening to a Russian broadcast in the back of the store? What is his mission?*

"Let us leave the lotus blossom as it is. It blooms when it blooms, it falls when

it falls, now it stands up in full blossom under the clear blue sky, the entire cosmoses reflected in it.
Neither the Buddha nor Kasyapa can touch that . . . nor can we. It simply greets us in the soft breeze and awaits our quiet and respectful smile."
Takeuchi Yoshinori

Letter of Commendation

Lieutenant McWherter is impressed with my good work ethics of supplying the snack bars with all the items needed to make it successful. The Lieutenant recognizes the compassion in my heart for the PX truck driver. I give the truck driver two nights off and I make the deliveries myself on those nights. I earnestly work late at night taking care of PX business.

It is nice of Lieutenant McWherter to give me a letter of commendation for outstanding dedication to sales, service, and compassion for others. *Even I am impressed! I proudly hang my Letter of Commendation behind the cigarette counter for all to see . . . what a good private can achieve.*

PX retail sales keep going up each week. Lieutenant McWherter receives an award for increased sales. He does not know why P X sales are increasing and he does not want to know why. Why ask questions when you have a good thing going? *You know what I mean.* His award will help get him promoted to captain. No doubt, Camp Haugen PX has the largest sales increase per capita than any outfit in the whole United States Army!

Lieutenant McWherter sure likes mama's peanut butter banana sandwiches. I keep mama's peanut butter banana sandwich recipe a secret. This secret recipe *is my job security. Besides, I have plans of someday of opening a drive-in coffee shop, the specialty: MAMA'S PEANUT BUTTER BANANA SANDWICHES. The coffee shop will be in the shape of a big ol' banana and the girl carhops, serving mama's peanut butter banana sandwiches will be on roller skates in their pretty peanut uniforms! The whole world should know that everybody likes peanut butter banana sandwiches and that I come from a long line of many generations of the finest peanut butter banana sandwich makers! My plan is the peanuttiest!*

I definitely know why PX sales are increasing, but I never have been one to give away trade secrets! These are . . .

'The Chocolate Bar Days' Aiko and I are doing well in our wholesale business. In fact, it is positively thriving as Aiko keeps stuffing our profits

into Japanese bank accounts. We are in love. We make our plans in the evenings or afternoons when we can be together. We are gonna' get married and have a big honeymoon in some foreign country, maybe like that there Mexico. I like tacos!

We are just not ready to tell anyone that we are gonna' get married. Generals don't like their privates marrying Japanese gals and they have issued all kinds of regulations to make sure we don't marry any of the local gals. Generals don't know nothing about love, they just go home at night to receive instructions from their wives for their next day's regulations!

In Japanese, the word for 'love' is, Ai. The word for 'child' is Kodomo. Put Ai and Ko together and we have the name Aiko, *child of love*. And, I truly love Aiko with all my heart!

"Love is the only reality and it is not a mere sentiment.
It is the ultimate truth that lies at the heart of creation."
Sir Rabindranath "Tagore" Thakur

My most popular and fast-moving wholesale product is tobacco. Lucky Strike cigarettes are number one on the list. Often, we are completely sold out, and I can't get enough to supply my weekly wholesale route. It is by far, the favorite brand that we sell.

Francisco De La Cruz

"My name is Francisco De La Cruz . . . my family and friends call me Pancho."

Pancho is a cook over in Service Company 511th. I have gotten to know Pancho, as I too, am assigned to Service Company while working in the PX. I am stationed behind the cigarette counter-my favorite place in the PX as I want to see who is buying what. I do not want any illegal competition to my wholesale business; someone might screw it up. Pancho is in line to buy his weekly ration of one carton of Chesterfields.

"Hey, Pancho, how's it going?"

"Not so good!"

"How come, Pancho?"

"They're shipping me out!"

Genuinely surprised, I say,

"Shipping you out?"

About this time, a lieutenant back in the line, *Now I am guessing that's the only time a lieutenant ever stood in line and that is to buy cigarettes,* yells at me ,

"Hey, Private! Move this line along! I want a carton of Lucky Strikes!"

Now, I wish this lieutenant hadn't said that! We privates are used to being yelled at by lieutenants. Being yelled at don't bother me none, like I said, I'm used to it.

What I wish he had *not* said was,

"I want to buy a carton of Lucky Strikes."

Lucky Strikes **. . .** is the best seller in my wholesale business. I am often out of Lucky Strikes and right now, I only have a few cases left. There are customers waiting for Lucky Strikes in downtown Hachinohe. My Japanese customers seem to like that red ball on the Lucky Strike package, just like that there red ball on their Japanese flag.

Here is this pushy lieutenant in the back of the line, this tobacco addict wantin' to reduce my Lucky Strike inventory! The Lieutenant don't know it, but Private Payne controls the tobacco market! *Lieutenants should not be smoking! This sets a bad example for us privates.*

"Sorry, lieutenant, sir; this is your unlucky day.

We are out of Lucky Strikes today and mighty sorry sir, we got no more Chesterfields, either. Better luck next time, lieutenant!"

As Pancho walks away, he pauses and says over his shoulder,

"Come over to my place tonight! Hanako is making gyoza fried dumplings. Bring Aiko with you. I am sure Hanako would like to see her."

"Ok, Pancho! We will be there!"

I am in control . . . The cigarette line moves on.

"Knowing when to move on is to control the market."
Joshiki

Happy Lane

Pancho and Hanako live down a little flagstone street well-worn with the foot prints of time. It is not too far from my snack bar at the dance hall. I call the little street, Happy Lane. Happy Lane is a wonderful, peaceful place. I have always liked to give names to my favorite places and Happy Lane is one of them. Out on the street, one can hear the shopkeepers calling out in their singsong voices,

"*Irasshaimase*", *Irasshaimase*" (Welcome, please come in!"). There are many little food shops with hanging red lanterns near the entrances. "Come in for yakitori, *(broiled chicken on little sticks)* bowls of hot ramen noodles, sushi, hot sake and large bottles of cold Sapporo beer." *Happy Lane is a happy place ... until today!*

I hold Aiko's hand as we slowly walk down the lane. A timid full moon slowly begins to rise over Hachinohe Bay, seeking to hide itself among the clouds. *Could it too, feel the unhappiness beginning to settle over Happy Lane?*

Aiko has chosen to wear a pretty *yukata* (summer kimono) with pink cherry blossoms. As we walk, her little wooden sandals tap out the rhythm of our arrival.

Pancho opens the door with a somber look on his face. I can sense that things have gotten real 'serces'. Pancho is a good soldier. He has obtained the rank of Buck Sergeant. Pancho and Hanako are very devoted to one another. They have two children, a boy Tadao who is two and a half years old and a little girl Yuki, a year old. *They are a family of love.*

As we sit on the *tatam*i mat, I can see the sadness that gently surrounds the family. The children are nestled against their mother; Hanako reaches for bites of the gyoza with her chopsticks for the little ones. I sip my beer, as Pancho says,

"They are going to send me home. I received my orders this morning. They say that me wanting to marry Hanako is against regulations. They are transferring me back stateside."

"What about Hanako? What about Tadao and Yuki?" I ask with much concern.

As I glance at Aiko, I see the sad look on her face. She too, is aware that we may soon be in the same situation.

"They will move back to Morioka and stay with Hanako's parents until I can find some way to bring them to the states.

I knew my time was running out. I want to . . . I must . . .

I just gotta' marry Hanako and that's against U.S. Military Government regulations." he says sadly. *Upon hearing of this military regulation, my heart feels wounded and a sigh fills my chest . . . I feel his pain deep within my heart.* Pancho continues,

"I wrote my Congressman asking for help. My Congressman sent my letter to Army Headquarters in Washington and it came all the way back down to General McArthur's GHQ, 8th Army, 9th Corp, our 7th division's commanding general, on down to our new regimental commander, Colonel John Jeffrey Hicks and he is furious.

He had our company commander, Captain Reno bring me to his headquarters' building."

"You know Pancho, I wonder if the officers and government people who make these regulations for us have ever been in love . . . *with a Japanese woman?*

It feels like those officers are always pointing their fingers and lecturing us privates not to get involved with Japanese gals, saying for us to control our emotions and our desires until we get back to the States, where there are nice American girls waiting for us . . . *so they say!"*

Aiko and I say our good-byes for the evening, and sadly leave Pancho and his family . . . a beautiful family to be torn apart by the cruelty of racial military regulations.

"When a finger points at the moon, the imbecile looks at his finger."
Chinese Proverb

The Seven Gods of Life

The moon is hesitantly hiding behind a low dark cloud gently sprinkling rain as if to shed tears of sadness on Happy Lane. I put my arm around Aiko as we slowly walk back to our home under the old pine tree. I scoop Aiko up in my arms-

carry her into our small room; she is overcome with sadness. I lay her head upon our pillow, kiss her gently and whisper,

"I love you so much . . . sleep for a while. I'm going to the Temple. I must speak to the Seven Gods of Life."

With sadness in my heart, I walk to the temple. With a few soft rings of the bell, I say in a quiet voice,

"Oh, Seven Gods of Life, please help this good family: Pancho, Hanako, Tadao and Yuki. They are truly in need of your help. They need each other. They are a happy family with two beautiful children. Please help those who make regulations understand that love for one's family is in the hands of the Gods." I ask this with all my heart.

Our regulations are now handed down to us by our new Commanding General of the 7th Infantry Division that has replaced our 11th Airborne Division. *This night, the Gods are silent.*

It Is Against Regulations!

\

Mrs. Hicks is President of the 32nd Infantry Regiment's Officers' Wives Club. She demands that her husband make an example out of this Mexican, who dared write his congressman that he wants to marry a Japanese girl.

The 7th Division General is unhappy with Colonel Hicks, our 32nd Regimental Commander, because Pancho is giving the division a bad name for violating the no marriage regulations. This makes Colonel Hicks a very unhappy man, which in turn, makes Colonel Hicks' wife a very, very unhappy woman!

At home in the evening, Col. Hicks tries to relax with a double martini. He is reading the Stars and Stripes newspaper when Mrs. Hicks storms into the room and angrily snatches the paper out of his hands and starts to yell:

"Listen to me, Colonel!" She waves her finger,

"You had better do something about that Mexican. Of all people, who does that Mexican think he is, Clark Gable? How dare that Mexican bring such disgrace to the regiment, wanting to marry a Jap woman? What a shame! There are many Mexican girls of his own kind back in the states just waiting to get married! You will not let it happen! Are you listening to me, Colonel? . . . Do you hear me, Colonel? How disgusting! This wetback wanting to marry a Japanese woman ... You must do something at once!"

Colonel Hicks softly replies,

"Yes, dear," as he pours himself another double martini.

We privates know that in the military . . . it is the officer's wives that make military policy.

Early the next morning to get out of the house before his wife wakes up to give him more instructions, Colonel Hicks heads to his office and clears his calendar. He arranges a very important meeting to take place. He calls

Captain Reno at Service Company and orders that Sergeant De La Cruz be brought to headquarters immediately.

Colonel Hicks is furious, and very worried as to how this issue may affect his promotion to one-star when the wives of generals hear about this request for a forbidden marriage being sent to a congressman for approval, and possible waiver of the regulation in place.

"Sergeant De La Cruz, stand at attention! What do you mean by writing to your congressman that you want to get married to a Jap? You know soldiers cannot get married to Japanese girls. It is against regulations to marry them. I ought to have you court-martialed for trying to marry this Jap gal! I am transferring you to another unit. Like a good soldier you will meet some nice Spic. Oh' ah, I mean some nice Mexican girl-get married and raise a family of little Mexican kids, instead of some little Jap half-breeds. Don't you know we have been at war with these Japs?"

"Captain Reno, get him out of here! I will have orders cut for Sergeant De La Cruz' transfer to Alaska right away ..

" Yes, Colonel . . . that should cool him off!"

As the door is closing, the Colonel is heard yelling,

"What's happening to this army, writing their congressmen?

Doesn't that wetback Mexican know anything? Congressmen don't know anything about military regulations, just ask my wife!"

The next day, at the officers' wives bridge party in the club, Mrs. Hicks, as she stuffs another chocolate bon bon in her mouth, lets all of the ladies of the club know just how proud she is of her husband.

"There will be no shame in our regiment! My husband, Colonel John Jeffery Hicks, Regimental Commanding Officer of the 32nd, has saved the honor of the 32nd Infantry Regiment. He has stood firm and reassigned that Mexican soldier to an artillery unit in Alaska. There will be no family marriage with a Japanese foreigner!"

"A person separated from the family, will be eaten by wolves."
Asian Proverb

Mrs. Hicks is all smiles, as she is well received by the ladies of the club with a big round of applause!

They ship Pancho back to the states with a deep wound in his heart, without a remedy, with a broken spirit. I am never to see Pancho again. A few years later, the marriage regulations, no doubt with the help of Pancho and others, are overturned.

"Do not look for help from someone other than yourself.
The remedy for your wound is the wound itself."
Rumi

Friends Are Not Forever

These are troublous times.

It is not trouble in my wholesale business that put an end to my wholesale business; it is trouble in the retail business that put an end to my wholesale business. *You know what I mean.*

Sometimes, when my snack bar is not very busy, I help behind the PX counter selling cigarettes. I feel very close to the tobacco business and I am always keeping an eye on things. Cigarettes are rationed- one carton of cigarettes per person, once a week. A ration card is required and it is punched when you purchase your weekly ration of one carton of cigarettes, and that is all you should get- one carton a week and no more! However, for a good friend one afternoon I sell him an extra carton of Camels. He says it is for his new girl to give to her grandfather for his birthday. Her name is Sachiko, and she is mighty pretty with a short pert haircut which shows off her pretty brown eyes. Her looks are so attractive that no wonder some of soldiers try to be her close friend.

That there Camel tobacco company puts good pictures into their advertising such as: "*More doctors smoke Camels than any other cigarette!*" Camel cigarettes are one of the best sellers in my wholesale business, and I thought one extra carton will just add to Lt. McWherter's sales record.

It is a setup . . . now, just why does Buck Sergeant Johnny Jardine's girlfriend, Sachiko have two cartons of Camel cigarettes when the MPs raid her house? Johnny told me later, because this MP First Sergeant by the name of Swinefine was Sachiko's fickle boyfriend for a while and that Sachiko dumped Swinefine for Johnny . . . *and that started a war with no end to peace! Swinefine trumped up a raid on her house and discovered the extra carton.*

"Fickle love finds no peace."
Joshiki

Here I am trapped in the middle. Private Payne has let Buck Sergeant Jardine buy another carton of Camels when Sergeant Jardine's ration card has already been punched for the week. The cigarettes are paid for, but that don't matter for Sachiko now has two cartons of Camels in her home and this is considered 'black market'. Black market is against military regulations *and this is something everybody should know!*

Sometimes helping a friend can get you into the stockade.

Ask me . . . I know!

Provost Marshal Major Hangington yells at Buck Sergeant Johnny Jardine.

"Sergeant Jardine, if you don't confess and sign a statement as to how your girlfriend got those two cartons of Camel cigarettes, I am gonna' bust you right down to a private!"

Johnny don't like that at all! *Now, I don't know why Johnny don't like that. It seems to me that I have been a private most of my life and it don't bother me none!*

Johnny takes the easy way out and confesses to stay out of the stockade. He signs a statement that Private Payne is the one that sold him a second carton of Camel cigarettes without punching his ration card and that statement he signed has got me, Private Payne, in *big trouble.* Things are real *serces,* not just serious, but I mean really, really *serces.*

The Promise

Now, I know that Johnny likes to shoot pool over at the Service Club. I don't waste any time. I double-time it over there and sure enough, there he is. With a nervous twitch of his shoulders he looks at me and attempts a big friendly smile

"Hi buddy, how you doing?"

He sets his shot up, still smiling at me.

I shake my fist up in the air and give him a hard mean look. Johnny gets that scared look on his face and his eyes widen with a look of anxiety . . . He knows I am mad!

"Hey, buddy . . . he finished his shot, cracking the balls over the table. How's it going?" He asks nervously, resting his hands on the cue.

"Johnny, what in the hell do you mean-how's it going buddy! You know where I'm ah going, you dirty rat and don't call me buddy! After the trial, I am going to the stockade!

I did you a favor to help you and your girlfriend! I believed it was for her grandfather's birthday.

Now, I know what you are going to do. You are going to sell those Camel cigarettes on the black market. Don't you know that black market is against army regulations?"

Johnny knows that I am real mad. He knows that I am about to haul off and knock his socks off. I do not care if he is a sergeant and I am a private, as those officers cannot bust a private down any lower than a private. Johnny cautiously moves over to the other side of the pool table near the door, where he thinks it is a little safer.

"Whoa, whoa, wait a minute!" Johnny waves his hand toward me.

"They made me do it, Ray. I'm sorry; I wish I hadn't signed that statement. If I had it to do all over again, I wouldn't sign it; I promise!"

Johnny relaxes a bit as he sees what he just said has put me at ease. Still, he stays on the other side of the pool table with one eye on the door . . . just in case.

"Johnny, you promise you won't sign another statement? They might just lose that statement!"

"Ray, I promise. I wish I had never signed that statement."

"Johnny, I'll talk to you later! Right now, I have some real important business to take care of. Don't forget, you promised! Remember, we are *buddies*! You have promised you will never sign another statement!"

Sergeant Johnny Jardine has long forgotten . . . the doable wonders of a private.

Johnny don't know it, but he said the right thing to me, for I know a private in the Provost Marshall's office, Scooter Hansail.

At a mean run, I go looking for Scooter. I know that Scooter don't take much stock in working in the Provost Marshall's office, so I go directly to my snack bar, knowing he is often hanging out with one of my snack bar girls . . . Scooter is in love! Scooter is ah friend of mine and as a private Scooter does not have much money. Sometimes as a favor, I give Scooter a free steak . . . Now it is time . . . for me to collect on that favor!

"Scooter, how would you like to have, five hundred dollars? You will be rich"

"Five hundred dollars, my God, Ray, that's almost a year's pay! What do you want me to do . . . rob a bank!"

And, just like that . . . Scooter became rich.

I bought Johnny Jardine's statement right out from under Major Hangington's nose for five hundred dollars and boy is he mad! Five hundred dollars is more than ten months pay for a private, but it is worth it to me as a good investment. I have made a lot of money in the wholesale business and I have Johnny's promise . . . *so I think!*

The MPs again round up Johnny and that Major Hangington stands Johnny at attention, yelling at Johnny, as if he is already talking to a private.

"Sergeant Jardine! I am gonna' bust you all the way down to a private! I am gonna' put you in the stockade! You will not see the light of day for many months if you don't sign another statement! Where did you get that extra carton of cigarettes?

Is this statement true? Private Payne sold the extra carton to me, Sergeant Johnny Jardine without punching my ration card. Sign now or you will be escorted to the stockade!"

This scares the hell out of Johnny! Provost Marshall Hangington is mad and most worried as he is in line to be promoted to Lieutenant Colonel. What if it is reported to Mrs. Hicks that Major Hangington is in line for a promotion? What will the Regimental Commander's wife instruct her husband, Colonel John Jeffery Hicks to do about the Provost Marshall's impending promotion?

Knowing the influential power of Mrs. Hicks, and fearing the loss of his promotion, Provost Marshall Hangington is all shook up.

"Now, listen to me well, Sergeant Jardine! Which would you rather have as punishment, lose one stripe and go free, or would you rather spend six months in my stockade doing hard labor? If you cooperate, tell me everything, sign a statement, you will go free. If you do not sign, you will go to the stockade. I will see to it that you will continue screwing up so that you will *never* get out of my stockade!"

I can sense trouble, learning from Scooter that the MPs had picked up Johnny. Scooter said he had seen Johnny arrive at MP headquarters handcuffed in the back of an MP jeep.

Scared half to death of that stockade, Johnny signs another statement; he does not keep his mouth shut.

Buck Sergeant Johnny Jardine loses a stripe and is now a Corporal. Sachiko goes back to First Sergeant Swinefine, her former boyfriend. Major Hangington is promoted to Lieutenant Colonel. Private Payne loses five hundred dollars and is off to the stockade . . . Scooter is rich. *These are indeed troublous times!*

"*Even a fish would not get into trouble, if it kept its mouth shut!*"
Korean Proverb

The Monkey House

Guilty . . . six months in the stockade; out in three months with good behavior; the judge slams down the gavel and they take me away to the camp stockade.

The 11th Airborne Division transferred back to the States. The 32nd Infantry Regiment, 7th Infantry Division, replaced my regiment the 511th. The 32nd Regiment is under-strength and those in the 511th Parachute Infantry Regiment that want to remain in Japan can transfer over to the 32nd. As much as I love the 511th, I love Aiko more, and we have money in the bank.

I transfer over to the 32nd and within this unit are the very ones that put me in the stockade. Before the trial, I explain the stockade to Aiko, jail bars and all.

"You go monkey house!" She says in disbelief, her eyes questioning this news. I hold her tightly and give her many kisses on her face, and tell her good-by for a while.

I begin my new life in an army stockade; it is no picnic. They work us hard every day, cutting grass and forcing us on long hikes with full field packs. When they say jump, we jump. When they say get down and eat dirt, we get down and eat dirt. *Stay out of trouble everyone, because if any one person does anything wrong, it is mass punishment for all.*

It is early evening; someone passes cigarettes through the barred window to their friends inside the stockade. To smoke the cigarettes, they huddle under a blanket, trying to hide the smell of the smoke. Soon, we others can smell the cigarette smoke and guess what? So do the guards! The guards enter the prison room, throwing buckets of water over the blanket, turning our bunks upside down yelling,

"You have thirty minutes to clean this mess up!"

It seems like only ten minutes go by before they return and again start yelling,

"Ok, thirty minutes are up; everybody out, into the street with full field packs! You are going on a nice little stroll with your full field packs!"

The nice little stroll turns out to be a long forced march. The guards do not carry full field packs and they set a mad pace.

We return to the stockade at sunrise, exhausted, dragging our feet, ready for another day of cutting grass. The ones that brought mass punishment upon all of us get their punishment in the dead of night. The guards pretend not to hear.

Aiko secretly sends a penciled message into the stockade through a friend of mine. After reading this sad news, I eat the message:

"Fujiwara no stay; you go monkey house; he close china shop right away. Where he go, nobody know. He no more stay Hachinohe. Last night, I go Moriyama's house. His old wife say old horse die; old Moriyama, he so sad, he too, die."

As if, things were not bad enough!

Three months of good behavior in this army stockade and I am out. I remember that day of freedom well, like the proverbial bamboo **...** bend with the wind. My three-year enlistment in the Army is up. I am shocked to learn that in the regulations to re-enlist, one must have six months in grade as a private first class. I come out of the stockade as a private. I have run out of time. It looks as if my career, as the longest serving private in the United States Army **...** is coming to an end.

"The tree that does not bend with the wind
will be broken by the wind."
Chinese Proverb

To conduct my wholesale business out in town, I always paid the PX the retail price. The PX has made money on my wholesale business with increased retail sales. While I was in the stockade, I wondered if Lieutenant McWherter was going bananas **...** without mama's peanut butter banana sandwiches? *I am the only one with mama's secret recipe . . . you know what I mean.*

I guess PX sales went down during my absence. I am wondering if they let Lieutenant McWherter keep his sales award, or if they even **...** let him stay on? Like the flow of water, Fujiwara has moved on; Moriyama and the old horse have passed on. As for my future with Aiko **...** our life together is uncertain.

"The flow of water and the future of human beings are uncertain."
Japanese Proverb

The clock is ticking . . .

Good Bye to the Chocolate Bar Days

After getting out of the stockade, I am given twenty-four hours to get my things ready for departure the next morning on the *Yankee Flyer*.

Under the faint glow of a new moon, I sneak through our secret hole in the fence, that only us privates know about. I run as fast as I can across the rows of farmers' rice paddies. I run down the little dirt trail that I know so well, into the cobblestone side street that leads to our little home. I must see Aiko.

Aiko is waiting. She sees me coming and runs to me. While holding me tightly with tears in her eyes, kissing my face, she whispers,

"You no more monkey house!"

She takes my hand and we go into our little home for the last time. *Our little one room home . . . we have wonderful memories of the days and nights gone by. Cherry blossoms in the spring, warm summer evenings, the coloring of the leaves of autumn, winter snowflakes falling softly against the window.*

The faint glow of the moon timidly peeks through the window, casting a soft light upon us as we hold each other lying on our *futon*, locked in an embrace that we do not want to end, not knowing where our future life may take us. I keep my arms wrapped around her with my face buried in her soft hair. I gently wipe away her tears and say,

"Don't cry for me; I love you, Aiko. I have a plan. You catch a train for Tokyo Ueno Station and then to Camp Zama. Each day I will look for you near the front gate of Camp Zama. I will be there for you!"

Looking out the window, I see streaks of light. It is time to go.

As I run back to Camp Haugen the fading song of the whippoorwill reminds me it is getting late; the sun is beginning its rise in the east, painting soft colors into the early morning sky. I must hurry. Quickly, I crawl through our secret hole in the fence for the last time.

I run to Service Company as fast as I can to pick up my duffel bag.

I throw the duffel bag over my shoulder and run for the road. I must not be late. At this moment, happiness fills my mind, Aiko and I will soon be together again to plan our future.

"Do not dwell in the past. Do not dream of the future.
Concentrate the mind on the present moment."
Buddha

Now Is the Hour

Dawn is breaking over Hachinohe bay; a small fading star twinkles softly through the branches of a dogwood tree. Across the valley, high up on the mountainside, comes the lonely melancholy cry of the fox.

Off in the distance, I can hear the faint sound of a motor-a sound that I recognize so well as it grows louder. It is the all too familiar sound of the ol' weapons carrier. *They are coming to take me away*. The screeching brakes' sound of the old weapons carrier signals it's time to say good-bye to Camp Haugen. The 32nd regimental MPs come to a halt at my designated place on the side of the road.

"Good morning, Private Payne! We are your escort.

This morning before leaving home, Colonel Hicks received instructions from his wife that you are not to miss your train.

By the way, a lieutenant came to our office early this morning and requested that we give you this letter."

I throw my duffel bag into the back of the weapons carrier and climb in with it. Resting my back on my duffel bag, I open the letter and slowly read the message.

Private Payne,

I wish you a safe trip; things have not been the same, now that you are gone. Please do not forget to send me your mama's secret peanut butter banana sandwich recipe. I will forever be indebted.

One of the officer's wives, whose husband works at Regimental Headquarters, told my wife that Colonel Hick's wife told her, that her husband Colonel John Jeffery Hicks Commanding Officer of the 32nd Infantry Regiment, following her instructions will transfer me, Lieutenant McWherter out of the PX and into a line company. Mrs. Hicks also related at the same time that there would be no promotion!

Well, Private Payne after the excitement at the Camp Haugen PX, it looks like I will be the longest serving lieutenant in the United States Army."

Sincerely yours,
Lieutenant Winfred Montan McWherter

The ol' weapons carrier, growling as if in recognition of a long lost friend, is slowly moving in low gear, grunting, belching smoke; it moves into second gear and then starts to hum in third gear as if singing to me a farewell love song. My old friend, the weapons carrier is carrying me for the last time down the winding dirt road to the 511th train station *Mutsu-Ichikawa.* Sadness comes over me as I brush away a tear.

I am happy to see that the 7th Division has not yet painted over the front bumper that is still stenciled 11 A/B Div. The ol' weapons carrier brings joy to my heart with the sounds of the engine that I know so well. The old pistons that have gone through the war, spent many a night looking for privates in off-limits places, are now tapping in rhythm as it winds its way down the road **. . .** *the road of no return.*

It is my ol' friend, the weapons carrier's gas tank that my friends and I had poured five pounds of sugar into one Saturday night. I thought to myself, *"Could the rhythm of the engine be a sweet love song of good-bye from an old friend that has spent many a night roaming the streets of Hachinohe looking for my friends and me?"*

Good-bye to my friends, good-bye to the beautiful girls of Tohoku, good-bye Hachinohe, good-bye to Camp Haugen, good-bye to those exciting days and nights with the 511th Parachute Infantry Regiment, good-bye to some of the most wonderful adventurous years of my life. Good-bye to the Chocolate Bar Days."

"We live in a wonderful world that is full of beauty, charm and adventure. There is no end to the adventures that we can have, if only we seek them with our eyes open."
Jawaharlal Nehru

I Must See Aiko

As I go out the front gate of Camp Zama, I anxiously look for Aiko. I see her waiting for me down the street away from the MP gate guards. After the "Monkey House", Aiko does not like MPs. She sees me, runs and throws her arms around me, whispering,

"I would have waited for you forever!"

Aiko and I are together for three wonderful days and nights before I am to ship out on the U.S.S. Breckenridge. We love each other so much!

I know that by going out of Camp Zama, it is a gamble- knowing a great number of troops are processing in and out. Not everyone is a good soldier. The barracks that I am assigned to has soldiers from all over Japan, strangers to me.

The strong desire to see Aiko is overwhelming; my love for her surrounds me with longing . . . I have to see Aiko!

It is getting near the time for me to leave; I go out the gate to find Aiko. Someone steals my duffel bag that has all of my possessions of three years in the 511th Parachute Infantry Regiment. Important parts of my life, memories of a lifetime are gone in an unguarded moment. They steal my soul and I feel deeply hurt.

Gone forever . . . lost in the shadows of the night; my duffel bag loss is a stinging tragic event in my life. Gone are all my photographs that I have taken of Aiko, except for the ones that I carry with me. Gone are the pictures and addresses of my good friends. As privates, we shared the most adventurous times of our lives . . . "*The Chocolate Bar Days.*"

"Beware of man's shadow and a bee's sting."
Burmese Proverb

Don't Cry For Me

Petals of soft white clouds drift across the sky, as summer gently passes into fall. Aiko and I spend much of the day among the fragrance of late summer flowers, sitting in a park planning our future.

In the evening, during the quietness of night, we hold each other, sharing our dreams and our fears promising our love for each other with tender words. We look into each other's eyes as we say, "I will love you forever and ever."

Aiko sobs herself to sleep softly saying,

"You come back."

I wipe away her tears and kiss her gently on the cheek.

"Sleep well, Aiko. I will come back. Don't cry for me."

The setting sun is casting its shadows into the lateness of the day. It is sprinkling rain as I look at Aiko standing on the dock holding in her hands the flowers I had picked for her in the park. The autumn rain is gently running down her cheeks, mixing with her tears. I want to wipe those tears away and hold her once more. She cries out to me,

"Come back, come back . . . I wait for you!"

Up on the deck of the Breckenridge, I wave and call to her,

"I will come back; you know I love you; I will come back; don't cry for me!"

With a melancholy wail, the U.S.S. Breckenridge slips away from the dock slowly moving out into the waters of Tokyo Bay. As the ship moves out of the twilight, into the darkness of the night, Aiko becomes lost in the distant mist.

"As the bee takes the essence of a flower and flies away without destroying its beauty and its fragrance, so let the sage wander in this life."
Joshiki, the Wandering Sage

The Passing of Time

Gone are the "chocolate bar days" of the occupation of Japan. The "chocolate bar days" will become a part of history as time passes by.

As the moon begins its slow rise over the lights of the city in the eastern sky, it casts its glow over the ripples of the ocean. I stand on the deck of the Breckenridge looking out at the twinkling of the city lights... until the last twinkle is lost to sight.

The ship moves further and further out into the Pacific; the lonely days and nights seem unending. I spend much of my time on the stern of the ship gazing back across the churning waters ... waters that are taking me further away from the love of my life- away from my Aiko.

Daily in the hold of the ship, I put to paper my love for Aiko, my loneliness, my sadness, and memories of those wonderful days and nights we had together in our little home near Camp Haugen. Precious memories of our love in those days and nights gone by flood my mind. I long to be again in our little wooden home under the old pine tree- to be once again with Aiko.

"Precious love is unending. Its memories flow with the currents of the oceans, unending in time."
Joshiki

As the U.S.S. Breckenridge sails under the Golden Gate Bridge, the city of San Francisco rises up to greet us. For many soldiers, it is a welcome sight to see as they crowd the railing, cheering and waving. I have nothing to cheer about, nor did I know that I would be going to Hawaii with my eldest brother and his new wife. The road for the tomorrows is unclear like falling cherry blossoms.

Letter of Good-bye

Aiko and I send our letters of love to one another.

Aiko asks with each letter,

"When are you coming back?"

My frequent answer to her:

"I am in Hawaii. I am trying to come back, but as Japan is under U.S. military occupation; I must have a letter of invitation and that letter I have not been able to get."

The rising of the sun and the twilight of the evenings, blend into the passing of time; the days grow into weeks, the weeks into months . . . Aiko's and my letters become less frequent.

I miss Aiko with all my heart. Not a day goes by that I do not think of her. With each day that passes, unable to return to Japan, I now realize that I have lost my Aiko forever.

"Don't cry for me." I had said,

"Aiko, I will come back."

With the passing of time and reality as it is, I now know that I will not return to Japan. The C*hocolate Bar Days* are over. I have new responsibilities. I am soon to be married and raising a family. With tears in my eyes and a lump in my throat, I sit down with a heavy heart filled with sadness and write my . . . letter of good-bye:

Dear Aiko,

You have brought much happiness to my life- precious days and nights- now gone by. I will always remember you- forever and ever- cherry blossoms in the springtime- new winter snow gently falling against the window- holding you in my arms- for the last time.

Aiko, please forgive me- I am getting married. We have a child on the way. We have come to the crossroads where we each must take a different path. Do not be sad, as we burn the bridges behind us. As painful as it is, we must say good-bye. I have left you with enough money to lead a comfortable life- for the rest of your life. You will get by. Do *not write back.*

Always remember . . . wherever you go, wherever you are, my heart is always with you.

With all my love,

Ray

I seal my letter of good-bye and light a candle. I take one last look at the memories of our life, one by one; I slowly turn our pictures, and Aiko's letters of love into ashes of the past.

I am never to see Aiko again.

"As we part at the crossroads of life,
we leave with our memories and our sadness.
Look down the road, as we must follow our own path."
Joshiki

Sequel: Private Payne: "THE WILD WILD EAST"